Silver in American Life

Catalogue No. 69 *(see pp. 93-94)*

Silver in American Life

Selections from the Mabel Brady Garvan and Other Collections at Yale University

EDITED BY BARBARA McLEAN WARD & GERALD W. R. WARD

DAVID R. GODINE, PUBLISHER
*in association with the Yale University Art Gallery
and The American Federation of Arts*

This exhibition and publication are supported by grants from the National Endowment for the Arts, the National Endowment for the Humanities, and the National Patrons of The American Federation of Arts.

The American Federation of Arts is a national, non-profit, educational organization, founded in 1909, to broaden the knowledge and appreciation of the arts of the past and present. Its primary activities are the organization of exhibitions which travel throughout the United States and abroad, and the fostering of a better understanding among nations by the international exchange of art.

First published in 1979 by
David R. Godine, Publisher, Inc.
306 Dartmouth Street
Boston, Massachusetts 02116

LCC 78-74920
ISBN 0-87923-288-9

Design & Typography
by Howard I. Gralla,
New Haven, Connecticut

Composition in the Sabon types
by Finn Typographic Service,
Stamford, Connecticut

Printed by The Meriden Gravure
Company, Meriden, Connecticut

Bound by Robert Burlen & Son,
Hingham, Massachusetts

IN MEMORY OF
CHARLES F. MONTGOMERY 1910-1978

Foreword

Silver in American Life was planned with a two-fold purpose in mind. Our primary goal was to share with communities across the nation a portion of the superb collection of some 1,200 pieces of American silver gathered at Yale University in the Mabel Brady Garvan and other collections. The secondary purpose was to tell the story of silver in as complete a manner as possible.

When Francis P. Garvan, a member of the Yale Class of 1897, gave his outstanding collection of Americana to the university in 1930, he expressed the hope that the objects could be "mobilized and circulated throughout the country" so that they "may be rendered more generally accessible." "Putting art on wheels" was the way Mr. Garvan phrased it. Through the assistance of The American Federation of Arts, this mandate has now been partially realized. This exhibition will visit twelve major art museums from coast to coast over three years, giving many people an opportunity to share the beauty and joy of Yale's collection.

Like many other collections of silver formed early in this century, the Garvan collection contains few objects made after 1825. To accomplish our second goal it was, therefore, necessary to rely on other collections at Yale, and our approach, which places silver objects in the context of American cultural life, would not have been possible without contributions from and the cooperation of the Peabody Museum of Natural History, the Numismatic Collection, the George J. Brush Mineral Collection, the Economic Geology Collection, and the Department of Athletics. Generous donors provided objects or funds to help us complete the story. Nevertheless, several lacunae still exist. The Yale University Art Gallery hopes to fill these gaps in the years ahead, to ensure the pre-eminence of the Yale collections as a teaching resource for the study of American art and history.

This exhibition and catalogue would not have been possible without the generous financial assistance of both the National Endowment for the Arts and the National Endowment for the Humanities. An initial study grant was provided by the NEH, which subsequently funded the short film and all the other educational materials which accompany the exhibition. The NEA grant enabled us to provide the show to the participating museums at a lower cost than would have otherwise been possible, and to make the catalogue available to the public at an affordable price.

Both of us wish to acknowledge the extensive and detailed efforts of our respective staffs who are responsible for making this project a reality. However, Barbara and Gerald Ward deserve a special word of praise. They had worked closely with Charles Montgomery in the early stages of planning. After his death, the Wards volunteered to carry on and complete the project as a memorial to their former mentor. We are sure that Charles Montgomery, who devoted so much of his boundless energies to teaching about and inspiring enthusiasm for American decorative arts, would have been pleased with the results.

WILDER GREEN
Director
The American Federation of Arts

ALAN SHESTACK
Director
Yale University Art Gallery

Acknowledgments

The humanistic interpretative scheme for this exhibition was largely a result of the imaginative, enthusiastic thinking of the late Charles F. Montgomery, our teacher and friend. The nature of the show and its integral components had been determined and our planning was well under way when Mr. Montgomery unexpectedly passed away in February of 1978. Whatever success or impact *Silver in American Life* may have is due to the creative and inspired vision which Mr. Montgomery brought to its conception. We have tried to see the exhibition through to completion in the same spirit in which it began, and we will always be grateful to Alan Shestack, Director of the Yale University Art Gallery, for courageously allowing us to do so.

This exhibition could never have been a reality without the untiring efforts of many individuals at The American Federation of Arts. Wilder Green directed the project and Jane Tai administered and coordinated our efforts with meticulous care. Susanna D'Alton scheduled the exhibition and obtained the cooperation of the participating museums. Melissa Meighan handled the many complex registrarial responsibilities involved with a traveling show of three years duration.

We are particularly indebted to William A. Lanford, John P. Burnham, Stephen K. Victor, and Martha Gandy Fales for preparing their essays which appear in this volume. These scholars also read all or part of the manuscript and served as our advisors in numerous other respects. In addition, Mr. Victor took part in the planning of the show during his year (1977-1978) as a National Museum Act Intern in the American Arts Office.

Kathryn C. Buhler, Patricia E. Kane, Brian J. Skinner, and Dr. Joe Ben Wheat also gave portions of the manuscript a critical reading, and their comments saved us from many an egregious error. Those which remain are our responsibility.

We are especially grateful for the assistance of Kevin L. Stayton, a doctoral candidate in the Department of the History of Art at Yale, who authored one-third of the catalogue entries and assisted in many other ways as the show was put together.

The following individuals and firms donated objects or made it possible for us to acquire others specifically for this exhibition: Mrs. Alfred E. Bissell, Mrs. Edward Leisenring, Mrs. Samuel Schwartz, Carl R. Kossack, Mr. and Mrs. Joseph A. Link, the David H. Clement family, George W. Pierson, Mrs. Florence M. Montgomery, Richard Surowiec of the Englehard Minerals & Chemicals Corporation, Sheila Sheehy of Handy & Harman, Stafford P. Osborn of Reed & Barton, and Thomas Mahalik of the Barden Corporation. Their vital contributions filled many gaps in our existing collection and enabled us to tell the story of silver in a more complete manner.

The cooperation of several departments within the University also made this exhibition possible. We would like to thank in particular Frank B. Ryan, Department of Athletics; Leopold J. Pospisil and Joan Cohen, Peabody Museum of Natural History; Horace Winchell and Eleanor Warren, Brush Mineral Collection; John P. Burnham, Numismatics Collection; Regina Staroles, President's House; Judith Schiff, University Archives; and Caroline Rollins, Yale University Art Gallery Associates.

A number of specialists from diverse fields, including Howard Lamar, Harry A. Miskimin, Cyril Stanley Smith, Robert Koch, Josephine Setze, Eugenia Herbert, Janet E. Buerger, Charles Carpenter, Sharon Darling, Margaret Craver Withers, Richard Baronio, Stuart Silver, Paul Williams, Jules D. Prown, William Howze, and Charles Belson, contributed their advice and suggestions during the planning stages of this exhibition. Mona Berman, a practicing silversmith, was unstinting in her efforts to help us locate and acquire examples of contemporary metalsmithing. J. Herbert Gebelein and Mr. and Mrs. Richard L. Davies of The Silver Institute also provided invaluable assistance, as did W. Scott Braznell and Cynthia Neely.

Representatives of the major silver companies, among them Mr. E. P. Hogan and Cindy Haskins of International Silver, David Rogers, Ann Holbrook, and Cheryll Greene of Gorham, and Duane Garrison of Tiffany & Company, were unfailingly helpful in our search for information. We would also like to thank Catherine Lippert for sharing her discovery of an English ceramic prototype for the Harvey Lewis inkstand (177).

In a seminar on American silver given by Charles Montgomery, preliminary research on many of the types of objects included in this exhibition was carried out by the following students: Joan Barrett, Robert Broadwater, Laura

Byers, Chiao-Hua Ching, David P. Curry, Ulysses G. Dietz, John Lamb, Thomas B. Lloyd, Nancy London, Katherine Mitchell, Dorothy O'Donnell, Marc Simpson, Janine Skerry, Kevin L. Stayton, Diana Strazdes, and Stephen K. Victor. Elizabeth Ely, Celia Betsky, and Edward S. Cooke, Jr., students in a previous seminar, also contributed valuable research.

As anyone who has ever tried knows, photographing silver is a time-consuming and difficult task. Therefore, we are pleased to acknowledge the efforts of Irving Blomstrann, who patiently and cheerfully took most of the superb photographs which appear in this book. We are equally indebted to Linda Peterson for undertaking the thankless task of editing a multi-author manuscript, and to Howard Gralla for his elegant book design and exhibition graphics. Charles F. Ryder designed the beautiful display cases which will travel with the exhibition.

This show could not have been prepared without the cooperation of the staff of the Yale University Art Gallery. Estelle Miehle processed much of the administrative work with her usual efficiency, and Fernande E. Ross deftly handled many difficult problems. Janet Saleh Dickson and Janet Gordon counseled us on the educational aspects of the show, and James D. Burke, Curator of Prints and Drawings, and his assistant Rosemary Hoffmann provided their expertise on silver and photography. Jane Krieger and Fronia Wissmann assisted in obtaining illustrations for the book.

The staff and students of the American Arts Office were instrumental at every stage of the project. Patricia E. Kane, Curator of American Decorative Arts, provided her guidance, knowledge, and support. Marion Sandquist impeccably typed the manuscript several times and, as always, contributed in many other ways. Nancy Idaka was involved in the exhibition from its inception and in addition to typing portions of the manuscript furnished many ideas and suggestions. Galina Gorokhoff helped to gather information on the paintings illustrated in the catalogue. Christine Bartolo, Thomas B. Lloyd, and Elizabeth Pratt Fox, a National Museum Act Intern during 1978-1979, helped with research and administrative problems. Thomas Michie, Linda Stamm, and Brooke Muhly were much needed volunteers.

American silver at Yale has had a great tradition, beginning with the magnificent gift of Francis P. Garvan in honor of his wife, Mabel Brady Garvan, in 1930. At every step of the way we have relied heavily upon the research and writings of those who have worked closely with the collection, including E. Alfred Jones, Josephine Setze, Charles Montgomery, and especially John Marshall Phillips. In addition, much of the information in this book is derived from the monumental catalogue of the Garvan and related collections written by Kathryn C. Buhler and Graham Hood. Published in 1970, this two-volume work is a cornerstone of any library on American decorative arts. Our attempt to carry on in the tradition established by all these people has been a humbling yet rewarding experience, and we have done the best we could to maintain their high standards.

BARBARA MCLEAN WARD

GERALD W. R. WARD

Table of Contents

'Smitten with the Silver Fever'

When Mark Twain visited the mining area of Nevada in the early 1860s, he and his companions quickly joined the locals in their rush for the precious metal that would make them all rich. Their full energies were soon absorbed as they were swept up in the frantic search for a mine with thick veins of ore, a "bonanza." As Mark Twain put it, they were "smitten with the silver fever."

Nevada in the 1860s was not the only time when Americans have been afflicted by this particular enthusiasm, this "silver fever." In many respects, this condition characterizes the role of silver in the American experience. For over three and a half centuries, silver has played a significant part in our history. The search for silver and gold was a driving force behind the settlement of this continent, and silver coins and silver objects have been an integral part of our domestic, religious, official, and economic life ever since. The impact of silver has been felt in events as momentous as the discovery of the massive wealth contained in the Comstock Lode, and as personal as the use of a silver basin in a baptismal service. Whether silver is used to create a shining teapot to be given as a wedding present, the Super Bowl trophy, a piece of fashionable jewelry, or a stunning photograph, the metal is interwoven into our culture, often in unexpected ways that largely go unnoticed.

Our major purpose in undertaking this project was to seek an understanding of this special and close relationship between silver and American life. We strove to examine silver in all its multi-faceted nature, in as broad a humanistic context as possible. This ambitious approach, which cast a net wide enough for several books, resulted in the essays and catalogue entries which follow. As our investigation proceeded, several themes seemed to particularly demand attention, namely, the attributes of silver as a metal, the role of silver in commerce and trade, the evolution of the silver-smith's profession, the way silver objects are made and how the techniques involved have changed over time, silver's symbolic role in society, and the importance of silver objects as a form of artistic expression. In exploring these themes, we have limited ourselves, with two exceptions, to objects in various collections at Yale University, principally those in the Mabel Brady Garvan and related collections in the Yale University Art Gallery. Throughout, we have attempted to focus attention on the objects themselves and the unique story each has to tell.

A related goal in preparing the various components of *Silver in American Life,* including the exhibition, this catalogue, a ten-minute film, and other related materials, was to bring silver to the attention of a wide audience of people, especially people with little or no previous exposure to the objects in Yale's collection. For too long silver has been considered as falling solely within the purview of the collector and connoisseur. This is certainly true, in part. But it is equally true that silver has also been a part of nearly everyone's existence at some point. In sharing this magnificent collection, therefore, we have tried to emphasize the universality of experience with the precious metal and the continuing tradition of silver in American life.

BARBARA MCLEAN WARD

GERALD W. R. WARD

Six Themes in American Silver

'A Mineral of that Excellent Nature'
The Qualities of Silver as a Metal

William A. Lanford

Silver is indeed "a Mineral of that excellent Nature."[1] White, lustrous, and nonreactive, silver is of all elements the best conductor of heat and electricity. Except for gold, it is the most malleable and ductile. Because of these properties, silver has played an important role not only in the history of the decorative and fine arts as illustrated by the objects shown in this volume, but also in the evolution of modern science and technology. The interest in silver and methods of assaying it was a prime motivation in the development of modern chemistry and quantitative analytical methods.[2] The electroplating industry, which grew from a desire for less expensive objects with the appearance of silver, led to the development of large electric generators.[3] The unit of electric charge, and, in turn, the unit of electric current and power are still defined in terms of the amount of silver deposited by a current passing through an electrolytic cell. And the contribution of silver to man's present understanding of his world through photography cannot be overstated, for photography provides a unique means of exploring nature, from the submicroscopic world of atoms, nuclei, and subnuclear particles to our own galaxy and even to the vast universe beyond. (See Figs. 1 and 2.)

The aim of this essay is to reveal the unity underlying the apparently diverse properties of silver by examining its atomic and microscopic structure. The general properties of silver derive both from those exhibited by single atoms of silver and from those characterizing macroscopic amounts of the metal. In the course of this discussion, we shall address the following questions: What special properties of this element are important in the extraction of metallic silver from its ores? Why is silver such an excellent conductor of heat and electricity, and what gives it its distinctive appearance? Why is silver such a malleable metal, and why does it become progressively harder and more brittle as it is worked under the smith's hammer? Why does annealing silver in a furnace render it soft again?

Silver, gold, and copper form Group Ib of the periodic table of elements. These elements are categorized together because each possesses a single valence electron outside a closed shell of electrons. They are therefore chemically similar, a fact which has intertwined their histories for thousands of years.

Perhaps the most important property shared by these three metals is their relative lack of reactivity, silver and gold being noble metals, that is, metals that do not undergo reaction with air as do all other common metals. Because they are chemically inert, all three are found in nature as native metals and as easily refined ores. As a consequence of their availability, they were known and widely used by the ancients. The early use of silver and gold, in particular, and the special value placed on these metals in the past account in part for the high esteem in which they are held today.

Figure 1
The use of silver in photographic plates has made an important contribution to the study of the atomic and subatomic particles that are the building blocks of all matter. Illustrated here is some of the first evidence for the existence of antimatter. When antimatter comes into contact with ordinary matter each annihilates, their masses being converted into energy as predicted by Einstein's formula $E = mc^2$. This photograph shows the path of an antiproton ($\bar{p}$) as it enters at the top right of the picture and annihilates in the lower center. The photographic plate also records the paths of several energetic particles created by the annihilation. (From C. F. Powell et al., eds., *Study of Elementary Particles by the Photographic Method* [New York: Pergamon Press, 1959], p. 411.)

Figure 2
Much of our knowledge of the universe derives from the use of photographic film to record astronomical objects by lengthy time exposures. Here the details of the Andromeda galaxy, two million light years from earth, are captured by the unique light-sensitive properties of silver-bromide photographic film. While the medieval notion that the earth was the center of the universe was dethroned long before the camera was developed, photography has allowed man to put the earth and our solar system in proper cosmological perspective.

As a result of their chemical similarity, silver, gold, and copper are commonly found together in ores. The geologic processes that concentrate these metals in ores rich enough to be commercially mined act similarly on all three elements. In fact, one of the largest sources of silver today is the refining of copper, which yields silver as a by-product.

The histories of the mining and refining of this triad of elements, particularly of the noble metals silver and gold, are also closely related. Alloys or combinations of these metals have been known and used for thousands of years, one of the earliest uses of silver being in the substance electrum, an alloy of gold and silver. And most "silver" articles have been and continue to be made not of pure silver but of sterling and coin silver, which are alloys of silver and copper.

Historically it has proved difficult to separate gold and silver completely because of their chemical similarity. While it was known as early as the eighteenth century[4] that commercial silver contained some gold, it was not then economically feasible to separate it out. As a result, all early silver objects contain trace amounts of gold. This continued to be true until the late nineteenth century, when effective methods of removing the gold were introduced. Analysis of the gold content in silver objects is therefore a convenient method for detecting restorations, improvements, and forgeries of pre-twentieth century silver.[5]

The history of the mining and refining of silver is a long and interesting one. Some of the major methods of refining metallic silver from its ore, illustrated in Figures 3 through 5, include cupellation, amalgamation, and the use of electrolytic baths. While these methods are quite different from one another, they all rely on the same chemical features of silver—namely, that silver is a noble metal which does not easily form chemical compounds and which is easily replaced in compounds (e.g., in its ore) by more reactive metals. The methods of separating gold from silver and silver from copper also rely on the relative reactivity of these metals, gold being the least reactive of the three and copper the most reactive. An age-old method of "parting" gold and silver is to beat the mixture into thin sheets and dissolve the sheets in nitric acid; the more reactive silver dissolves, while the less reactive gold remains behind. The colorful language of a report in an issue of *Harper's New Monthly* describes the process accurately: "Another divorce of the alloys shows a sharper trial and more poetic parting, as when gold and silver beaten by hammers into a sheet are plunged in boiling acid—the silver dissolves in the limpid acid—seeks apparent extinction in the embrace of its fiercer lover; and the gold, resisting the onset of the acid, remains behind, a colder virgin, torn, distracted but absolutely pure. The acid, clear and limpid, holds the silver fast till in new reactions the silver escapes and reappears, first as a filmy dust, and finally as solid metal."[6]

The metal silver consists of aggregates of individual silver atoms arranged in the orderly geometric shape of a crystal lattice. While the general chemical properties of silver and appropriate methods of refining it are determined

Figure 3
This illustration from Georgius Agricola's famous sixteenth-century text on metallurgy, *De re metallica* (Basel, 1556), shows the details of a working cupellation furnace. A method of separating silver from its ore widely used since classical times, cupellation was based on the fact that gold and silver are the only common metals that do not oxidize in air, even when heated. Hence when the silver ore was heated in air above its melting point, the impurities in the ore were oxidized. Lead was then mixed with the ore, and the oxidized impurities dissolved in the lead and were absorbed in the porous cup or "cupel" in which the heating took place. Cupellation was eventually replaced by refining methods based on amalgamation with silver.

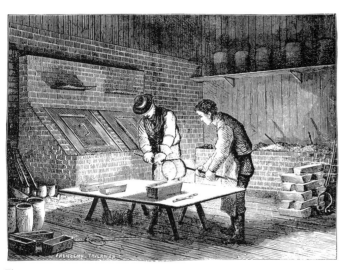

Figure 4
From its introduction in Mexico in 1557 until the end of the nineteenth century, amalgamation with mercury was the most important method of separating metallic silver from its ore. Here is a contemporary description of silver refining as practiced in the American West: "The cars containing the mingled stone and metals rise swiftly in the shaft and roll out on a platform at the top of the silver mill, and are then dumped into bins or spouts leading directly to the stone-crushers. . . . The next step in the process is the grinding and amalgamating in circular tanks. . . . Quicksilver [mercury], salt and sulphate of copper are added to the slime as it is grinding. Hot steam comes to add heat and turmoil to the boiling mass, and the strange loves of the metals begin. The silver and gold part with their original forms, and in chemic union with the mercury are lost to sight and touch. . . . At last the product may

be gathered up in canvas bags and, on submitting these to pressure, a portion of the quicksilver trickles through the fabric in silver tears—literally a "quick" or live metal. The rest, still stubbornly clinging to its treasures, remains behind: a curious pasty mass, resembling neither gold, silver nor mercury. . . . How can we win back the silver and gold to their metallic state? Let them be torn by fire. The mingled quicksilver and metals are placed in retorts and under the influence of cherry-red heat the quicksilver springs up as vapor and flies away through pipes on invisible wings. . . . The precious metals, unheeding the fire, remain behind till, in a fiercer heat, they flow together in solid bars" (*Harper's New Monthly Magazine* 58 [December 1879]: 80). This illustration shows the final stage described above, the casting of silver into bullion. (From *Harper's Weekly*, 30 May 1874, p. 457.)

Figure 5
Today silver is recovered both directly from silver ores and as a by-product of the refining of other metals such as copper and lead. The electrolytic method of refining silver, shown here, makes use of an electrolytic bath containing two electrodes, one composed of partially refined silver, the other a thin sheet of very pure silver. As the refining proceeds, silver from the partially refined metal electrode

dissolves, forming ions in the electrolytic solution. These ions, driven by electric force, pass through the electrolytic bath and are plated out on the other electrode as very pure silver. Any gold present in the partially refined metal will not dissolve in the electrolytic solution, and is thus recovered. (Photograph courtesy of Handy & Harman Company, New York.)

by the qualities of individual silver atoms, the appearance as well as many of the physical and electrical properties of bulk silver result from the crystalline nature of the material. The arrangement of the silver atoms in their crystal lattice, shown schematically in Figure 6a, allows the closest possible packing of identical spherical atoms. These atoms are bonded together by the action of their valence electrons. Upon crystallization, the single outermost electron associated with a particular atom becomes free to move anywhere within the crystal. These free electrons constitute a negatively charged "electron cloud," leaving the individual silver atoms which have lost one electron positively charged. It is the strong attraction between the negatively charged electron cloud and the positively charged silver atoms that binds the crystal together. Such "metallic bonding" is shown schematically in Figure 6b.

Figure 6a
All silver objects are made up of silver atoms arranged in a crystal lattice known as the "face centered cubic crystal," schematically illustrated here. While most of the chemical properties of silver are fixed by the properties of individual atoms, many of its physical properties result from its microcrystalline structure. (Drawn by Joan Levy.)

Negative Electron Cloud

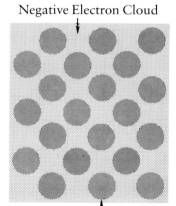

Positive Silver Ion

Figure 6b
Atoms in metallic silver are held together by metallic bonding, illustrated here. Upon crystallization, each silver atom gives up its outermost electron to form a negatively charged electron cloud of free electrons, in the process becoming positively charged and creating an attraction that binds the crystal together.

The free electrons within solid silver are responsible for several of its important qualities. For example, these electrons carry electrical current and therefore make silver a substance with high electrical conductivity (See Fig. 7.) They also provide the principal mechanism for thermal conductivity and for reflection of light.

The most immediately striking property of silver is its shiny, almost pure white appearance. White is generally considered not properly a color in itself but rather the superposition of all colors. A metal such as copper appears red because, although it is generally a good reflector of light, it does not reflect the color complement of red as well as it does other colors. Silver, on the other hand, reflects all colors of light well. Again, it is the free electrons that are principally responsible for this high reflectivity. Because they are free within the metal, it is difficult for them to absorb energy from the light waves; instead they reflect it. Objects made of silver and gold maintain their bright appearance because they do not oxidize in air. Most other metals become oxidized on their surfaces; the oxides tend to absorb light, dulling the surface.

In a metallic crystal, all atoms with the exception of those on the surface are surrounded by the same number and type of atoms. As a result, each atom feels the same forces. Consequently, if a whole plane of atoms "slips" a distance equal to the separation between atoms, very little is changed. (See Fig. 8.) This is exactly what happens when silver is worked by the smith. The combination of its particular crystal structure, which allows "slips" in several directions, and its metallic bonding makes silver particularly malleable.

This crystal structure of silver, so important to properties of the metal, is, however, seldom evident in finished silver artifacts such as those illustrated here. These articles are made not of a single crystal of silver but of many small crystals. The polycrystalline structure can be seen under an ordinary microscope if the surface of the silver is properly prepared. (See Fig. 9.) By studying what happens to the "grain structure" of these small crystals as silver is worked, we gain insight into why the silver hardens and becomes brittle as the smith shapes it under his hammer, and why annealing this silver in a furnace makes the metal again soft and malleable.

Figure 7
Silver was put to rather unusual use in the development of nuclear weapons during and after the Second World War. For this project, large powerful electromagnets were needed, and silver, as the best known conductor of electricity, was well suited to this use. Starting in 1942, fifteen thousand tons of silver were transferred from the U.S. Treasury's West Point depository and formed into electrical conductors from which magnet coils were then made. Shown here are some of these silver coils being dismantled before being returned to the Treasury. While most of the silver was returned soon after the war, some, including that shown here, was in use until 1969. (Photograph courtesy of Union Carbide/Oak Ridge Y-12 Plant.)

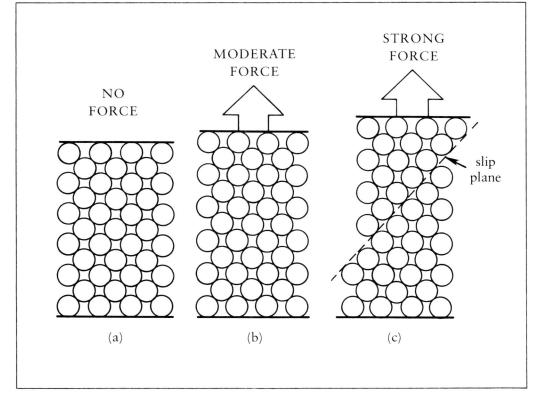

NO FORCE

MODERATE FORCE

STRONG FORCE

slip plane

(a)   (b)   (c)

Figure 8
Silver objects are made up of many small crystals of silver. If a moderate force is used to stretch silver, as shown in (b), the spacing between silver atoms changes only slightly and the silver will snap back to its original shape when released. If stronger force is applied (c), the silver crystals can be permanently deformed by the slipping of whole planes of silver atoms. It is through many such slips that silver is shaped under the metalsmith's hammer. The stresses created by the deformation of silver's microcrystalline structure cause hardening and embrittlement, which can be relieved by annealing in a furnace. (Drawn by Sandra Sicignaro.)

The grain structures of the crystals in a cast silver ingot are rather regular in shape, as Figure 9 demonstrates. Hammering deforms these crystals and creates internal stress that causes the silver to harden and become more brittle. However, heating silver makes the atoms mobile, and during the annealing process these atoms move again to form into more regularly shaped crystals, relieving the internal stress and making the metal once more soft and malleable. While a small amount of hammering may be beneficial because of the hardening it causes, repeated deformation of the crystals by the smith's hammer—for example in raising the sides of a tankard or a teapot—would result in extreme brittleness and cracking were not frequent annealing part of the process. In making the body of a tankard (13), the silver may be annealed dozens of times.

Pure cast silver is too soft to be practical for most uses. While the use of silver-copper alloys may originally have been a chance occurrence or simply due to some convenience associated with the refining process, it has long been known that an alloy of silver with about 10 percent copper is harder and more durable than pure silver. Benjamin Silliman, one of America's most famous nineteenth-century scientists, recognized this quality: "this alloy being harder and firmer than silver, [it] wears longer, and receives a more perfect impression in coinage. It is still very malleable and ductile."[7] Silliman goes on to note that the standard for British silver was 8.3 percent copper, while that for silver made in America was 10.8 percent copper. This difference in national standards is now being used as a clue to the national origin of pieces of undocumented silver.[8]

This silver-copper alloy has some disadvantages. One well-known inconvenience is that while silver does not oxidize in air, copper does, resulting in discoloration. This condition was cleverly avoided by the silversmith who, upon finishing an object, did a little "refining" of his own. Again in the words of Silliman, "the beauty of fine silver is given to the surface by boiling the silver in a copper vessel containing very dilute sulphuric acid which dissolves out the copper of the alloy and leaves the silver of dead white; it is then burnished and exhibits its proper beauty of color and lustre."[9] Hence the smith was able to make an object with the strength and hardness of the alloy but with the appearance of pure silver. Repeated polishing of old silver can remove this surface layer of pure silver, exposing a dark oxide "fire scale" which is not removed by the usual silver polishes. Fire scale is commonly seen on early American silverware.

A second problem with the silver-copper alloy, its tendency to embrittle with age, does not become apparent until hundreds of years after manufacture and consequently was unknown to early artisans. The hardening caused by the alloying of silver is similar to that caused by hammering; that is, it is caused by internal stress. In the case of alloying, this stress results from the fact that silver and copper atoms are different sizes. When a copper atom replaces a silver atom in its crystal structure, it does not quite "fit," causing stress and stress hardening. Over a period of centuries, the copper atoms migrate out to the surfaces of the individual crystals, resulting, partly through corrosion, in a weakening of the metal along these grain boundaries. This problem is of minor practical importance except to curators of ancient silver, and might be avoided by the choice of a different silver alloy.[10]

In summary, we see that William Badcock was indeed accurate when in 1679 he characterized silver as "a Mineral of that excellent Nature." Its special combination of qualities has made it accessible, workable under the existing technology of early metalsmiths, and suitable for the manufacturing of useful and durable wares. Most important, as the illustrations in this volume show, products made of silver have a remarkable and enduring beauty that has made silverware desirable for thousands of years.

Figure 9
As molten silver gradually cools and
solidifies, many small silver crystals
begin to form. As the so-
lidification approaches completion
these initially separate crystals join,
forming solid silver with a microcrystalline structure like that shown
in this photograph of a cast silver
ingot examined under a microscope. (Photograph by author.)

1. William Badcock, *A New Touchstone for Gold and Silver Wares* (1679; reprint, New York: Praeger Publishers, 1971), p. 7.
2. Anneliese Grunhaldt Sisco and Cyril Stanley Smith, trans. and ed., *Lazarus Ercker's Treatise on Ores and Assaying* (Chicago: University of Chicago Press, 1951), pp. xv-xix.
3. Cyril Stanley Smith, "Reflections on Technology and the Decorative Arts in the Nineteenth Century," in Ian M. G. Quimby and Polly Anne Earl, eds., *Technological Innovation and the Decorative Arts* (Charlottesville, Virginia: University of Virgina Press, 1974), pp. 1-64.
4. Benjamin Silliman, *Elements of Chemistry*, 2 vols., (New Haven, Connecticut: Hezekiah Howe, 1831), II, 362; and Pierre Joseph Macquer, *Elements of the Theory and Practice of Chemistry* (London: A. Millar and J. Nourse, 1758), pp. 346-347.
5. Victor Hanson, "The Curator's Dream Instrument," in *Application of Science in Examination of Works of Art* (Boston: Museum of Fine Arts, 1970), p. 27.
6. "Silver," *Harper's New Monthly Magazine* 58 (December 1879): 82.
7. Silliman, *Elements of Chemistry*, II, 343.
8. Hanson, "The Curator's Dream Instrument," pp. 24-27.
9. Silliman, *Elements of Chemistry*, II, 343.
10. Cyril Stanley Smith, "The Interpretation of Microstructures in Metallic Objects," in *Application of Science in Examination of Works of Art* (Boston: Museum of Fine Arts, 1965), pp. 35-37.

'You Shall Not Crucify Man on a Cross of Gold' Silver and Money in America

John P. Burnham

The hope of discovering silver and gold was among the many motivations of the explorers who charted the unknown vastness of the New World from the sixteenth century on. The Spanish achieved practical success in their search for El Dorado, the legendary kingdom said to be fabulously rich in precious metals and jewels. If the English, French, and Dutch did not find such wealth in North America, in the end the bounty of their colonies proved far greater and longer lasting than all the silver of New Spain.

The conquests of the Aztecs in Mexico by Hernando Cortés in 1521 and of the Incas in Peru by Francisco Pizarro in 1532 are the most famous of many exploits which yielded great treasures of silver and gold. The *conquistadores* of Peru must have felt their hazardous ventures well repaid when they viewed 1,300,000 ounces of gold in one heap, and when the king of this rich realm offered them a personal ransom of a roomful of gold ornaments. The loot was shipped home to Spain, but this supply was already exhausted by the 1540s. An even greater source of bullion supplanted the original booty. In 1545 an enormous mountain of silver was discovered at Potosí in Peru, the largest deposit ever found up to that time. Fabulously rich mines at Zacatecas and Guanajuato in Mexico, as well as lesser diggings in a hundred other places, were also found. The flow of gold, and especially silver, had a profound economic impact upon not only Spain but on the whole of western Europe.

Between 1521 and 1660 about 18,000 tons of silver and 200 tons of gold were officially imported into Spain from the New World. Compared to the quantities of precious metals produced today, these amounts seem insignificant. But in the sixteenth and seventeenth centuries, the economic consequences of this traffic for Europe were both significant and unsettling. The influx of bullion made Spain the richest and most powerful nation of the time. The great price inflation that occurred in Spain was transmitted to all the countries with whom Spain had commerce, as the Spanish kings repaid the foreign bankers who had financed their grandiose schemes and settled up the excess of Spain's imports over her exports. While inflation rates varied from place to place depending on individual circumstances, prices in general rose to up to 300 percent of what they had been in 1521.

The gold arrived at Spain in the form of ingots. The silver was usually coined, however, according to the Spanish standard. Mints were established at Mexico City in 1535, at Lima in 1565, at Potosí in 1574, and later at Cuzco, Bogota, Popayan, and Santiago de Chile. The Spanish population in New Spain was increasingly large. It was absurd to ship metal to the mother country to be coined and then shipped back to the colonies. At first neatly made (Fig. 10), the coins became crude lumps or "cobs" destined to be remelted and transformed into the coins of France, the Netherlands, and other countries. In 1732 a slight lowering in fineness of the silver coin was marked by the introduction at the Mexico City mint of an elegant new design featuring the pillars of Hercules (Fig. 11). These new pieces of eight or "pillar dollars" (and the fractional pieces of one half, one, two, and four reales) were "milled," or machine made, with a protective edge design as a guard against the fraud of clipping. The striking of "cobs," called *macuquinas,* continued at Potosí and other mints for varying lengths of time. In 1772 a further reduction of 1½ percent in the silver coinage was indicated by the substitution of coins bearing the bust of a Spanish monarch (Fig. 12) for the pillar type.

Substantial quantities of the product of the Spanish colonial mints found their way to the North American colonies as a consequence of normal trade. Along with coins from various European mints, they constituted what little coin circulated. In many of the colonies economic life was such that little, indeed, was needed, but the New England trade with Africa and the Caribbean—the so-called "triangular trade"—brought a motley supply of coins to the colonies which contributed to the decline of barter exchange, at least along the seaboard.

Figure 10
Mexico, Two Reales, Charles and Johanna, Mexico City Mint. An example of the first coinage struck in the Americas. Numismatic Collection, Yale University.

Figure 11
The familiar milled "pillar" type of
Spanish colonial coinage struck in
denominations of one half, one,
two, four, and eight reales.
Numismatic Collection, Yale University.

The presence of coins of differing weight and standard, some worn, some clipped, some counterfeit, created a confusing and unsatisfactory situation, especially in centers of trade such as the Massachusetts Bay Colony. In 1652 the Massachusetts General Court directed that a mint be established to produce silver coins (15) more acceptable than the various foreign coins then circulating. Shillings and their fractions were to be coined to the sterling standard, although of lesser weight. The Massachusetts silver coinage, including the famous "pine tree shilling," was struck from 1652 to 1682. In 1684 the coinage was spoken of as a thing of the past. Cecil Calvert, Lord Baltimore, had silver coins struck in England in 1658 for use in Maryland, but—with the exception of two small private issues by John Chalmers in Annapolis in 1783 and Standish Barry in Baltimore in 1790—no other silver coins were struck in North America until after the establishment of the United States Mint in 1792.

The shortage of coin was a constant complaint throughout colonial times. To a degree this dearth was alleviated by the issuance of paper money, a practice which Americans raised to a high art. The increasingly prosperous colonists, intent on raising their standard of living, wanted to buy more English and Continental goods than they could afford. For this they needed gold and silver, the base of the money supply. What their complaints about money shortage really meant was that they wanted to import more goods rather than keep a better money supply. Nonetheless, coin did circulate and was saved. And most was foreign, especially Spanish-American. Estate inventories in probate records indicate the great diversity of money holdings. The 1676 estate of one James Browne, perhaps of Salem, included

four pieces of gold (£15.12.6) as well as both English money (£19.12.6) and New England money (£1.11.6). The 1677 inventory of the worldly goods of Nathaniel Mighill of Salem recorded New England money valued at £23.4.0, "Old England" money of only £2.2.0, a single English guinea worth £1, and "ten fifty nine pieces of eight and six Rayalls" (Spanish reales) valued at £16.7.6. New England coins accounted for over 95 percent of the money in a 1678 estate in Essex County, Massachusetts, while a 1763 estate from the nearby town of Dorchester included only one New England shilling.

In a hoard of nearly 2,000 coins buried in about 1704 and uncovered at Castine, Maine, a witness reported that "the French money largely predominated; next, the old Spanish 'cob' dollars. . . . There were quite a number of Belgic and Portuguese coins. The most interesting of all were the Massachusetts pine-tree shillings and six-pences, all of the date 1652, and in number about twenty-five or thirty. I saw but two English coins, shillings—worn nearly smooth." An eighteenth-century hoard found at Windsor, New York, consisted of about 650 "Spanish dollars," an English crown, a French coin, and a Spanish gold medal. Not only in colonial times, but on into the nineteenth century, foreign coins would dominate American issues in circulation.

One of the blessings bestowed upon the newly independent United States of America was the sovereign right of coinage. Fierce debate was waged about the establishment of a new coinage, within the limits evolved in history: that money meant the precious metals silver and gold, and that the intrinsic value of a coin's metallic content should equal its monetary value. Thus the stage was set in the waning years of the eighteenth century for the monetary controversies and confusions of the nineteenth.

In the end, the basic recommendations of Thomas Jefferson were adopted. Jefferson had pointed to the Spanish dollar as the coin "most familiar of all to the mind of the people." He suggested that the dollar be made the basic monetary unit of the Republic, and that a decimal system be used. Jefferson's proposals were advanced by Alexander Hamilton as Secretary of the Treasury and embodied in the legislation finally passed by Congress in 1792. By the Coinage Act of 1792 the dollar was officially made the American unit of account (Fig. 13). The silver dollar was to contain

Figure 12
Mexico, Eight Reales, 1805,
Mexico City Mint.
The introduction of the "bust" type
in 1772 signaled a reduction in the
weight of Spanish colonial silver
coinage. These eight reales and their
fractions were a familiar part of the
circulating medium in the United
States in the nineteenth century.
Numismatic Collection, Yale University.

Figure 13
Obverse designs of all standard
silver dollars issued by the United
States.
Numismatic Collection, Yale University.

371.25 grains of pure silver, a figure arrived at by a sample test of Spanish dollars. A freshly struck piece of eight contained more silver, but naturally the coins circulating in the United States were considerably worn. The silver half dollar, quarter, dime, and half dime were also authorized, along with both copper coins and gold. It was not until 1794 that the first silver coins struck at the Philadelphia mint, the first public building erected by the United States, made their appearance.

The United States was placed on a bimetallic standard by the 1792 law. Free and unlimited coinage of both gold and silver was authorized. Gold and silver were both made full legal tender. The mint ratio for the two precious metals was specified at 15 to 1, i.e., an ounce of pure silver was worth 1/15 of an ounce of pure gold at the mint. If the market values of the two metals were always 15 to 1, there would be no difficulty in maintaining a bimetallic standard. But mint ratios and market ratios have never remained the same for long. History furnishes ample evidence that it is one thing to adopt bimetallism formally, and another thing to maintain it as a standard.

When a mint ratio of 15 to 1 is adopted, a government in effect agrees to exchange one ounce of gold for fifteen ounces of silver, and vice versa. While 15 to 1 was approximately the market ratio in 1792, it gradually rose in the 1790s to about 15.5 to 1. The mint was therefore overvaluing silver (or undervaluing gold). The shrewd trader could buy an ounce of gold at the mint for 15 ounces of silver, sell the gold in the market for 15.5 ounces of silver, and return to the mint to repeat the process, making a profit of half an ounce of silver for each round trip.

The saying "bad money drives out good money," a popular rendition of Gresham's Law, may be restated in this case as "money overvalued at the mint tends to drive out of circulation money undervalued at the mint." And so it was with the United States coinage. American gold coins were exported or hoarded. Curiously, the silver dollar was exported also, to the West Indies, where shiny new dollars could be exchanged for dull Spanish dollars which contained a small but profitable extra amount of silver. In 1804 the coinage of the gold eagle or ten dollar gold piece was suspended. In 1806 Secretary of State James Madison ordered the director of the mint not to coin anything larger

than the half dollar, thus suspending the striking of silver dollars.

In 1834 a new mint ratio of approximately 16 to 1 was adopted. Now gold was overvalued at the mint, and gold coins slowly began to replace silver, which was either hoarded or exported. Through this turmoil, as in earlier years, the country had to depend on foreign coins and other substitutes for a significant part of its money supply. It was not until 1857 that a law was passed repealing "all former acts authorizing the currency of foreign gold or silver coins, and declaring the same a legal tender in payment of debts."

The discovery of gold in California in 1848 vastly increased the supplies of gold available, lowering its price and making silver even more undervalued at the mint. Silver coins were increasingly removed from circulation to be sold abroad as bullion. In an effort to keep silver coins circulating, the weights of the half dollar, quarter, dime, and half dime were lowered almost 7 percent in 1853. As subsidiary coins, they were to be struck only for the account of the government and were made legal tender in amounts up to five dollars. The standard silver dollar, which had reappeared in 1840, continued to be coined at the old weight standard. The small quantities minted were largely melted by bullion dealers.

The consequences of the great discoveries of silver in Nevada and other Western territories from 1859 on were hidden among the economic events surrounding the Civil War: the introduction of federal paper money or "greenbacks" to finance the conflict, rapid inflation, and the suspension of specie (i.e., gold and silver) payments. The aftermath of the war saw a losing thirty-year battle on the part of debtor groups to maintain prices at high wartime levels. The postwar decline in prices was partly the result of a monetary policy aimed at contracting the paper currency and resuming specie payment. Even before the resumption of specie payment in 1879, inflationists—Populists and other debtors—had arrived at the view that higher price levels could be attained by injecting silver into the monetary system at an inflated ratio.

The price of silver remained at levels higher than that implied by the mint ratio until 1874, however. It did not pay to have silver coined into silver dollars when that silver was worth more than a dollar as bullion. No one noticed, there-

fore, the elimination of the standard silver dollar from the coins authorized to be struck by the Coinage Act of 1873. Although the 1873 law, which simplified the coinage, provided for the inclusion of a new coin, the trade dollar (19), silver was effectively demonetized. The metal could no longer be taken to the mint for coinage into a silver dollar of unlimited legal tender status; the trade dollar was legal tender only in amounts up to five dollars, as were the subsidiary coins. The trade dollar was intended for use in Chinese port cities by importers no longer willing to pay the premium demanded for Mexican dollars, the coins most favored by the Chinese. Its weight was 420 grains compared to 412½ grains for the standard silver dollar, and its pure silver content of 378 grains represented an advantage of three fourths of a grain over the Mexican coin.

Within three years the situation had changed. Silver had commenced on a long, and frequently precipitous, decline in price as a result of the discovery of new, immensely rich silver mines in Nevada and the adoption of the gold standard (and demonetization of silver) by western and southern European nations. The previously ignored provision of the 1873 act removing the standard silver dollar from the coinage list became known as the "Crime of '73." The Populists and other inflationists cried conspiracy and demanded the restoration of free and unlimited coinage of silver dollars at the old 16 to 1 ratio.

The best the silverites could obtain was the passage of the Bland-Allison Act in 1878 and the Sherman Silver Purchase Act in 1890, the first stipulating that the Treasury buy fixed amounts of silver monthly to be coined into standard silver dollars, and the second providing for the monthly purchase of silver to be used as backing for new issues of paper money in the form of silver certificates and treasury notes. Despite these efforts, the price of silver continued to fall, the money supply continued to decrease, and the decline in farm prices was not reversed.

As a curiosity it might be observed that in 1873 the United States mint had produced two silver dollar coins, both legal tender, both .900 fine, but one of 420 grains and the other of 412½ grains. In 1878 two silver dollar coins were again struck, but the heavier trade dollar was not legal tender, having been demonetized in 1876, while the lighter standard silver dollar had full legal tender status.

The panic of 1893 was brought about by the heavy redemption for gold of treasury notes issued under the Sherman Silver Purchase Act. When the gold reserve fell below the critical $100,000,000 minimum, Congress was forced to repeal the Silver Purchase Act. The repeal led to the climax of the free silver controversy in the election of 1896 when a mighty Populist upsurge brought William Jennings Bryan—with his stirring exhortation "You shall not crucify man on a cross of gold"—to the brink of the presidency. Bryan's second defeat, at the hands of William McKinley in 1900, was anticlimactic. On 14 March 1900 Congress had passed the Gold Standard Act, making the gold dollar the sole standard unit of value and formalizing the adoption of the gold standard which the country had effectively been on since the 1870s. Silver was dead as a dominant political issue as a consequence of new gold discoveries and the long-awaited reversal of the downward trend in prices that followed.

Except for a brief period during and immediately after World War I, the price of silver continued its decline. In 1932, during the depths of the Great Depression, it reached a low of 24.25 cents an ounce, a price at which the standard silver dollar was intrinsically worth less than 19 cents. (From the beginning in 1792, the standard silver dollar was defined as having 371.25 grains of pure silver. Thus for the intrinsic value of the metal to be equal to the monetary value of the coin, the price of a fine ounce of silver would have to be $1.293.)

In 1933 and 1934 the old combination of inflationist pressure and the interests of silver producers brought about new silver purchase legislation. Until the 1950s, the market price for silver continued to be below the price at which the government would purchase newly mined silver. Again, the enactments of Congress failed to achieve their goals of higher prices for silver.

Eventually the market accomplished what a century's legislation could not. Demand for silver for industrial uses—in photography, electrical equipment and electronics, brazing alloys and solder, and storage batteries—coupled with a tremendous increase in the use of silver for coinage to meet the needs of a vigorously growing economy, drove the price of silver up as new supplies failed to fill the gap. Now the pressure was from consumers of silver to keep the price down. To stretch out supplies, silver was eliminated from the coinage in 1965, although the half dollar continued to be 40 percent silver until 1970. The last silver coins minted to the old standard were dated 1964.

By means of its stockpile, augmented by the metal released from use in coins, the government was able to maintain the price of silver at $1.293 from 9 September 1963 through 18 May 1967. When the Treasury could no longer continue to hold down the market, the price of silver immediately rose to $1.60 an ounce, threatening the subsidiary silver coins still in circulation; at a value of more than $1.3824 an ounce, the silver in a dollar's worth of half dollars, quarters, or dimes was worth more than $1.00.

The result is plain to the eye. The new economics of silver as an industrial commodity, and the time-tested workings of Gresham's Law, have turned American coinage a lifeless dull gray characteristic of its new copper-nickel "sandwich" composition. Perhaps as poetic justice, the Treasury, left with a stock of silver dollars coined under the Bland-Allison Act of 1878 – 2.9 million of them minted at Carson City, Nevada – auctioned off hundreds of thousands of these coins at thirty dollars apiece. So ended a monetary tradition for silver stretching back over the millennia.

Bolles, Albert S. *Industrial History of the United States.* Norwich, Connecticut: The Henry Bill Publishing Company, 1881.

Buttrey, T. V., Jr., ed. *Coinage of the Americas.* New York: The American Numismatic Society, 1973.

Crosby, S. S. *The Early Coins of America.* Boston: Estes and Lauriat, 1878.

Friedman, Milton, and Schwartz, Anna J. *A Monetary History of the United States, 1857-1960.* Princeton, New Jersey: Princeton University Press, 1963.

Grunthal, Henry, and Sellschopp, Ernesto. *The Coinage of Peru.* Frankfort am Main: Numismatischer Verlag P. N. Schulten, 1978.

Nesmith, Robert. *The Coinage of the First Mint of the Americas at Mexico City, 1536-1572.* Numismatic Notes and Monographs, No. 131. New York: The American Numismatic Society, 1955.

Newman, Eric P., and Doty, R. G., eds. *Studies on Money in Early America.* New York: The American Numismatic Society, 1976.

Noe, Sydney P. *The Castine Deposit: An American Hoard.* Numismatic Notes and Monographs, No. 100. New York: The American Numismatic Society, 1942.

_____. *The New England and Willow Tree Coinages of Massachusetts.* Numismatic Notes and Monographs, No. 102. New York: The American Numismatic Society, 1943.

_____. *The Oak Tree Coinage of Massachusetts.* Numismatic Notes and Monographs, No. 110. New York: The American Numismatic Society, 1947.

_____. *The Pine Tree Coinage of Massachusetts.* Numismatic Notes and Monographs, No. 125. New York: The American Numismatic Society, 1952.

Porteous, John. *Coins in History.* New York: G. P. Putnam's Sons, 1969.

Stack, Norman. *United States Type Coins: An Illustrated History of the Federal Coinage.* New York: Stack's, 1977.

Vermeule, Cornelius. *Numismatic Art in America.* Cambridge, Massachusetts: The Belknap Press of Harvard University Press, 1971.

Wagner, Kip, and Taylor, L. B., Jr. *Pieces of Eight.* New York: E. P. Dutton & Co., Inc., 1966.

Willem, J. M. *The United States Trade Dollar – America's Only Unwanted, Unhonored Coin.* Racine, Wisconsin: Whitman Publishing Co., 1965.

'The Most Genteel of Any in the Mechanic Way'
The American Silversmith

Barbara McLean Ward

Since the Middle Ages the profession of the gold- or silver-smith has been regarded variously as an art, a craft, and an industry. The first English and European silversmiths who settled in the American colonies came from the artisan class. Through diligence, wise investments, and family connections many of these craftsmen made large fortunes as merchants and became leaders in their communities. During the nineteenth century, however, the metamorphosis of silversmithing from a craft to an industry reduced many of the producers of silver objects to the level of common laborers. Many others became general shopkeepers and retailers of the works of the large factories, making little or no silver themselves. Just before the turn of the century the Arts and Crafts movement, with its celebration of the noble qualities of handwork, began to help restore the independent American craftsman to an honorable and profitable position. Since 1940 the profession of metalsmithing has entered a new phase, gaining academic sanction and becoming a regular part of the curricula of colleges and universities throughout the United States. This trend may indicate that the silversmith is once more emerging as a creative artist whose work will again influence all of the arts.

In medieval times the silversmith was the principal innovator in the arts and "the most highly honoured of all artists . . . because he worked in the most precious metals."[1] Declining church patronage following the Reformation and the economic inflation of the sixteenth century, however, resulted in the gradual decline of the silversmith's status as an artist. The value of his works became little more than equal to the value of the gold and silver of which they were fashioned, and many examples of the silversmith's skill and workmanship were melted down when economic necessity required it. Increasingly the silversmith became an imitator of the stylistic innovations in the other arts, and by the seventeenth century he was regarded by his contemporaries as one of the mechanical artists.[2]

Although the court goldsmiths of seventeenth- and eighteenth-century Europe were still able to exercise considerable influence on the other arts through their privileged positions, the average silversmith designed for the marketplace. His trade consisted largely of interpreting the latest styles into utilitarian objects for the lesser nobility and the bourgeoisie.

This was particularly true in America, where there were no kings or aristocrats to serve as patrons of the arts. In a frontier region, where painters and artisans alike were treated as useful technicians, it is little wonder that the silversmith's art was valued principally for its technical excellence and practical utility. It has been suggested in nearly every book written about early American silver that objects made from the metal had a special appeal for Americans because they represented a practical way of using one's wealth and saving it as well. Since plate could easily be converted to cash, it represented money in the bank while displaying the tastefulness of its owner. And the latter point is crucial to the status of the silversmith in early American society, because the silversmith was able to act as an arbiter of taste in a provincial society eager to emulate the latest London styles. The colonial silversmith was regarded by his contemporaries merely as a useful craftsman, but his trade was the craft closest to the fine arts, being "Kindred to Sculpture and Statuary." In short, "his Employment [was] the most genteel of any in the Mechanic Way."[3]

It is very difficult to generalize about the social position of the eighteenth-century American silversmith, for as Carl Bridenbaugh has noted, "the fact is that craftsmen could be found in every rank from that of the privileged urban gentry all the way down to that of the white indentured servants and Negro slaves. They constituted a vertical, not a horizontal, section of colonial population."[4] However, judging from the available evidence it seems clear that above all the silversmith was expected to be an honest man of reputable family. Apprentices were not often taken from the lower classes of society, and advertisements like the one placed in the *New Jersey Journal* by Benjamin Williams of Elizabeth Town in 1788 usually requested boys who could be "well recommended."[5] In addition, the large amount of money needed to set up in business probably prevented the poorest men from becoming master craftsmen. Although conditions varied from one region to another, in seventeenth-century Boston many in the trade came from the leading families of the colony. When Jasper Danckaerts visited the city in 1680 he took it as a symbol of declining piety and incipient materialism that the sons of four clergymen were apprenticed to goldsmiths,[6] but this trend also indicates that Bostonians held the craft of silversmithing in high esteem.

The mystery surrounding the techniques of refining and working gold and silver contributed to both the respect accorded the honest craftsman and the suspicion of unknown craftsmen. Some silversmiths apparently made objects which were far below the sterling standard in quality, and several were convicted as counterfeiters.[7] It is probably significant that the first consumer protection laws in England were those passed in the year 1300 to specify the correct alloy to be used in the objects, commonly called plate, made by the goldsmith. Dishonest practices persisted, however, and when William Badcock wrote *A New Touchstone for Gold and Silver Wares* (London, 1679), he did so in an effort to teach buyers how to tell the difference between the proper alloys of gold and silver and their baser counterparts. A goldsmith himself, Badcock hoped "to procure an honest Reformation in the making of Gold and Silver Works . . . [that] they would truly be the Ornament and Riches of this Kingdom."[8] In the colonies, no assay offices existed to certify the quality of the metal in a given piece, and a man's touchmark was his personal pledge that the metal he used was of the proper alloy. His success in the business probably depended a great deal on his reputation for integrity and honest dealing.

In considering the place of the silversmith in the community, then, it is hard to overemphasize the importance of personal relationships between the silversmith and his patrons. As Brock Jobe has pointed out in his study of the Boston furniture industry of the early eighteenth century, much of a man's success in his trade came as the result of family connections or the recommendation of a former master.[9] Although family ties were no guarantee of success, many of the most prosperous silversmiths of early America appear to have been native sons or men with close links to the community, particularly in the larger northern cities of Boston, New York, and Philadelphia. Charles Le Roux of New York is an example of one of the many native craftsmen who achieved professional success and earned the trust of his community. Le Roux served the city in a number of public offices and was chosen by its Common Council to produce official presentation silver.[10] Immigrants who arrived in America at a young age, like Philip Syng, Jr., whose father was also a silversmith, seem to have fared better in business than their fathers. Philip, Jr., who came to America

from Ireland when he was only eleven years old, grew up in Philadelphia and married a local girl named Elizabeth Warner in 1730. A friend of Benjamin Franklin, he was a member of Franklin's intellectual circle, the Junto, as well as many other prominent organizations. It is interesting to note that when he retired and left his business to Richard Humphreys, Syng placed a notice in the newspaper recommending Humphreys "as a person qualified to serve [his former customers] on the best terms."[11] Many immigrants, however, are known only by a single advertisement and can not be connected with any surviving works. Whether these men served as journeymen for several years or quickly turned to other trades when they found the environment inhospitable to their ambitions is not known.

It is interesting that in the South, where settlements were few and most wealthy planters ordered their silver directly from England, fewer of the sons of prominent people were trained as silversmiths. This may be because in this region, where the wealthiest men were gentlemen landowners rather than merchants, the trades were held in generally lower esteem than they were in Pennsylvania, New York, and New England. As a result, a larger percentage of silversmiths were slaves and indentured servants. Master craftsmen often moved from one Southern town to the next seeking a sufficient market for their goods, and evidence suggests that only a very small number of these craftsmen were able to make a suitable living from silversmithing alone.[12]

The most accomplished masters of the craft were those who worked in cities, where the luxury market was large enough to bring them a substantial amount of business. The best of these urban craftsmen were responsible for turning out a large number of the pieces of silver which survive from colonial times. Although nearly any trained goldsmith could be trusted to make small items or to do repairs, important public commissions seem to have gone to the same craftsmen year after year. This pattern indicates that certain silversmiths were acknowledged by their communities as the leaders in their field.

Such master craftsmen probably employed a number of journeymen and apprentices. Although guilds for regulating the trades did not exist in the colonies as they had in the mother country, the first American silversmiths practiced

Figure 14
Workroom, silversmith's shop, ca. 1771. (From Denis Diderot, *Receuil de Planches* [Paris, 1771], vol 8.)

their craft in the traditional English manner and learned their trade through the apprenticeship system. Usually bound to a master for seven years, the young student began his training by performing menial tasks such as polishing finished objects, tending the forge, pumping the lathe, and drawing wire on the bench. Gradually he assumed more responsibility, and during the last years of his term he probably made whole objects entirely by himself.[13]

All plate produced in the shop was made under the supervision of the master craftsman and received his touchmark. In addition to his apprentices the master usually employed journeymen, or day laborers, who were often well-trained men with a full range of skills who lacked the financial means to set up their own shops. In America many journeymen were recent immigrants, and it appears that indentured servants and slaves also worked at silversmithing and the allied crafts. References to slaves in the trade indicate that a large percentage of the journeymen working in Charleston, South Carolina, during the eighteenth and early nineteenth centuries were enslaved blacks.[14] In 1784 John Le Telier advertised for the return of "A negro man named John Frances . . . by trade a goldsmith" who had run away from his shop.[15] Similar references make it clear that slave craftsmen worked in Philadelphia and New York as well as in the South.

Many of the journeymen working in America were specialists in a particular branch of the goldsmith's trade, such as chasing, engraving, or watchmaking. For instance, when ordering plate from England in 1698, William Fitzhugh of Virginia asked to "have no letters engraved upon them nor Coats of Arms, having a servant of my own, a singular good engraver, and so can save that money."[16] In 1760, John Paul Grimke advertised in the *South Carolina Gazette* that "having now a journeyman who is an extraordinary fine chaser, those who are inclined to have their old plate beautified, may have it chased in the newest taste at small expence."[17]

Little is known of the men who served as journeymen to the trade, apart from those who were employed as journeymen before going into business for themselves. Some others may have been those same men who appear so frequently in advertisements only to disappear within a few years—perhaps they found it impossible to make a living working independently and were forced to turn to day labor for their livelihood. In his book *Maryland Silversmiths*, J. Hall Pleasants studied a group of fourteen London-trained silversmiths who came to Baltimore as indentured servants between 1773 and 1775. Of these, not one worked as a master craftsman in the area after receiving his freedom.[18] In a highly competitive market there was scant hope for the foreigner with little or no capital.

Journeymen and apprentices worked alongside the master in most silversmiths' shops. When making an object to order, the silversmith usually received at least a portion of the metal needed for the piece from the customer. This silver was weighed and credited against the final cost of the finished plate. The silversmith determined the kind of object his customer desired and created an appropriate design. The first step in making the piece was to melt the scrap silver in a crucible and cast it into an ingot, or it could be cast into a disc of the size and thickness the silversmith wanted. An ingot would have to be flattened by hammering until it reached the desired thinness. During this process the metal hardened, and it was necessary to return it to the fire and anneal it several times to keep it workable. Once the silversmith had a sheet of silver he would raise it into a vessel using small hammers and stakes held fast in a vice (Fig. 14), (24). Cast pieces were soldered onto the body and ornament was added by chasing, embossing, or engraving.[19] Although there are no known representations of the interior of an early American silversmith's shop, European prints provide a reasonable approximation of the appearance of such an establishment. Because the seventeenth- and eighteenth-century silversmith was a retailer as well as a manufacturer, his shop was often divided into two parts, the workroom (Fig. 14) and the display area (Fig. 15). As mass-produced items became more readily available after 1840, many silversmiths became primarily retailers of silver objects, serving in much the same capacity as the commercial jeweler of today.

Figure 15
Display area, silversmith's shop, ca. 1771. (From Denis Diderot, *Receuil de Planches* [Paris, 1771], vol. 8.)

To some extent, even in the seventeenth century, every silversmith was a merchant. When retail merchandising or investment in land and shipping proved more lucrative than their craft, silversmiths often became full-time merchants and left the actual silversmithing to others. John Hull, for instance, became very prosperous as the result of his investments and his role as joint mintmaster for the colony of Massachusetts. He seems to have spent most of his time administering his many business ventures and serving the community in public office. Robert Sanderson, his partner, was probably responsible for the daily workings of their silversmith shop. Sanderson apparently felt comfortable and content as a craftsman, for he trained his three sons to follow him in the trade.[20] Edward Winslow (1669-1753), another well known early American silversmith, became a prominent public servant who lived to see his sons become prosperous local merchants. His portrait, painted by John Smibert about 1730 (Fig. 16), shows a humble man of means. In his early years Winslow produced some of the most magnificent of all American objects made in the baroque style, but by the end of his life his business activities and duties as Judge of the Inferior Court of Common Pleas for Massachusetts so consumed his time that when he died he owned only £4 worth of goldsmith's tools.[21]

The majority of silversmiths in cities and towns alike appear to have dabbled in a number of trades. The market for luxury objects was always somewhat limited, and even in cities such as Boston and Philadelphia it was necessary for men to supplement their incomes by diversifying their business activities. William Cowell of Boston and James Chalmers of Annapolis are just two of the many silversmiths who kept taverns, and one enterprising Maryland silversmith named John Inch plied several trades at once, as his advertisement indicates: "John Inch, Silver smith, Hereby gives notice, That he still carries on his Silversmith's and jeweller's Business, buys Gold and Silver, and keeps Tavern as formerly, and has provided himself with a very good House Painter and Glazier lately from London who shall work for any Person very reasonably. He also keeps good passage-boats, and has now of his own and others, Vessels that are fit to carry grain etc. to and from any part of Chesapeake-Bay he also has for sale, a convict-servant Woman's Time, lately imported, who is a good Stay-maker; a great quantity of Oakum, Ship Bread Delph and Stone ware of divers sorts, too tedious to mention."[22] Even well-known and prolific master craftsmen like Paul Revere branched out into other fields, making such items as false teeth and brass bells. Many silversmiths also added the watch- or clockmaker's trade to their business.

By the middle of the eighteenth century more and more prosperous silversmiths seem to have been content to encourage their sons to carry on in the family business. For many, the goldsmith's trade had brought self-respect and material comfort, advantages which they sought to pass on to their sons. Some of the best-known families of craftsmen include the Richardsons of Philadelphia; the Adamses of Alexandria, Virginia; the Galts of Williamsburg and Yorktown, Virginia; the Moods of Charleston, South Carolina; the Moultons, Reveres, and Burts of Massachusetts; and the Van Dycks and Le Rouxs of New York. That the profession of the goldsmith ceased to be an upwardly mobile one is not really surprising, for as the population of America increased, social mobility generally decreased and class lines tended to become more static. However, the sense of community was still strong and class divisions were probably not keenly felt.

During the first years of the nineteenth century the silversmith continued to function within his community very much as he had in the eighteenth and the growth and prosperity of the young republic were reflected in the large numbers of artisans, including even at this date a few women, who engaged in some branch of the silversmith's trade. By 1840 the discovery of the technique of electroplating had led to the rise of large companies which produced silverplate for mass consumption. Although these companies did not eliminate the individual craftsman from the market, they greatly reduced his importance. Increasingly, the roles of producer and retailer became divided. It was not unusual for craftsmen like Edward Moore and William Gale of New York to produce objects to be sold through big retail establishments such as Tiffany & Company. As John Langdon has described the situation in Canada: "Previously the buyer of silver negotiated directly with the maker, but in the second quarter of the nineteenth century there grew up an in-

Figure 16
John Smibert (1688-1751)
Edward Winslow (1669-1753)
Oil on canvas, 1730
Mabel Brady Garvan Collection
1935.153

termediary—the dealer—and the silversmith gradually, but surely, lost his identity as a craftsman known to the public and became a maker to the 'trade.'"[23]

As in the eighteenth century, many continued to ply several trades at once, and as the big companies grew to engulf the small craftsmen the latter adapted to the new circumstances. Many left the trade entirely, and those who did continue to work as silversmiths appear to have been primarily retailers and repairers after 1840. Although some companies maintained handcraftsmen to do specialized tasks such as chasing and engraving, factory workers began to be trained only in one small phase of silver production. By the end of the century the merger of many companies into large corporations such as the Gorham Manufacturing Company and International Silver Company further depersonalized the industry.

The handcraft tradition among the Indians of the American Southwest, however, began to flourish during this period. Because silver and gold were not available to the natives of North America until Europeans introduced the metals through trade and gifts, American Indians did not begin to produce silver objects themselves until the eighteenth century. Many small brooches of Iroquois and Seminole manufacture are known, and by the middle of the nineteenth century the craft was being practiced by the Plains tribes as well. The Navajo first learned silversmithing about 1860, and they in turn passed their knowledge on to the nearby Pueblo tribes. At first silversmithing was only a part-time occupation for these peoples, but as white visitors to the region began to be interested in the jewelry worn by the natives, local traders encouraged Navajo and Pueblo smiths to make large numbers of items for the tourist trade.

By the 1920s and 1930s numerous Indian men and women were working as full-time silversmiths to fulfill this new demand. When John Adair studied the people working in the trade in the 1940s he found that these craftsmen were respected by the other members of the tribe because they were able to make a substantial income from these endeavors. Working at simple forges with both handmade tools and tools provided by the traders (Fig. 17), these craftsmen made objects for other members of the tribe as well as for the tourist trade.[24] Although the pressure to produce quantities of jewelry reduced the quality of Navajo and Pueblo work in the 1950s, recent interest in returning to the earlier traditions has resulted in the revival of exquisite craftsmanship in the jewelry made by native Americans of the Southwest.

In the country as a whole the first indication of a major resurgence of self-consciously handcrafted silver came with the introduction of a special order line of handwrought silver articles by the Gorham Manufacturing Company in the late 1890s. Known by the trademark Martelé (after the French *Martelé,* "hammered"), these pieces were left with evidence of hammer marks in homage to the beauty of handwrought silver (53, 188). It was hoped that putting the worker back in touch with the creative process would reduce the dehumanizing nature of factory work.[25] The tenets of John Ruskin and William Morris were adopted with enthusiasm by Americans as Arts and Crafts societies proliferated during the first years of the twentieth century.

Many small firms dedicated to handcraftsmanship were established during this period. It is interesting to compare craftsmen of the Arts and Crafts period with their colonial predecessors. Although much more quantitative data is needed for both groups, some broad trends are apparent. First of all, in the early twentieth century there were fewer craftsmen working in proportion to the total population than had been the case in the eighteenth century. At least 20 percent of the craftspersons working independently at the turn of the century were born in Germany, Denmark, Sweden, Scotland, and England, and at least 22 percent were women. A new type of craftsperson, the hobbyist, is also evident at this time. Gentlemen and ladies took up the craft for the sheer fulfillment of creating something with their own hands. Perhaps the most significant difference between the silversmith of the Arts and Crafts period and his or her eighteenth-century counterpart is that the former made handcrafted silver out of choice, whereas the latter did so because there were no more efficient ways of working available to him. As the fervor of the Arts and Crafts movement began to wane during the First World War, however, the temptation to use modern manufacturing techniques often became too great for even the most dedicated silversmiths, and many firms turned to spinning and die stamping in an effort to make more objects at lower cost to the consumer.[26]

The economic difficulties of the 1930s, followed by the shortages of the war years, served to destroy many of the small shops which made fine handwrought silver, but some firms continued in operation for twenty or thirty more years and a few are still in business today. Since the Second World War, however, the great growth in the field has been not in the traditional craft area but rather in the realm of the academically trained artist-craftsperson.

This change has radically altered the nature of the silversmith's craft. The organization of the Society of North American Goldsmiths in 1969 is just one indication of the renewed vigor and increasing professional awareness in the field. Today most metalsmiths have received training in art schools and university art departments and many have master's degrees in the specialty. Since the early 1950s the number of programs in metalsmithing has increased to the point where nearly every large university in the United States offers such courses. Many of the most prominent of today's craftspeople hold teaching positions in these universities, a fact which allows them an artistic freedom in their work which is not possible in production work. Fully half, and possibly more, are women, and probably 50 percent concentrate their energy on the production of jewelry. Because of the investment in time and money which hollow ware requires, most modern silversmiths make such objects only on commission.

What has created the fundamental change in the craft in recent years is the acceptance of work in precious metals as a branch of sculpture. As one writer recently observed: "metal [work] has been . . . moving away from functional/decorative considerations to non-functional decorative approaches."[27] This freedom is most evident in jewelry, where pieces have become primarily studies in form. Experimentation with new techniques for manipulating metal has accelerated in the last few years, so much so that the late 1960s and early 1970s are coming to be known as the "technocraft" period in American metalsmithing. Without the restrictions of the ancient guilds and regulatory laws which have hampered contemporary silversmiths in some European countries, the American silversmith has been free to experiment not only with techniques but with interesting combinations of materials (58). Consolidation of these new ideas in the 1970s and a renewed stress on fine craftsmanship and careful finishing in the teaching of the skill are helping to increase the pride and validity of the profession in the world of contemporary art.[28]

Although contemporary shop practices are akin to those of the seventeenth century, the attitudes and values of the people practicing the art have changed significantly. Silversmiths still produce useful objects, but metalsmithing is more and more becoming an art for its own sake, independent of utilitarian considerations. The personal statement has replaced the functional purpose of the early American silversmith's work, as the craft returns to the status of an art.

Figure 17
Navajo Silversmith, ca. 1920.
Museum of New Mexico.

1. Hugh Honour, *Goldsmiths and Silversmiths* (New York: G. P. Putnam's Sons, 1971), p. 20.
2. Eva M. Link, *The Book of Silver*, trans. Francisca Garvie (New York: Praeger Publishers, 1973), p. 47.
3. R. Campbell, *The London Tradesman* (1747; reprint, Newton Abbot, England: David and Charles, 1969), pp. 141-142.
4. Carl Bridenbaugh, *The Colonial Craftsman* (Chicago: The University of Chicago Press, 1961), p. 156.
5. Carl M. Williams, *Silversmiths of New Jersey, 1700-1825* (Philadelphia: George S. MacManus Company, 1949), p. 56.
6. Bartlett Burleigh James and J. Franklin Jameson, eds., *Journal of Jasper Danckaerts, 1679-1680* (New York: Charles Scribner's Sons, 1913), pp. 274-275.
7. Kenneth Scott, *Counterfeiting in Colonial America* (New York: Oxford University Press, 1957), pp. 210-235.
8. William Badcock, *A New Touchstone for Gold and Silver Wares* (1674; reprint, New York: Praeger Publishers, 1971), p. 48.
9. Brock Jobe, "The Boston Furniture Industry, 1720-1740," in Walter Muir Whitehill, ed., *Boston Furniture of the Eighteenth Century* (Boston: The Colonial Society of Massachusetts, 1974), pp. 11-14.
10. Phoebe P. Prime, *Three Centuries of Historic Silver* (Philadelphia: Pennsylvania Society of the Colonial Dames of America, 1938), p. 52; and Kathryn C. Buhler, *Colonial Silversmiths, Masters and Apprentices* (Boston: Museum of Fine Arts, 1956), pp. 22-23.
11. Prime, *Three Centuries of Historic Silver*, pp. 94-97.
12. This information is gleaned from George Barton Cutten, *The Silversmiths of Virginia* (Richmond, Virginia: The Dietz Press, Incorporated, 1952); E. Milby Burton, *South Carolina Silversmiths, 1690-1800* (Charleston, South Carolina: The Charleston Museum, 1942); J. Hall Pleasants and Howard Sill, *Maryland Silversmiths, 1715-1830* (1930; reprint, Harrison, New York: Robert Alan Green, Publisher, 1972); and Jennifer Faulds Goldsborough, *Eighteenth- and Nineteenth-Century Maryland Silver* (Baltimore, Maryland: The Baltimore Museum of Art, 1975).
13. Martha Gandy Fales, *Joseph Richardson and Family, Philadelphia Silversmiths* (Middletown, Connecticut: Wesleyan University Press, 1974), pp. 62-67.
14. Burton, *South Carolina Silversmiths*, pp. 207-210.
15. Alfred Coxe Prime, comp., *The Arts and Crafts in Philadelphia, Maryland, and South Carolina* (The Walpole Society, 1929), p. 79.
16. "Letters of William Fitzhugh," *Virginia Magazine of History and Biography* 6, no. 1 (July 1898): 71.
17. Prime, *The Arts and Crafts in Philadelphia*, p. 64.
18. Pleasants and Sill, *Maryland Silversmiths*, pp. 278-281.
19. William deMatteo, *The Silversmith in Eighteenth-Century Williamsburg* (Williamsburg, Virginia: Colonial Williamsburg, 1961), *passim*.
20. Hermann Frederick Clarke, *John Hull, A Builder of the Bay Colony* (Portland, Maine: The Southworth-Anthoensen Press, 1940), pp. 113-114.
21. John Marshall Phillips, "Edward Winslow, Goldsmith, Sheriff, and Colonel," *Bulletin of the Associates in Fine Arts at Yale University* 6, no. 3 (June 1935): 45-46; and Helen Comstock, "Silver by Edward Winslow of Boston, 1669-1753," *Connoisseur* 108, no. 482 (December 1941): 205-209.
22. Prime, *The Arts and Crafts in Philadelphia*, p. 75.
23. John Emerson Langdon, *Canadian Silversmiths and Their Marks, 1667-1867* (Lunenberg, Vermont: Privately Printed by The Stinehour Press, 1960), p. xvi.
24. John Adair, *The Navajo and Pueblo Silversmiths* (Norman, Oklahoma: University of Oklahoma Press, 1944).
25. John S. Holbrook, *Silver for the Dining Room, Selected Periods* (Cambridge, Massachusetts: Printed for the Gorham Company by the University Press, 1912), pp. 112-119.
26. The American Federation of Arts, *American Art Annual*, vols. 17 (1920) and 27 (1930); Margaretha Gebelein Leighton, *George Christian Gebelein, Boston Silversmith, 1878-1945* (Boston: Privately Printed, 1976), pp. 107-109; and Sharon Darling, *Chicago Metalsmiths* (Chicago: Chicago Historical Society, 1977).
27. C. E. Licka, "The 1977 Metalsmith Exhibit: Historical Critique of Metalsmithing Developments," *Goldsmiths Journal* 3, no. 4 (August 1977): 2.
28. *Ibid.*, pp. 2-6; Robert Ebendorf, "The Art of Gold and Silversmithing," in *Precious Metals, The American Tradition in Gold and Silver* (Miami, Florida: Lowe Art Museum, University of Miami, 1976), p. 13; John Prip and Ronald Hayes Pearson, "The New American Craftsman: First Generation, Metals," *Craft Horizons* 26, no. 3 (June 1966): 29-31.

'From the Shop to the Manufactory' Silver and Industry, 1800-1970

Stephen K. Victor

Before the end of the eighteenth century, silversmiths began to adopt mechanical processes to supplement and substitute for certain handcrafting techniques. The use of mechanical and industrial processes would affect the manufacture of silver in several important ways between 1800 and the present. Both the style of silver objects and the patterns of consumption of silver goods would undergo major changes with the shift from shop to factory production. The development of factory production techniques would also transform the working methods and conditions of the silversmith.

Mechanization took place because of the benefits it could provide. For the silversmith, any reduction in the amount of labor or materials that go into a piece of silverware means a decrease in cost. Those savings result in greater profits for the maker or lower prices for the consumer and, in turn, a much wider use of silver goods. Provided quality is maintained, both the maker and user of silver objects stand to benefit from mechanization. Those benefits remained unquestioned for almost a century until an appreciation of the special virtues of handwrought silver appeared.[1]

The earliest mechanical advances introduced into silversmithing did not require the use of power sources other than manual effort and did not demand a shop organization beyond the traditional one of master, journeyman, and apprentice. After the early nineteenth century, the application of water or steam power became increasingly widespread as more powerful machines were put to use. As shops grew into large manufacturing concerns, the increase in the number of workers permitted the efficiency of specialization.

Some of the effects of technological development can be seen in the silver objects manufactured with the aid of new techniques. Indeed, the objects themselves are primary documents of the adaptation of these techniques, which revolutionized the way silver was both shaped and decorated, and gradually came to exert a strong influence on style and taste. While many of these processes were developed specifically for silver, techniques evolved for shaping and forming other metals were often equally applicable to this extremely malleable and ductile substance.

One of the earliest and most important innovations in silver manufacture was the production of flat sheets of silver by rolling (Figs. 18 and 19). Rolled sheets of silver were available in England by the middle of the eighteenth century.[2] The use of rolled sheet silver is apparent in this country by about 1790, but it may have been available as early as the 1730s.[3] The octagonal and cut-corner rectangular forms and smooth surfaces popular in the Queen Anne style of the early eighteenth century were more readily produced from sheets of silver than by raising from an ingot. Signs of construction by cutting and soldering rather than by raising can be seen, for example, in the octagonal pepper box (158) made by William Cowell, Sr., of Boston in about 1710-1720.

Other evidence suggests that the use of this new process spread quickly in America. Joseph Richardson of Philadelphia is involved in correspondence about "rowlers for a flating mill" in 1760; his comments indicate that he had used such a mill previously.[4] In 1789 the American Bullion and Refining Office advertised to sell "flatted metals," presumably sheets of silver and gold, to goldsmiths.[5]

Figure 18
(1) Stamping the trimmings; (2) safe where dies are kept; (3) rolling the plates. (From Randolph T. Percy, "The American at Work, IV: Among the Silver-Platers," *Appletons' Journal* 5, no. 31 [December 1878]: 483.)

FIG.1.

FIG.6.

FIG.4.

FIG.5.

A.

FIG.3. A B

FIG.2.

FIG.8.

FIG.7.

24

Figure 19
Steps in the manufacture of silver in the late nineteenth century: (1) melting; (2) flattening; (3) flatware blanks in two stages of manufacture; (4) roll for forming flatware; (5) flatware blank with handle formed; (6) drop pressing; (A) tin die for drop pressing spoon bowl; (7) polishing room; (8) pitcher formed of spun forms, die-rolled ornament, and cast handle. (From "The Manufacture of Silverware," *Scientific American* 36, no. 19 [12 May 1877]: 287.)

By the late eighteenth century forms were commonly produced by soldering pieces cut from thin sheet silver, a process equally well suited to the clean lines of the new neoclassical style (172). In addition to saving the time and effort of raising a form from an ingot, the cutting and soldering technique produced a smooth surface without planishing, the tedious hammering out of dents. Even for those forms still produced by raising, starting with a uniform blank of rolled silver rather than an ingot saved the silversmith considerable effort.

A technique closely related to roll-flattening of silver produced beading, pierced strips, and more complicated relief ornament (Fig. 18). Appearing in the late eighteenth century, beading and pierced galleries are characteristic of silver from the Philadelphia area (32). The frequency of beaded edging on Philadelphia silver of this period hints that a machine for producing such ornament was used. This "gadroon mill," as it was sometimes called, would have employed either a roller or a press to form beading and other ornament by pressing appropriately shaped dies onto a very thin sheet of silver. Charles F. Montgomery has suggested that pierced banding was made by a Philadelphia firm and sold to others in the same region, and there is evidence that the same company that was supplying sheet silver in 1789 was trying to purchase a piercing press.[6] It is not clear whether this press used rollers or was a stamping press. In either case it would have pressed shaped dies onto sheet silver; some such machine was probably in use in Philadelphia by that time.

Various kinds of mechanically produced banding and ornament are also found on silver of the late Federal or Empire period, in the characteristic neoclassical style of the time. The teapot by William Heyer (178), the presentation urn by Fletcher and Gardiner (73), and the inkstand by Harvey Lewis (177) are punctuated with stamped or rolled ornament. The types of ornamental banding found in this period include Greek key, egg and dart, lattice, leaves—laurel, oak, olive, or grape—and many other designs. Each of these patterns required a separate die or set of dies for pressing the ornament. Since very thin silver was customarily used for these trimmings, fine resolution of detail could be obtained, even with moderate pressure. The indentations behind the pattern were filled with silver solder to support

Figure 20
The spinner at work. (From "The Manufacture of Silverware," *Scientific American* 36, no. 19 [12 May 1877]: 290.)

the design in the thin metal.[7] The mills and probably the dies used in them were imported from England.[8]

The use of banding on silver and plated goods continued to increase all through the Victorian period, as may be seen in the Gorham water pitcher (49) and soup tureen (184) and in the tilting water set (52) made by Simpson, Hall, Miller, and Company.[9] These strips were not only decorative but functional; as we shall see below, decorative banding was used to hide joints in hollow ware formed in parts.

The shaping of curved silver forms by spinning on a lathe was another important innovation in silverware production. In spinning (Fig. 20), a circular blank of metal is held in a lathe against a wooden pattern or chuck. As the metal

CASTING

BURNISHING

PLATING

SATIN FINISHING

SOLDERING

Figure 21
Reed & Barton's silverplate works at Taunton, Massachusetts. Upper left, casting; upper right, burnishing; center, plating; lower left, satin finishing; lower right, soldering; upper vignette, silver-plated goods; lower vignette, the factory complex. (From "American Industries, No. 22: The Manufacture of Silver-Plated Ware," *Scientific American* 41, no. 19 [8 November 1879]: 287.)

turns, pressure is gradually applied to it with a burnisher, forcing the metal to conform to the shape of the wooden pattern. This technique was adopted quite early by manufacturers of Britannia ware; the date of its first use in the American silver industry is not known.[10] Since the pattern had to be removed after the piece was spun, spun forms were usually limited to simple, open-ended shapes.[11] No fluting or gadrooning was possible, since spinning demands a smooth circular path for the burnishing tool. In spite of these limitations, spinning was widely used because of the great ease of the process compared to raising by hammer. The use of a pattern yielded great uniformity, essential to an industrialized process. Closed shapes were often made by soldering together several spun pieces; the joints were hidden by decorative banding (Fig. 19),[12] a practice probably responsible for the horizontal emphasis of much Victorian silver. For example, the Gorham Renaissance revival water pitcher (**49**) and the Tiffany Etruscan pitchers (**182**) have bodies formed by spinning and have a definite horizontal feel.

Another new technique that rapidly produced dish-shaped forms was the pressing or stamping of metal with large dies (Fig. 19). The pressure was applied either gradually, by means of a screw, or suddenly, in a drop press. Forms made in this way need not be round and may be fluted or otherwise irregular.[13] Although stamping requires less labor than spinning, the machinery and dies used in stamping are quite expensive.[14] The process of stamping was used very early, perhaps as early as 1801, for forming the bowls of silver spoons.[15]

Rolling and stamping were used not only for shaping silver and forming decorative bands, but also for surface ornamentation. A shallow pattern could be applied rather easily to a flat sheet of silver, or to the base metal in the case of electroplate, by rolling; a pattern on a relief die was transferred to the flat metal as it rolled under the die (Fig. 18). By stamping a piece of silver with a series of dies of increasing depth, an imitation of repoussé work could also be accomplished by machine,[16] although the high cost of making dies seems to have prevented the widespread use of this kind of deep ornamentation. Drop stamping could also be used to impress a surface pattern, even on shaped metal.

Another kind of surface decoration produced by machine, one very popular on silver and silverplate in the last part of the nineteenth century, was the satin finish, a stipple or matte surface applied by a device consisting of rotating jointed steel wires (Fig. 21). As the object to be satin-finished was held against the moving wires, their ends struck the surface in rapid succession, producing a very fine stippling. In plated goods, the "finish" was applied before the plating. The contrast between the bright sheen of burnished silver and the matte surface of satin finish provides the interesting textural variety of much Victorian silver (**182**) and silverplate.

Yet another sort of surface ornament, often used in the same period, was engine turning or machine engraving (Fig. 22). Engine turning is a process by which a geometric pattern is scratched on the surface of a metal object; again, in the case of plated ware the design is incised before plating. The object to be engraved is attached to a device that moves it up and down and back and forth, following the pattern of a template, until a large number of lines are scratched by a stationary engraving tool. The lines may be straight or wavy depending on the form of the template. Reed & Barton sent their wares from their shop in Taunton, Massachusetts, to Boston for engine turning until they installed their own machine in about 1860.[17] With engine turning an overall engraved pattern is produced on the surface of an object with considerable precision and speed. Some engine turning is rather stiff, but the best of it yields complex patterns that add considerable life to the object. Sometimes engine turning was combined with hand engraving to produce more complex effects (**48**).

All of these methods of decoration used in the Victorian period, and later in the twentieth century, provided a substitute for the traditional forms of ornamentation applied by hand, such as engraving, chasing, and repoussé. The newer techniques required far less labor and yielded a highly ornamented form at a moderate price. They were used especially in conjunction with plated goods meant to be sold at low prices. The taste for an exuberance of ornament, indeed an emphasis on decoration often to the neglect of form, may be seen as a hallmark of late nineteenth-century American design and is undoubtedly related to the development of the mechanical processes of rolling, stamping, and engine turning to produce inexpensive ornament.

Figure 22
Engine turning. (From Randolph T. Percy, "The American at Work, IV: Among the Silver-Platers," *Appletons' Journal* 5, no. 31 [December 1878]: 489.)

The industry of electroplating metals with silver was established in the United States in the 1840s, soon after the initial development of the technique in England.[18] The process relies on an electric current to transfer atoms of silver from a solution to the object to be silver-plated. Most of the early electroplated ware in this country was made with Britannia metal as a base; thus it was natural for the Britannia companies, such as Reed & Barton (Fig. 21), to become the first major American producers of silver-plated ware. Indeed, these companies offered the same products either plated or unplated into the 1850s.[19] The techniques for spinning, stamping, and casting Britannia and silver were so similar that silver forms could be imitated rather easily in Britannia and hence in silver-plated wares. The cost of silver-plated goods was considerably lower than that of sterling, and the use of electroplate became widespread.[20] The lower cost of plated goods made them available to many who could never afford silver before. "Formerly the costliness of solid plate confined the luxury of a beautiful and well furnished table to the wealthy; but since the advent of electroplated ware, almost any one may possess needed articles of table furniture having the most elegant of modern designs and being equal in appearance to the solid silver ware."[21]

Although electroplated flatware was widely produced by the early 1850s, the increased labor costs and silver shortages accompanying the Civil War made silver-plated hollow ware a desirable and affordable commodity. Consumers were presumably pleased to have electroplated ware with "all the splendor and durability of the best plate, at about one-fourth the cost."[22] By 1859 United States production of plated ware had surpassed that of solid silver, and in 1869 about three times as much plated ware as solid, in dollar value, was produced.[23] Given the lower cost of individual items of plated ware, the larger production value indicates a prodigious use of electroplate—$8.14 million in 1869 when the population was about 39 million, or 21 cents worth of plated goods per person in a year when the best plated teaspoons cost about six cents.[24]

The history of silver manufacture is a history of increasing distribution and use of silver goods. In 1810, the value of total manufactures of gold and silver, including jewelry, was $1.07 million; by 1859 silver and plated ware production, excluding jewelry, reached $7.25 million; and in 1899, silver goods production was $26.11 million.[25] That growth has continued to the present, with some decline during the Depression; the industry produced $377.40 million worth of hollow and flat ware, including stainless, in 1972.[26]

Part of the increase in the use of silver in the later nineteenth century is undoubtedly due to the ready source of silver in the mines of the West. The great silver discoveries of the Comstock Lode and elsewhere were being exploited by the 1870s.[27] New sources of silver, new techniques of mining and refining, and the declining demand for silver as a basis for European monies all combined to lower the price of the metal. The traditional preciousness and scarcity of silver aided the growth of silverware consumption in the later nineteenth century. Lower silver prices encouraged those who previously could afford only plated goods to acquire tableware of more fashionable solid silver. To meet the enlarged demand for solid silver, factory methods were rapidly adopted, and silversmiths increasingly became silver manufacturers.[28] By 1899 the value of solid silverware produced in the United States again surpassed that of plated goods and remained ahead until after 1914.[29] Total production of silverware continued to grow, and by 1937 Americans manufactured and used about half the world production of silver goods.

Production and distribution on this scale would not have been possible with the limited manufacturing and marketing techniques of the colonial or Federal periods; the small population and the status of silver as a luxury item in the eighteenth century provided little or no incentive for the development of mass-production techniques. But with the burgeoning of both population and demand, silver manufacturers entered the realm of modern industrial production, with its characteristic large size, widespread use of power machinery, and extensive specialization.

A certain degree of specialization had existed in silversmiths' shops even in the colonial period, when journeymen and apprentices performed some of the more menial tasks. A larger shop could, of course, operate with more specialization than a smaller one. Certain early nineteenth-century firms employed many craftsmen and used them to perform specialized tasks. For example, by 1815 Fletcher and Gardiner had a shop or factory consisting of sixteen apprentices, probably four journeymen, and two burnishers.[30] The economic benefits of specialization had been known since the days of Adam Smith,[31] and the larger manufacturers had begun to take advantage of this knowledge by the middle of the nineteenth century. Reed & Barton's factory, producing Britannia and electroplated wares, had achieved a high degree of specialization before the Civil War. It had groups of fitters, solderers, polishers, platers, spinners, and burnishers, each with a foreman and separate working areas or rooms (Fig. 21).[32]

Certain manufacturers reaped the benefits of specialization by producing only a small range of silver objects. For example, when Jabez Gorham began manufacturing silverware in 1831, his production consisted largely of silver spoons and other small wares.[33] Thus a few workers could devote their energies to making a few items that had a large market. Another possible reason for specialized production like Gorham's was the fact that different types of machinery and tools are used for flatware than for hollow ware. By limiting production to flatware, Gorham was able to keep his investment down.

The adaptation of machinery to the production of silver goods meant that less skilled workers could be employed in some parts of the manufacturing process, although great skill was still needed in others. For example, a skilled die-sinker had to make the dies for stamping ornamental banding or for drop stamping spoons. Once the dies were made, however, a less skilled operator could run the rolling press or drop stamper to produce large quantities of a given item. The different skills and degrees of skill required for various operations also encouraged specialization within the factory, just as it had between masters and apprentices in the traditional silversmith's shop. By the 1870s, twelve distinct trades were exercised by the 450 employees of the Gorham factory, including flatware making, designing, die-cutting, pattern-making, stamping, molding, embossing, engraving, chasing, plating, burnishing, and polishing.[34] The differentiation and specialization of tasks encouraged manufacturers to hire women to perform certain tasks such as burnishing, engraving, and chasing. Women at Tiffany & Company's shop in the 1880s were paid the same wages as men but worked in a separate room.[35]

The cost of the increasingly complex and expensive machinery and dies and the diversity of skills needed to produce silver made ever larger firms advantageous. Expansion of some silver and electroplate manufacturing firms was possible through merger. The International Silver Company was formed through the merger of seventeen firms in 1898.[36] In 1869, 258 firms were engaged in silver and plate manufacture; by 1899 that number had declined to 169, to rise slightly in this century, to 179 in 1929 and 189 in 1972. Those same companies employed 5,050 persons in 1869, 12,205 in 1899, 15,735 in 1929, and 13,100 in 1972.[37] Thus the size of individual companies increased dramatically in the latter years of the nineteenth century to take advantage of the economies of scale, permitting them to acquire the best and most specialized machinery and to employ staffs of specialists.

The principal technological developments of the industry in the twentieth century have been in the direction of automation. Automatic buffing, polishing, and soldering machines were introduced at International Silver in the 1920s. Since these machines are set up to operate on certain shapes, their use has made the production of a smaller range of products advantageous. Plating is another area in which automation now plays an important part; racks of unplated objects hanging from a moving belt are carried from tank to tank where they are dipped, on command from a programmed control panel, in various cleaning and plating baths for certain predetermined times.[38]

The manufacturer derives no benefit from his large and specialized production unless his goods can be sold. The eighteenth-century American silversmith normally sold his goods at his own shop.[39] If a shop was to produce large quantities of a single item, a means of distributing those goods was needed. Thus, with the increase in the size of a manufacturer, one finds a corresponding development of marketing methods. At first Jabez Gorham sold most of his products either to peddlers or to retailers in Boston.[40] By the 1850s, many silver manufacturers were producing catalogues of their goods. Retailers could order by mail or by telegraph; orders came to the New England manufacturers from the Midwest and West.[41] The combination of catalogues and salesmen's visits to jewelers has remained the principal method of distribution; wholesalers are seldom used in the silverware industry and not extensively in the plated goods industry.[42]

The shift of silver production from "the . . . *shop* to . . . the *manufactory*"[43] over the last two hundred years is closely related to changes in the role of silver in American life, as well as to the evolution of style and taste in silver. The most striking development is the vastly increased consumption of silverware, amounting to a virtual democratization of silver. Silver maintained its lure as a precious metal while simultaneously becoming available to a broad public, as the discovery of massive new sources for the metal and new manufacturing techniques combined to produce less expensive wares. Many of those goods were not solid silver, of course, but silverplate; still, they had the appearance of the more expensive article. Since the late nineteenth century, the middle classes have been able to have a sense of the luxury or at least to create the image of the luxury of silver at a moderate cost.

Associated with the increased production and consumption of silver is the emergence of a new set of aesthetic principles based on the virtues of the machine-produced silver object. The techniques of mass production encouraged new attitudes toward ornament, the quality of surfaces, and standardization, influencing both style and taste. The increased emphasis on variety of ornament and surface texture described above is typical of the effect on design of the fresh possibilities introduced by machine techniques. In satisfying the new taste for ornament, silverware designers of the late nineteenth century drew their inspiration from a wide range of sources: "All beauty is akin. . . . All . . . accumulations of grace and beauty, may be useful to those whose business it is to cover with grace and beauty the tables of mankind. . . . All that ancient art, tradition, and literature have of elegant, grotesque, or curious, as well as all that modern life has to suggest of striking and novel—here you behold it, in brilliant silver and burnished gold."[44]

Standardization and the related quantity of production were held up as signs of the progress of the times, as commentators of the period belittled the small production of earlier silversmiths and the lack of uniformity of their work: "It is a literal truth that four thousand men, working in scattered shops by ancient methods, could not accomplish more than four hundred men who work under one roof and one direction, aided by modern machinery; nor could the ware hammered out by these scattered mechanics bear a moment's comparison with the uniformity of perfection produced by a well-regulated manufactory."[45] Although most of the changes accompanying industrialization eliminated the evidence of the craftsman's hand in the finished object, Americans of the Victorian age seemed little concerned; labor was being saved and greater quantities of goods were available to a greater number. The vision of the silversmith as a craftsman guided by his muse and his art seems not to have figured greatly in the nineteenth century's appreciation of beauty. The idealization of the craftsman gained currency only with the Arts and Crafts movement as the century drew to a close.

The mechanization of silver-making meant that the role of the machine constantly expanded, while that of the craftsman declined. One may bemoan the loss of craftsmanship in industrialization, but in doing so one must realize that without mechanical aids to production silver would have remained a perquisite of the very rich and played a much smaller part in American life.

1. The Martelé line of the Gorham Manufacturing Company (53) and the silver of the Arts and Crafts movement (54) are examples of that renewed appreciation. It is not clear whether these represent a reaction to the quality of industrial design or a willingness to pay for handwork as a sign of wealth.
2. R. Campbell, *The London Tradesman* (1747; reprint, Newton Abbot, England: David and Charles, 1969), pp. 141-142. English patents for rolling metals exist from the early eighteenth century, and rollers were used in the production of soldered plate by 1743 at Sheffield.
3. The inventory of Cesar Ghiselin listed a flatting mill in 1735. See Harold E. Gillingham, "Cesar Ghiselin," *The Pennsylvania Magazine of History and Biography* 57 (July 1933): 248.
4. Martha Gandy Fales, *Joseph Richardson and Family, Philadelphia Silversmiths* (Middletown, Connecticut: Wesleyan University Press, 1974), pp. 232, 239, 282-283.
5. *Pennsylvania Packet*, 23 October 1789, quoted in Alfred Coxe Prime, comp., *The Arts and Crafts of Philadelphia, Maryland, and South Carolina, Part II, 1786-1800* (1933; reprint, New York: Da Capo, 1969), p. 143.
6. Henry J. Kauffman, *The Colonial Silversmith* (Camden, New Jersey: Thomas Nelson Inc., 1969), p. 99, holds beaded edges to be a "Philadelphia bench-mark." Montgomery, in Charles F. Montgomery and Patricia E. Kane, eds., *American Art, 1750-1800: Towards Independence* (Boston: New York Graphic Society, 1976), p. 56, finds pierced galleries limited to Philadelphia, Wilmington, Baltimore, and Annapolis; the advertisement for a piercing press appeared in the *Pennsylvania Packet*, 23 October 1789, quoted in Prime, *Arts and Crafts*, p. 143.
7. Donald L. Fennimore, "Elegant Patterns of Uncommon Good Taste: Domestic Silver by Thomas Fletcher and Sidney Gardiner" (master's dissertation, University of Delaware, 1971), p. 41.
8. *Columbian Centinel* (Boston), 25 December 1805, cited in Fennimore, "Elegant Patterns," p. 39.
9. "The Manufacture of Silverware," *Scientific American* 36, no. 19 (12 May 1877): 290, reports that Tiffany & Company made ornamental banding by rolling strips of silver between engraved rolls. No mention is made of filling with solder in this article, perhaps because thicker strips could be rolled with the heavier machinery of the Victorian period.
10. Britannia is a tin alloy better adapted to making thin sheets and to spinning than pewter, to which it is similar. The Taunton Britannia Company spun its forms as early as 1832, according to George S. Gibb, *The Whitesmiths of Taunton* (Cambridge, Massachusetts: Harvard University Press, 1943), p. 72. The technique is readily adaptable to silver because of its great ductility. Gorham Manufacturing Company's use of spinning lathes occasioned no notice as a novelty in 1868; see "Silver and Silver Plate," *Harper's New Monthly Magazine* 37, no. 220 (September 1868): 444.
11. A sectional chuck that collapsed for removal from a closed form was developed in the 1870s. See Gibb, *Whitesmiths*, p. 261.
12. "The Manufacture of Silverware," p. 290.
13. The screw press technique was used by Babbitt & Crossman for forming Britannia in 1827; see Gibb, *Whitesmiths*, pp. 31-32. Drop forming was established by the same company in 1829; *ibid.*, pp. 40-41.
14. Dorothy T. and H. Ivan Rainwater, *American Silverplate* (Nashville, Tennessee: Thomas Nelson Inc.; Hanover, Pennsylvania: Everybodys Press, 1968), p. 39. See also Andrew Ure, *Dictionary of Arts, Manufactures, and Mines* (New York: D. Appleton & Company, 1842), p. 1,007.

15. Deborah Dependahl Waters, "From Pure Coin, The Manufacture of American Silver Flatware," in Ian M. G. Quimby, ed., *Winterthur Portfolio 12* (Winterthur, Delaware: The Henry Francis du Pont Winterthur Museum, 1977), pp. 27-29.

16. Randolph T. Percy, "The American at Work, IV: Among the Silver-Platers," *Appletons' Journal* 5, no. 31 (December 1878): 486.

17. Gibb, *Whitesmiths*, p. 131.

18. Experiments were begun by J. O. Mead in Philadelphia in 1837. Mead came to Hartford and established Rogers & Mead in 1845; the partnership dissolved, Mead reestablished his business in Philadelphia, and the Rogers Brothers of Hartford became leading producers of electroplate. See Edmund P. Hogan, *An American Heritage: A Book about the International Silver Company* (Meriden, Connecticut: International Silver Company, 1977), pp. 32-41, and Gibb, *Whitesmiths*, pp. 126-127.

19. Gibb, *Whitesmiths*, pp. 129-131; see also Nancy Goyne (Evans), "Britannia in America: The Introduction of a New Alloy and a New Industry," in Milo Naeve, ed., *Winterthur Portfolio II* (Winterthur, Delaware: The Henry Francis du Pont Winterthur Museum, 1965), pp. 160-196.

20. By 1859 the value of U.S. production of plated ware surpassed that of solid silver and remained higher (except for the period 1899-1919) at least until 1937, according to the Census of Manufactures, as summarized in tables in United States Tariff Commission, *Silverware, Solid and Plated* (Washington, D.C.: United States Government Printing Office, 1940), pp. 32-33, 48-49. Since plated goods are considerably cheaper than solid, these figures based on value alone indicate that the production of plated ware, in terms of numbers of objects, far surpassed that of solid goods. More recent statistics for the relative production of solid and plated wares are unavailable, because after 1929 the Census of Manufactures combined the plated and solid classifications.

21. "American Industries, No. 22: The Manufacture of Silver-plated Ware," *Scientific American* 41, no. 19 (8 November 1879): 296.

22. "Silver and Silver Plate," p. 445.

23. U.S. Tariff Commission, *Silverware*, tables, pp. 32, 48.

24. *Ibid.*, table, p. 48; United States Bureau of the Census, *Historical Statistics of the United States, Colonial Times to 1970* (Washington, D.C.: United States Government Printing Office, 1975), part 1, p. 8; for the price of spoons see Noel D. Turner, *American Silver Flatware, 1837-1910* (South Brunswick and New York: A. S. Barnes, 1972), p. 45.

25. Tench Coxe, *A Statement of the Arts and Manufactures of the United States of America for the Year 1810* (Philadelphia: A. Cornman, Junr., 1814), p. 14; U.S. Tariff Commission, *Silverware*, tables, pp. 32, 48.

26. United States Bureau of the Census, *Census of Manufactures, 1972, Subject Series: General Summary* (Washington, D.C.: United States Government Printing Office, 1975), p. 1-50.

27. U.S. Bureau of the Census, *Historical Statistics*, part 1, p. 606; T. H. Watkins, *Gold and Silver in the West: The Illustrated History of an American Dream* (New York: Bonanza, 1971), pp. 79-80, 98, 164-167.

28. Gibb, *Whitesmiths*, pp. 213-215.

29. U.S. Tariff Commission, *Silverware*, tables, pp. 32, 48.

30. Fennimore, "Elegant Patterns," p. 43.

31. Adam Smith, *An Inquiry into the Nature and Causes of the Wealth of Nations*, ed. Edwin Cannan (New York: Modern Library, 1937), pp. 4-5.

32. Gibb, *Whitesmiths*, pp. 150-151.

33. J. D. Van Slyck, *Representatives of New England: Manufacturers* (Boston: Van Slyck & Co., 1879), p. 251.

34. *Ibid.*, pp. 254-255; "Silver and Silver Plate," p. 443.

35. "How Skilled Work Remunerates Women: In Silversmiths' Shops," *Harper's Bazaar* 16, no. 33 (18 August 1883): 514.

36. Hogan, *An American Heritage*, p. 43.

37. U.S. Tariff Commission, *Silverware*, tables, pp. 32, 48; U.S. Bureau of the Census, *Census of Manufactures, 1972*, p. 1-50.

38. This automatic transport and immersion system was adopted at International Silver in 1957.

39. Martha Gandy Fales, *Early American Silver* (New York: E. P. Dutton and Company, 1972), pp. 207-212.

40. Van Slyck, *Representatives*, p. 250.

41. Rainwater and Rainwater, *American Silverplate*, pp. 62-63.

42. U.S. Tariff Commission, *Silverware*, pp. 62-63.

43. "Silver and Silver Plate," p. 436.

44. *Ibid.*, p. 443.

45. *Ibid.*, p. 436.

'An Handsome Cupboard of Plate'
The Role of Silver in American Life

Gerald W. R. Ward

If you ask most people what they think of silver, their response is liable to include some mention of the fact that silver is a nuisance to keep clean. Keeping silver free from tarnish is indeed a time-consuming task, despite the claims made through the years by manufacturers of silver polish (Fig. 23). Leaving aside this generally shared dislike of silver polishing (which may be, incidentally, one reason why silver is not as popular in these servantless days), it is possible to arrive at a few tentative conclusions concerning more important aspects of the role of silver in American life over the past three centuries.

It seems clear that the basic role of silver has changed remarkably little since the seventeenth century; it is still used to mark important occasions in life from the cradle to the grave, and its ownership still connotes a certain standard of financial success and social pretension. The major change which seems to have taken place has been not a shift in attitudes toward silver, but rather a general lessening in the intensity of meaning behind those same attitudes. Silver objects of the past, reserved for the very few and made by skilled craftsmen who were among the leaders of society, carried a greater cachet and fascination in their own time than silver has commanded since the middle of the nineteenth century. Easily convertible into cash and recoverable when stolen, silver objects in the colonial period also had an important economic role which has largely dissipated, although speculation in silver in bullion form continues. In the following few pages, some of these elements of continuity and change in the place of silver in our society will be explored.

In the colonial period, the ownership of silver objects was clearly an important indication of social status, and their display was an ostentatious means of communicating the owner's wealth and position in the world. The power of silver in this regard was well established in English tradition, in both official and domestic life. For example, English ambassadors of the early eighteenth century were encouraged to spend approximately £3,000 on silver plate, so that they might entertain in a fashion suitable to a representative of the crown.[1] On the domestic level, a similar attitude prevailed. Samuel Pepys of London, writing in 1664, noted in his diary after a dinner party that his guests "eyed mightily my great cupboard of plate, I this day putting my two

Figure 23
Advertisement for silver polish.
(From *The Jewelers' Circular and Horological Review* 38, no. 23 [5 July 1899]: 46.)

flaggons upon my table; and indeed it is a fine sight, and better than ever I did hope to see my owne."[2] Throughout his diary, Pepys makes numerous references to his "very handsome cupboard of plate," a phrase which also appears in the oft-quoted letter written in 1688 by William Fitzhugh of Virginia: "I esteem it as well politic as reputable to furnish myself with an handsome cupboard of plate which gives myself the present use and credit, is a sure friend at a dead lift without much loss or is a certain portion for a Child after my decease."[3] Such an attitude was still prevalent a century later. After a visit to the Connecticut mansion of Colonel Wyllys in 1791, Mrs. Anstis Lee recalled that she "had never seen so much silver service and it was regarded as an evidence of wealth and family."[4]

Wealth *and* family—in other words, silver communicated more about the owner than merely his or her financial success. Sometimes a specific object seemed to have connotations which are now lost to us. What did it mean, for example, when Samuel Sewall of Boston in 1728 gave his sister-in-law "a Silver Cup with one ear, weighing about 3 ounces and 12 grains," commenting that "a Minister's Wife . . . ought not to be without such a one"?[5] In all likelihood, the ownership of such an object conveyed something of what the Sterling Silversmiths Guild of America would have us believe the ownership of silver has *always* signified, namely "wealth, prosperity, purity, happiness, temporal and spiritual well-being," to say nothing of "propriety, of subdued richness, of beauty, [and] of faultless taste."[6] In a recent advertisement evocative of the seventeenth-century attitude of Pepys and Fitzhugh, the Guild stated that "only sterling puts you in a class by yourself. It's a subtle touch of elegance that tells the rest of the world where you're going (or that you've arrived). Sterling reflects your success and the pride you take in your home."[7] Although such an advertisement is self-serving and overstates the significance of silver in the contemporary world, where there are so many other ways of displaying one's status and wealth, it has an element of truth and serves to illustrate the relative lack of change in the attitude toward silver in the home over the past three and a half centuries.

Although silver's meaning may be percieved in much the same way, its role as social barometer and status symbol has undeniably diminished. One reason for this may be that fear of theft has largely eliminated the practice of openly displaying silver on cupboards, tea tables, or sideboards which was prevalent up through the nineteenth century. The impact of silver, both visual and social, was undoubtedly heightened by this custom, especially in the seventeenth century, when the cupboard (77-84) formed the focal point of the home's main living space, or in the late nineteenth century, when massive sideboards groaned not only with the latest silver, but with the family's accumulated treasures as well. Unfortunately, many families in this century of necessity keep their silver stored away or locked in a bank vault.

Another key to the relatively diminished place of silver in modern life is the widespread ownership of silver, and especially silver-plated goods, in comparison with the colonial period. It has been estimated that only about 5 percent of the population owned silver in any quantity during the seventeenth and eighteenth centuries, and this limited ownership of the precious metal undoubtedly accounted for a great deal of its allure.[8] With the opening of the great silver mines in the American West in the 1850s, and the arrival of electroplating techniques in this country at about the same time, the ownership of silver became much more commonplace. By 1868 it could be stated that "there is more solid silver plate owned in the United States than in any other country of the world. . . . There are few families among us so poor as not to have a few ounces of silver plate, and forlorn indeed must be the bride who does not receive upon her wedding-day some article made of this beautiful metal."[9]

The manufacture of vast quantities of silver-plated goods also had a tremendous impact on the meaning of silver. In the years before such companies as Reed & Barton, the Meriden Britannia Company, and the Rogers Brothers Company began their extensive production of silver-plated hollow ware and flatware, "the costliness of solid plate confined the luxury of a beautiful and well furnished table to the wealthy; but since the advent of electroplated ware, almost anyone may possess needed articles of table furniture having the most elegant of modern designs and being equal in appearance to the solid silver ware."[10] In fact, *The Silver Standard* of 1912 reported that in a survey of over two thousand homes conducted by the *Hoard's Dairyman*, described as "one of the leading agricultural publications in the country," 79.5 percent of those interviewed said they owned "Rogers Bros. Silverware." Whether this particular poll has any validity is questionable, but there is no doubt that the abundance of silver, its relatively low cost, and the rise of a large silver and silver-plating industry centered in New England took silver out of the province of the few and made it accessible to the many. This nearly universal ownership of silver can be considered as one element of the material abundance which led the historian David Potter to characterize Americans as a "people of plenty."

Beyond its role as a status symbol, silver has long been used to lend dignity to the rituals of everyday life and to add significance to various communal events, be they secular or religious. The use of silver—the "gift metal" as it has often been called—was particularly prevalent in the domestic life of the Dutch in colonial New York, who exchanged silver presents at births, christenings, engagements, weddings, birthdays, anniversaries, holidays (of which there were eight or more every year), and deaths.[11] Silver objects played an important role in the ritual of serving tea in the eighteenth century (85-92), and an equally important role at meals in every period. A writer for *Harper's New Monthly* noted in 1868, for example, that silver should be used for dining, because "it is a duty we owe ourselves and one another to glorify and refine eating and drinking, so as to place an infinite distance between us and the brutes, even at the moment when we are enjoying a pleasure which we have in common with them."[12] (It is perhaps worth noting that silver chamber pots and bidets also exist, perhaps for the same reason.)[13] Silver has been used to make hundreds of different small forms, such as snuff boxes, tobacco boxes, patch boxes, boatswain's whistles, toys, inkstands, thimbles, hooks, wine funnels, coffin plates, bells, napkin rings, bottle tickets, mustard pots, nutmeg graters, pipe lighters, snuffers, strainers, and toast racks—in addition to the larger items of the tea and dining table. The choice of silver for these small objects gave them a special stature that the same forms in pewter, brass, or some other material lacked.

In 1651, the Massachusetts General Court expressed its "utter detestation and dislike, that men or women of mean condition should take upon them the garb of gentlemen, by wearing gold or silver lace, or buttons, or points at their knees, or to walk in great boots, or women of the same rank to wear silk or tiffany hoods or scarves which, though allowable to persons of greater estates or more liberal education, yet we cannot but judge it intolerable in persons of such like condition."[14] This remarkable piece of sumptuary legislation is an early indication of the ubiquitous use of silver for objects of personal adornment, such as buttons, buckles (36), pins (109), and necklaces (60, 196), throughout the last three centuries. Native American silversmiths, in fact, fashioned silver jewelry (112-114) to the virtual exclusion of other forms.

It has long been traditional to use silver for presentation pieces awarded to individuals for acts of heroism (74), superior athletic achievement (75, 190), deeds of military or civic importance (69, 73), or for nearly any conceivable reason or on any possible occasion. The supreme (or at least the largest) presentation piece made in this country may well be the enormous loving cup made by the Gorham Manufacturing Company in 1899 for Admiral George Dewey, "the Hero of Manila." The raw material for this incredible object (Fig. 24) was provided by 70,000 dimes contributed by people from all over the country, and the design was supplied by William C. Codman. The cup stands some 8′4″ high and abounds with nationalistic symbols, including a portrait medallion of Dewey himself.[15] Although different from the Tyng cup (69) in scale and style, it shares the same underlying spirit.

Figure 24
Loving Cup, Providence, Rhode Island, 1899
Designed by William C. Codman (1839-1921)
Gorham Manufacturing Company
Chicago Historical Society, bequest of George Goodwin Dewey

Figure 25
Torah bells, New York, 1772
Myer Myers (1723-1795)
Kahal Kadosh Mikveh Israel in the
City of Philadelphia

Silver has also played a central part in the rituals of the major religious faiths in America. Different faiths use different forms (61-68) to conduct these rituals, but the use of silver has been widespread among those congregations that could afford it. In the Catholic Church, the theory of transubstantiation accounts for the use of silver and gold liturgical vessels; only vessels of precious metal were considered appropriate for receiving the body and blood of Christ. This theory is not part of the Protestant or Jewish faiths, yet both churches and synagogues have long used silver objects in their ceremonies, and it is clear that objects such as the torah bells, or *rimonim*, made by Myer Myers for the Congregation Mikveh Israel of the city of Philadelphia (Fig. 25) hold great meaning. The diary of Samuel Sewall provides several clues to the special connotations silver objects had among Congregationalists in the early eighteenth century. In 1708, Sewall records that Thomas Chiever, a Boston schoolmaster, drew on Psalm 66 in encouraging him to bear with fortitude "the Afflictions of God's people, [for] God by them did as a Goldsmith, Knock, knock, knock; knock, knock, knock, to finish the plate; It was to perfect them not to punish them." Six years later, Sewall's notes on a sermon he heard in Portsmouth, New Hampshire, were as follows: "Christians of the greatest excellency are compar'd to vessels of Gold. Are pure, precious, will endure the Fire. Are fill'd with all the Graces of God's Spirit. Christians that do not excell are compar'd to Silver; persons of Lesser piety, though truly piety. Use. Labour to be Vessels of Gold, or at least of Silver."[16] As this passage indicates, the purity and perfection of silver clearly have had strong symbolic meaning for the major religious faiths. This tradition continues today; some of the most ambitious works undertaken by modern silversmiths are works commissioned by churches.

One aspect of silver that has appealed to people over the centuries is its ability to give a sense of permanence and continuity. Modern advertising emphasizes that "the fine Sterling Silver Tableware you buy to-day will not only glorify your own home but will become a lasting symbol to future generations of your good taste and love for worthwhile possessions."[17] Silver objects often become a family's most treasured possessions, handed down from generation to generation. The will of the wealthy Elizabeth Curwen of Salem, made 23 December 1717, specified the following distribution of her silver:

TO	OBJECT
Son Henry Gibbs	*Great Silver Tankard which his grandfather Sir Henry Gibbs sent me as a present; Great Silver Salt sellar*
Grandson Henry Gibbs by my son Robert	*Silver sugar box which his great-grandfather Sir Henry Gibbs sent me also as a present*
Grandson Henry Gibbs by my son Henry	*my least Silver Salt Cellar*
Grandson Jona. Curwen	*silver scallop & basin*
Grandson Sam. Curwen	*lesser Tankard & lesser salver*
Grandson George Curwen	*Great silver salver*
Granddaughter Mary Gibbs	*silver caudle cup*
Granddaughter Mary Gibbs	*silver sucking bottle*
Granddaughter Margaret Gibbs	*silver mustard pot & silver knobbed spoon*
Granddaughter Mehitable Gibbs	*least silver porringer & two silver knobbed spoons*
Granddaughter Elizabeth Lindall	*silver Goblett cup & my biggest silver porringer*
Granddaughter Mary Lindall	*Scallopt Silver Cup with a foot to it & my lesser silver porringer.*[18]

The descent of a silver bowl by Bartholomew Le Roux (**142**) through eight generations of the same family is recorded on the object itself. Made for Joseph and Sarah Wardel of New Jersey, who were married in 1696, this bowl was handed down to their daughter Sarah, and to seven other Sarahs down to "Sarah McCalmont Lewisson, great great great great great great granddaughter of Joseph and Sarah Wardel, Boston 1904."

As the interest in collecting antique American silver grew in the years following the Centennial, much old family silver, such as the Le Roux bowl, found its way into private collections and museums. John H. Buck's *Old Plate*, a study published by the Gorham Company in 1888, and the 1906 exhibition of early American silver at the Museum of Fine Arts in Boston were pioneering ventures in a continuing series of publications and museum exhibitions which stimulated the collecting and study of colonial silver. Francis P. Garvan (Fig. 26), shown with his two-handled covered cup made by Edward Winslow of Boston about 1710-1715, was in the vanguard of collectors who amassed their treasures

Figure 26
Augustus Vincent Tack (1870-1935)
Francis P. Garvan (1875-1937)
Oil on canvas, ca. 1930
Mrs. Francis P. Garvan

during the first few decades of this century, as interest in antique silver intensified. The demand for old silver, of course, also produced a good many forgeries, particularly of the work of Paul Revere. In the last decade, there has been a renewed interest in nineteenth- and twentieth-century silver, and collecting silver, whether it be eighteenth-century teapots or modern souvenir spoons, is an avocation pursued by enthusiasts from all walks of life.

Although silver's role in society has diminished to the point where it is only a glimmer of its former self, its symbolic value remains very much what it was three hundred years ago. Silver is still used on traditional occasions in traditional settings for traditional purposes, and the precious metal seems inextricably fused into the alloy of our American culture.

1. J. F. Hayward, *Huguenot Silver in England, 1688-1727* (London: Faber and Faber, 1959), p. 78.
2. Robert Latham and William Matthews, eds., *TQHE Diary of Samuel Pepys*, 11 vols. (Berkeley and Los Angeles: University of California Press, 1971), V, 266.
3. "Letters of William Fitzhugh," *Virginia Magazine of History and Biography* 2, no. 3 (January 1895): 271.
4. Quoted in John Marshall Phillips, *American Silver* (New York: Chanticleer Press, 1949), p. 115.
5. M. Halsey Thomas, ed., *The Diary of Samuel Sewall, 1674-1729*, 2 vols. (New York: Farrar, Straus and Giroux, 1973), II, 1063 (hereafter cited as *Sewall*).
6. Jean Parker, "Your Sterling and You," in *The Story of Sterling* (New York: The Sterling Silversmiths Guild of America, 1947), pp. 7, 48.
7. *The New Yorker* 53, no. 35 (17 October 1977): 29.
8. Graham Hood, *American Silver: A History of Style, 1650-1900* (New York: Praeger Publishers, 1971), p. 12.
9. "Silver and Silver Plate," *Harper's New Monthly Magazine* 37, no. 220 (September 1868): 434.
10. "The Manufacture of Silver-Plated Ware," *Scientific American* 41, no. 19 (8 November 1879): 296.
11. Celia Betsky, "The Dutch and Their Domestic Silver in America (1686-1750)," seminar paper, Yale University, 1975.
12. "Silver and Silver Plate," p. 434.
13. See Walter Muir Whitehill, "Tutor Flynt's Silver Chamber-pot," *Publications of the Colonial Society of Massachusetts* 38 (Transactions 1947-1951): 360-363.
14. Quoted in Bernard Bailyn et al., *The Great Republic* (Boston: Little, Brown and Company, 1977), p. 103.
15. Sharon S. Darling, "Admiral Dewey's Loving Cup," *Silver* 9, no. 1 (January-February 1976): 10-12.
16. *Sewall*, I, 599; II, 757.
17. Parker, "Your Sterling and You," p. 9.
18. Curwen Papers, Essex Institute, Salem, Massachusetts, vol. 4.

'As Good As Sterling'
Art in American Silver

Martha Gandy Fales

The person who taught me to enjoy silver as a work of art was Charles Montgomery. When he looked at an object, he mentally devoured it. He wanted to know *everything* about it: how it came into being, why, where, who made it, who used it, and especially why it looked as it did. His questions were astute, acute, and endless. Those who glance passively at what they see and do not ask questions never learn what these objects actually represent. Having no questions, they have no answers.

Each piece of American silver we look at has its own special artistic expression and a great deal to tell us about its origins. Our judgment of its aesthetic quality is affected by our ability to distinguish one stylistic interpretation from another. It is essential to recognize individual preferences for certain designs and forms on the part of a silversmith or his patrons in a particular area of the country. By knowing what is prevalent one is able to discern what is special.

The same stylistic trends which affect painting, architecture, and all the arts are apparent in silver. Understanding how the silversmith was able to translate major aesthetic movements into utilitarian objects and how his expression differs from the source of its inspiration is one of the great rewards of studying or collecting American silver.

In this country, where useful objects find the greatest patronage, the silversmith has often been in the advance guard in bringing an expression of the latest style into existence. As a result styles change quickly in silver. American silver has kept pace, and clearly shows the influence and development of the major artistic movements abroad. In fact, it is no exaggeration to say that in the colonial period, silver represented a fine art in the new country and progressed more rapidly and with greater patronage than the arts of architecture, painting or sculpture. "In the newest fashion" was the promise universally made by silversmiths advertising their wares.

Equally common was the boast of the American silversmith that his product was "as good as sterling," meaning not only that the metal was as pure as the guaranteed sterling standard of English silver, but implying also that it was as well made and as well designed. The amazing fact is that in general the product of the American silversmith who made this claim *was* as good as sterling. When John Hull and Robert Sanderson began working in Boston in the mid-

dle of the seventeenth century, their products even then reflected the late Renaissance tradition which still lingered on in the artistic expressions current in England and on the Continent. The design of their silver had its origins in the Renaissance movement of Italy and therefore was architectural in nature, with basically rectilinear forms, like the cluster-column candlesticks made by their apprentice Jeremiah Dummer (138). Decoration consisted of paneling, heraldic motifs, baluster shapes, and simplified ornament.

In looking at silver it is helpful to begin by learning about its chronological and stylistic development, at the same time studying the techniques used to achieve current modes of design. A tiny dram cup (134) made about 1651 exhibits a central rosette and paneled decoration enclosing stylized fleur-de-lis, just as did contemporary English-made versions. In chasing the design into the silver the silversmith took advantage of the metal's natural tendency to oxidize, knowing that tarnish building up in these areas would accentuate the pattern. The bowl's ear-shaped handles, formed of twisted wire, likewise depend upon the contrast of light and shade for their flair.

Engraving also enhances silver because it breaks up the shining surface into a myriad of hairline reflections of light. New York silversmiths, influenced by the high reputation for excellence in engraving of their Dutch counterparts, made abundant use of engraved decoration. New York beakers (136) are gracefully embellished with characteristic seventeenth-century strapwork, scrolled vines, and rosettes. The beaker also reveals the silversmith's sophistication in controlling the amount of outward flare at the top of its long tapering sides. Another nicety of New York silver seen in beakers as well as tankards and other forms is the applied cut-card border, borrowed from Dutch prototypes, which accentuates the base and gives it a substantial feeling.

Boston silversmiths at the end of the seventeenth century used bold floral engraving to relieve smooth circular silvery areas. John Coney, in making a curvaceous covered cup (135) with a superbly rounded body, embellished it with an elaborately engraved coat of arms featuring a spotted leopard in its crest. Following seventeenth-century style, he employed cast silver for bold caryatid handles with graduated studded embossing on the sides, providing another dimension to the metal surface.

Figure 27
Sugar Box, Boston, ca. 1700-1710
Edward Winslow (1669-1753)
Mabel Brady Garvan Collection
1935.152

Contrasting foreign influences in American silver can be seen at work in a Portuguese-inspired New England bowl and in New York bowls inspired by Dutch prototypes (**141, 142**). The floral design was chased into the metal, either in circular scrolling patterns or contained in compartmented panels. The bowls are further enhanced by the metal's ability to be wrought in repoussé lobes around the top, which adds to the embossed appearance. Critical to the appearance of a bowl, and other objects as well, is the size of the handles in proportion to the body. In some cases, the handles are not quite adequate to the scale of the object, being too small or obviously made up of castings from two separate molds the silversmith had on hand rather than from a specially designed mold.

Silver was unusually well suited to the extravagances of the baroque style which developed in the arts at the end of the seventeenth century. Because of its malleability, silver could be shaped into bold moving lines with curves and reverse curves. It could be cast into florid three-dimensional details. Its surfaces could be worked in such a way that smooth areas could be contrasted with rich repoussé ornamentation. The recessed areas of gadrooning could be intentionally oxidized to achieve startling effects of light and shade. By the end of the seventeenth century American silversmiths were capable of producing some brilliant baroque expressions (Fig. 27). Admittedly based on examples imported from England or the Continent, with details selected from emblem books or illustrations in literature published at the time, the American examples are as lavishly executed as their Old World cousins.

Among the outstanding examples produced during this period is a type of covered cup made by several New York silversmiths (143) which delights the eye in many ways, as any masterpiece should. While it derives not from a Dutch prototype, as one might expect in New York silver, but from an English one, its form is peculiar to its native area. Its robust repoussé is a counterpoint to the mirror-smooth planished surface above the leaves which appear to nestle around the bowl. This surface in turn is highlighted by an expertly engraved coat of arms massively contained by mantling which adds to the curving, swirling motion of the handles and lid. The leaf design in relief on the base and lid is brought to full round in the cast handles, whose knob finials are repeated on the lid to unify the design. In truth, it seems the silversmith has spared no technique or tool available to him in producing this piece. A dotting punch has even been used to granulate certain areas of the decoration, giving further texture and yet another tonal quality to the object.

John Coney used a diversity of techniques in making a masterful monteith (146) for a Boston patron. Equal to its English predecessors, this unique American expression of the baroque makes use of narrow bands of unrelieved sheen juxtaposed with brilliant faceting of flattened fluting to provide a perfect foil for the extraordinary crested rim. Chased leafage surrounds cast and applied urns enframed with cast scrolled pediments and punctuated by cherubs' heads, producing a bold silhouette that invites the eye to wander over its fascinating surface.

Of equal grandeur is the chocolate pot (149) made by Edward Winslow. Although slightly marred by the addition of a later spout, the chocolate pot is superbly designed with three different kinds of fluting, full proportions to the body, and cut-card ornamentation on the lid. Applied ornament, gadrooning, repoussé, and engraving of baroque inspiration made artistic expressions of less presumptuous forms as well, such as canns, casters, salvers, and even snuff boxes.

In the early eighteenth century a reversal of the trend toward massive heavy ornamentation developed in the early rococo (sometimes called Queen Anne) period. Silver was equally adaptable to the new stylistic emphasis on line, plain shiny surfaces, and rhythmic curves. Circular and octagonal shapes predominated, as in the pear-shaped octagonal teapot so handsomely forged on the anvil of Peter Van Dyck (152). The vertical faceting of the sides of the silver refracts the light in a most pleasing way, while the horizontal moldings and fillets emphasize the shape and give tensity to the design. There is an exaggerated and spirited profile to the S-curved spout and handle in keeping with the robustness of the body. New England globular teapots (153) are more restrained examples of early rococo silver. Like the best silver of the second quarter of the eighteenth century, they depend largely upon their outline and intricately engraved arms and borders for their beauty. Both pear-shaped and globular teapots were well chosen for the brewing of tea, since their shapes ensured that a maximum amount of hot water would be in contact with the tea leaves, which settle to the bottom of the pot while steeping.

While there was a regional preference for globular teapots in New England and for pear-shaped teapots in New York, both forms closely followed English silver precedents. Most tea-table objects ultimately derived from Chinese porcelain forms, since both tea and the equipment for serving it were introduced to the Western world from China. One of the most satisfying transformations of Chinese porcelain into silver was performed by Simeon Soumain in a small sugar bowl (154). Its serene circularity is proclaimed from the top of the reel on its lid, through intricate ciphers and shining body, down to its reel-shaped foot.

An especially successful blending of the octagonal and circular designs of early rococo silver is achieved in a salver by Jacob Hurd (160). Here the ability of an outstanding silversmith can be seen in the remarkably smooth, even surface (not easy to accomplish by hand-hammering), the sophisticated outline of the molded border with just the slightest incurving of the long sides, and the engraved inner border composed of shells, rosettes, and diapering which forms a lobed enclosure for the central coat of arms.

In seeking the answer to what constitutes a masterpiece in the expression of any of the arts, one must determine how well an object expresses the current style. It is crucial that the object be well-made from a technical point of view and, in the case of utilitarian objects, that it perform its intended function satisfactorily. The material the object is made of should also be appropriate to both its function and its design. It is possible for even the smallest object to be a masterpiece, but the outstanding masterpiece is the one that aspires to greatness through a monumentality of concept and design.

In silver it is the presentation piece that most often fulfills the latter criterion. In early rococo American silver, the two-handled covered cup was such an object. Following English examples, Jacob Hurd's presentation cup (69) is divided into sections of pleasing proportions. Although a large object, it is given gracefulness through the simplicity of its curvilinear form. The expanse of the large body is broken up by the central focal point—the engraved cartouche—which reveals the occasion of the cup's presentation. Where the midband is placed on the body of the cup is the dividing line between the success or the failure of the design. Hurd had a discerning eye and managed to place the horizontal accent in precisely the right place. The molded lid and a banded finial highlight his judgment. Furthermore, the handles are of sufficient proportion to enhance the design rather than detract from it. In any successful work of art each component of the design must be essential to it.

As the rococo style progressed, silver became more asymmetrical in shape and more elaborately embellished. Lines that were once simply curved became doubly curved in the third quarter of the eighteenth century. C-scrolls became broken C-scrolls, and symmetrical scallop shells became tattered asymmetrical shells. It is usually in the superficial ornamentation of an object that the first traces of a new style make their appearance. Applied decoration and handles could be cast in a sand mold impressed with a pattern of decoration or a handle taken from a newly made London piece. In this way English designs quickly penetrated the American silversmith's repertoire. American-made candlesticks were also cast in molds for the most part, and are virtually indistinguishable from their English counterparts.

One of the chief tenets of rococo design is a feeling of lightness and delicacy. By piercing silver in a variety of patterns, the silversmith could create this desired airiness in forms such as a chafing dish (165) or a dish ring (164). At the same time, the piercing served a practical purpose in dissipating the heat between the dishes these forms supported and the tables on which they stood.

Repoussé ornamentation replete with rococo motifs added to the effect of richness. Floral borders were often embossed on body and lid, but of even greater sophistication was the profuse use of repoussé over the entire surface of a piece, as in the case of Joseph Richardson's remarkable tea kettle on stand (Fig. 28). The naturalistic element of the rococo style can be seen in fantastic repoussé at the top of the swirling cartouche. This imposing object does what most masterpieces do: it makes use of many processes to achieve its statement. The combination of chasing, engraving, repoussé, and cast ornament is so well accomplished that the viewer is not aware of where one technique stops and another begins. In other words, the various areas of design are deftly joined together and the transitions smoothly executed. In addition, the basic form itself has assimilated the rococo style, being an inverted pearshape ("double-bellied," in the silversmith's parlance), doubly curvilinear, and delicately poised on a garlanded and scrolled frame. Beautiful objects like this sit well in space, and the spaces they enclose

Figure 28
Tea Kettle on Stand, Philadelphia,
ca. 1745-1755
Joseph Richardson (1711-1784)
Mabel Brady Garvan Collection
1932.93

are as well designed as those they occupy. The space framed by the tea kettle's handle is as satisfying to look at as the shape of the piece itself.

The period of the Revolutionary War ushered in an artistic upheaval as well as a political one. Our new nation turned to classical Rome as a source of inspiration for both its form of government and its stylistic expression. Robert Adam, working in England in the third quarter of the eighteenth century, popularized the new movement in architecture and the decorative arts, restoring simplicity, symmetry, refinement, and regularity to these arts. The tall, elegant classical urn (176) became a decorative symbol of the age and invaded such forms as coffee pots and sugar bowls, not only as the basic shape of the body but also as decorative finials. Cream pots took the outline of an inverted Roman warrior's helmet. Restrained elegance was essential for the successful interpretation of this style. Pearling and beading replaced the rococo gadrooning in borders. Pierced rims or reeded and fluted galleries were added to edges to achieve the repetition and orderliness of this Roman revival.

Simultaneously, there was a revolutionary change in the process of making silver. New machinery was developed which led to the industrialization of the craft and drastically affected the stylistic design of silver. Rolling mills made it possible for the silversmith to buy sheets of silver, so that it was no longer necessary for him to flatten the metal himself through the long and difficult process of hammering. No longer did he have to raise up the body of an object through course after course of hammering. Now he could simply seam flat pieces of metal together. As a result, in the design of Federal silver one can see everywhere the flat pieces of metal from which an object was made. From this time on, man became more and more dependent for his designs upon what the machine could do, whereas previously he had designed an object and then developed the equipment to achieve that design.

In looking at silver in the neoclassical style, it becomes important to see how well the silversmith used his new machinery and how successfully he was able to unify the final design using parts which were often mass-produced. Beading could be bought by the yard, and as the period progressed milled borders could be bought in the same way,

so that more and more some silversmiths became assemblers of parts. This technology played its role in the general tendency for regional characteristics to become less pronounced in the period of national unification. Patterns of milled borders varied in the different centers of production, however, so that in the beginning silver wore telltale signs of certain locales much as Federal furniture did with its mass-produced bands of inlay.

This technological change was just beginning when Paul Revere made his fluted tea sets (172). The reflections created by the fluting gave a most pleasing repetitive effect to each different form in the set. The delicate engraving of classical festooning added to the aura of refinement. Even when left perfectly plain and outlined only by a simple band of molding just the right width, the fluted form provided an elegant expression of the neoclassical taste.

As this fashion progressed, its interpretation became bolder and more strongly stated. The inspiration shifted from Italy to the more monumental antiquities of Greece and Egypt. Scale increased, forms became larger, and the gauge of the flattened silver used by the metalworker became heavier. The emphasis was on the horizontal axis of the design rather than on the vertical axis, as had previously been the case.

A handsome example of the monumentality of the antique style is a small inkstand made by Harvey Lewis (177). So substantial is its design that it would be equally successful if it were 3½ feet rather than a mere 3½ inches high. One of the most important achievements of this period is typified in the beautifully sculpted cast ornament used for its caryatid supports. In order to disguise the use of mechanically-made ornament, more than one type of milled border was often used, as here, on a single piece of silver. A tea set (178) of the same period includes a selection of several different bands of varying width, while the sides of the bodies of the pieces are embossed into big reflective lobes to make them appear more massive than they actually are. By knowing the stylistic goals of the silversmith working in any given period, we are better able to assess his success in achieving those goals.

As the nineteenth century progressed, not only the size of silver objects increased, but also the number and variety of forms. Entire dinner services were made, complete with silver plates, dishes, and pitchers of graduated sizes. The silversmith had to consider more than just the shape and decoration of a single piece; he had to endeavor to make a whole assemblage of forms harmonious. With an increased market for his wares and more frequent use of mechanization, the silversmith resorted to a greater use of superficial ornamentation to disguise and cover up his machine-made product. Fortunately, as silver manufacturing firms came into being there were some which still employed silversmiths who designed and worked in the traditional way and were able to control the new technology, using it to their own advantage.

By the middle of the nineteenth century a desire for constant innovation resulted in the well-known Victorian eclecticism. Rapidly changing stylistic revivals occurred, proceeding from the antique style through the rococo revival to Louis XVI, Renaissance, and then to a series of fads for the exotic—Moorish, Persian, East Indian, and Japanese. In looking at nineteenth-century silver it is more important than ever to try to discern what each particular artistic style was trying to express in order to determine how successful an individual silversmith was in creating a specific piece of silver. Revivalists of styles tried to achieve goals never even contemplated by the original creators of those styles. For instance, a pair of salts (179) made about 1840 obviously derives from rococo inspiration, being supported on a scrolled cast shell by a naturalistic dragonesque bough. However, the dishes of the salts, with the greater precision of their lobes and the distinctive cutting of their upper edges, belong entirely to the middle of the nineteenth century rather than the middle of the eighteenth century.

Artistic attitudes toward such subtleties as relationship of parts and sense of scale are delicately fluctuating matters of taste, and an individual piece of silver can only be judged on its own terms, by its own aesthetic standards. By eighteenth-century standards, the handles of nineteenth-century pitchers (182) and pots (181) would have been too thin and rigid. But the nineteenth-century examples were inspired by antique models which in turn were created in an aesthetic atmosphere which favored greater contrast between parts. The difference must be acknowledged, respected, and indeed cherished, as one looks at various artistic interpretations in silver.

Figure 29
Vase, New York, ca. 1875
Designed by James H. Whitehouse
Tiffany & Company
The Metropolitan Museum of Art;
gift of William Cullen Bryant, 1887

Representative of the best qualities of the Victorian period in general and the Renaissance revival period in particular is the William Cullen Bryant vase (Fig. 29). Produced in 1875 by Tiffany & Company and designed by James H. Whitehouse, the Bryant vase is classically Greek in form. The surface is so intricately modeled with strapwork and medallions that it gives the appearance of deep carving. The details, however, are not blindly copied from classical models. They have been thoughtfully selected from the repertoire of American flora and fauna in honor of Bryant's contemplation of nature. It is Bryant's bust and the wildlife mentioned in his poems that adorn the medallions, not some anonymous images from a classical bas-relief. The borders are not stock milled bands but carefully designed borders repeating the motifs of the deep reliefwork in a slightly different dimension, thereby giving unity to the whole design.

A burgeoning interest in naturalism coincided with the exploration of new areas of the world. Expeditions to the Arctic region were reflected in punch bowls modeled in icy chunks of silvery coldness. Increased traveling to the seaside created an interest in marine forms and resulted in the popularity of silver designs such as the Whiting and Company bowl (187), which gives the appearance of a salt-water pool along a rocky coast, its upper watery surfaces shimmering in the golden sunlight.

As the nineteenth century closed, an original new artistic movement called art nouveau came to the fore. This style was best expressed in silver by the Gorham Company in its Martelé line, a name given by William C. Codman to silver produced entirely by hand methods. These creations (53, 188) were characterized by free-flowing organic lines and naturalistic motifs—flowers, waves, sea nymphs, fish, shells, and even clouds, smoke, and flames. To emphasize the handcraftsmanship, the hammer marks were not entirely planished out as they had been traditionally. Pitchers, hand mirrors, and cigarette boxes became vehicles for the imaginative and fanciful expressions of art nouveau. The surface of silver became almost liquid in appearance and was frequently adorned with the head of a woman with dreamy eyes and flowing tresses.

A similar concern for the beauty of the hand-hammered surface is evident in the work of individual American silversmiths at this time. With the Arts and Crafts movement, which flowered in the United States around the turn of the twentieth century, a number of silversmiths produced functional modern designs (54) as well as reviving the simple "colonial" styles of the eighteenth century.

Periodically there has been a revival of interest in reproducing historic American silver. In the second quarter of the nineteenth century the first major attempts were made at reproducing eighteenth-century objects for their own beauty and not simply to replace lost pieces or augment sets. The simplicity and functionalism of these early styles led craftsmen like George C. Gebelein, Arthur Stone, and their associates to produce exact reproductions of early objects (76).

In evaluating the quality of a reproduction one must discard the usual criteria. There should be no improvement of technique or deviation from the design on the part of the copyist. Exactness and faithfulness to the original are the desired properties. Few craftsmen are able to subject themselves to the required strictures and resist the temptation to improve upon the original.

Silver in the twentieth century has continued to reflect changing styles. New alloys, easier to care for, have replaced silver for ordinary tablewares, but there is still no substitute for silver for important and traditional pieces. Due to its innate properties, it is equally adaptable to the exotic and decorative designs of the art deco period or to the streamlined, stripped-down, functional forms produced by Denmark's Georg Jensen and his followers.

Throughout the changing whims of fashion, American silversmiths have accepted and rejected certain designs. To the original source of their inspiration they have added regional, national, or perhaps even personal elements. Their choices have resulted in a distinctive artistic expression, and their best work exemplifies the finest qualities of their age. It is our pleasure to look inquiringly at their silver in order to appreciate which examples of their art are lasting in beauty, craftsmanship, and usefulness, and which, among all these splendid creations, are truly masterpieces.

Silver in American Life

Unless otherwise noted, objects are in the
Yale University Art Gallery

Short Title List

Buhler and Hood
BUHLER, KATHRYN C., AND HOOD, GRAHAM. *American Silver, Garvan and Other Collections in the Yale University Art Gallery,* 2 vols. New Haven: Yale University Press, 1970.

Clayton
CLAYTON, MICHAEL. *The Collector's Dictionary of the Silver and Gold of Great Britain and North America.* New York: The World Publishing Company, 1971.

Fales, *Early American Silver*
FALES, MARTHA GANDY. *Early American Silver.* New York: E. P. Dutton and Company, Inc., 1973.

Fales, *Richardson*
FALES, MARTHA GANDY. *Joseph Richardson and Family, Philadelphia Silversmiths.* Middletown, Connecticut: Wesleyan University Press, 1974.

Flynt and Fales
FLYNT, HENRY N., AND FALES, MARTHA GANDY. *The Heritage Foundation Collection of Silver, With Biographical Sketches of New England Silversmiths, 1625-1825.* Old Deerfield, Massachusetts: The Heritage Foundation, 1968.

McClinton
McCLINTON, KATHARINE MORRISON. *Collecting American Nineteenth-Century Silver.* New York: Charles Scribner's Sons, 1968.

Montgomery and Kane
MONTGOMERY, CHARLES F., AND KANE, PATRICIA E. (eds.). *American Art, 1750-1800: Towards Independence.* Boston: New York Graphic Society, 1976.

Nineteenth-Century America
Nineteenth-Century America: Furniture and Other Decorative Arts. New York: The Metropolitan Museum of Art, 1970.

Phillips, *American Silver*
PHILLIPS, JOHN MARSHALL. *American Silver.* New York: Chanticleer Press, 1949.

Turner
TURNER, NOEL D. *American Silver Flatware, 1837-1910.* New York: A. S. Barnes and Co., 1972.

Vermeule
VERMEULE, CORNELIUS C. *Numismatic Art in America: Aesthetics of the United States Coinage.* Cambridge: The Belknap Press of Harvard University Press, 1971.

Silver: Its Sources and Uses

1   **Native Silver**
Mollie Gibson Mine, Aspen, Colorado
W. 4 9/16″ (116 mm); WT. 64 oz, 13 dwt (2004 gm)
Donated by Samuel L. Penfield to the George J. Brush
Mineral Collection, Yale University

Silver occurs in nature as a pure metal as well as in compounds such as silver sulphide and chloride. In addition it is
often carried, in trace amounts, in minerals in which it replaces copper and lead by atomic substitution. Silver minerals are not found in common rocks but are formed under
special and infrequent circumstances. Under certain conditions saline solutions circulate deep into the earth's crust,
become heated, and react with the surrounding rocks, ex-
tracting silver and other metals. These metals are then trans-
ported in the solution and are deposited in channels which
we see today as veins. Silver minerals are usually found
embedded in quartz and other valueless minerals which are
also deposited from the solutions.

Rock from which it is profitable to separate the silver
minerals is called silver ore. Rich ores with high silver con-
tents have been mined for centuries, but it is only in the
twentieth century that mining and extraction techniques
have made it feasible to extract silver from very low grade
ores. Some of the richest ores ever discovered contain a high
percentage of pure silver metal which requires very little
refining. Ores of this type have always been comparatively
rare and few remain to be mined today. This particular
specimen was mined in Aspen, Colorado, at the Mollie
Gibson Mine, which was active during the late nineteenth
and early twentieth centuries. As can be seen from the rough
sides of this piece, silver is usually gray or blackish in the
natural state, which probably explains why it was sometimes discarded by inexperienced prospectors in favor of
tiny grains of glittering gold. This specimen has been polished to reveal the pure, shiny metal underneath. An ore
mineral of this type usually contains some gold as well as a
little copper or lead and ranges from 80 to 90 percent silver.
Although native silver does not often occur in large chunks,
the largest single piece ever mined was found in the Cobalt
district of Ontario and weighed over 1,500 pounds.

Refs.: Brian J. Skinner, *Earth Resources* (Englewood Cliffs, New Jersey:
Prentice-Hall, Inc., 1969), pp. 51, 66-67. J. H. Watkins, *Gold and Silver in
the West: The Illustrated History of an American Dream* (New York:
Bonanza Books, 1971).

2   **Argentite**
Austin, Nevada
W. 2 11/16″ (68 mm); WT. 4 oz, 1 dwt (126 gm)
George J. Brush Mineral Collection, Yale University

3   **Polybasite**
Comstock Lode, Nevada
W. 3″ (76 mm); WT. 4 oz, 2 dwt (127 gm)
George J. Brush Mineral Collection, Yale University

4   **Proustite**
Francisca Mining District, Asientos, Mexico
W. 2 5/16″ (59 mm); WT. 3 oz (93 gm)
Donated by W. J. Linn to the George J. Brush Mineral
Collection, 1910, Yale University

Three of the major silver sulfide minerals, argentite, polybasite, and proustite, were all found in the mines of the Western United States during the bonanza days of the late nineteenth century. Both argentite (Ag_2S) and polybasite ($Ag_{16}Sb_2S_{11}$) are a dark bluish-black in color, a fact which caused them to be referred to as that "blasted blue stuff" when they clogged the pans of the early prospectors searching for placer gold in the river beds of Nevada. It was only in 1859, through the knowledge of a few miners with experience in Mexican mines, that the heavy bluish-black silver minerals were recognized for what they were. By 1861, when Mark Twain arrived in Virginia City as a young employee of the new territorial government of Nevada, silver minerals were being hunted in earnest. He found the whole area "smitten with the silver fever" and soon took to the hills himself. Until 1900 the mines of Nevada, Colorado, and Arizona were the scene of frantic activity and wild living. Fortunes were made and lost within a matter of days and mining stocks passed as currency. It is interesting that in a country so rich in silver very little of the metal itself actually exchanged hands. Locked in complex ores, the silver was accessible only through heavy capital investment and advanced technology.

Proustite, a beautiful glittering red mineral (Ag_3AsS_3) known to miners for centuries as "ruby silver," was found in the American West in beautiful crystals similar to this example from Mexico. Although proustite does not figure as prominently in mining lore as argentite and polybasite, it too is an extremely rich ore mineral, containing approximately 65.4 percent silver. Argentite contains approximately 87 percent silver and polybasite is about 75 percent silver.

Refs.: Alan M. Bateman, *Economic Mineral Deposits* (New York: John Wiley & Sons, Inc., 1950), pp. 454-474. Dan de Quille, *The Big Bonanza* (1876; reprint, New York: Thomas Y. Crowell Company, 1947). Mark Twain, *Roughing It* (1872; reprint, New York: New American Library, 1962). Willard Lincoln Roberts, George Robert Rapp, and Julius Weber, *Encyclopedia of Minerals* (New York: D. Van Nostrand Reinhold Company, 1974), pp. 6, 33, 93-94, 110, 488, 493-494, 561-562.

5 Silver-lead Ore
Leadville, Colorado
W. 5¾" (146 mm); WT. 13 oz, 3 dwt (408 gm)
Economic Geology Collection, Yale University

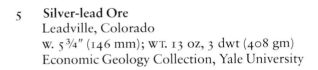

In 1874 the hills surrounding Leadville, Colorado, were found to contain a silver-rich lead carbonate ore, and well into the early part of the twentieth century the area's mines produced as much as $12,500,000 worth of silver in one year. Today, however, silver is generally a by-product of other mining operations, and the mines of Leadville are no longer of significance in the production of silver. The type of lead ore displayed here, in which silver has replaced lead in the mineral galena (PbS), would yield less than one ounce of silver for every ton of ore mined. Nevertheless, modern mining techniques have made it possible to mine such huge tonnages of ore that silver is now extracted in larger quantities as a by-product than was possible in straight silver mining in the past.

Refs.: Alan M. Bateman, *Economic Mineral Deposits* (New York: John Wiley & Sons, Inc., 1950), pp. 452-474. Rodman Wilson Paul, *Mining Frontiers of the Far West, 1848-1880* (Albuquerque, New Mexico: University of New Mexico Press, 1963), pp. 109-134. J. H. Watkins, *Gold and Silver in the West: The Illustrated History of an American Dream* (New York: Bonanza Books, 1971), pp. 95-98.

6 Ingot, 1878-1880
Free American Mine, Georgetown, Colorado
Joseph Reynolds and General James I. Gilbert, Proprietors
L. 2 15/16" (75 mm); WT. 7 oz (217 gm)
American Arts Purchase Fund   1978.80

This small souvenir ingot is an evocative memento of the late-nineteenth-century silver mining boom in Colorado. It is made of silver from the Free American Mine, located on

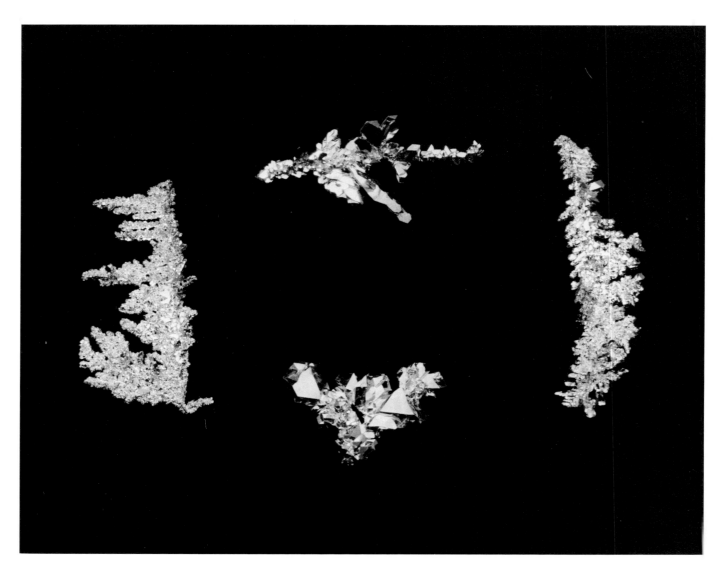

Red Elephant Mountain near Georgetown, Colorado. This valuable mine was opened in late 1876 and produced $100,000 worth of silver the next year. Joseph Reynolds of Chicago and General James I. Gilbert, speculators who invested in several mines together, purchased the Free American in the spring of 1878 and sold it in March of 1880. Gilbert, a successful businessman who moved to Colorado in 1876 in order to invest his capital in mining, was an important figure in the development of the Clear Creek County mines. For many years this ingot belonged to the Boston silversmith George C. Gebelein (76).

Ref.: *History of Clear Creek and Boulder Valleys, Colorado* (Chicago: O. L. Baskin & Co., 1880), pp. 326-327, 511-515.

7 **Silver Crystals**, 1978
Refined by Handy & Harman, Fairfield, Connecticut
L. approx. 1⅝″ (41 mm)
Gift of Handy & Harman

Today, the silver contained in various silver ores (2-5) is generally obtained as a by-product of the refining of lead, zinc, or copper by various methods. These beautiful silver crystals emerge near the end of the long and complicated process of refining electrolytic copper slimes, a common means of recovering silver (see Fig. 5). The silver crystals are deposited on the cathodes in an electrolytic bath consisting of a dilute solution of silver nitrate and copper nitrate in which doré anodes have been placed. After the crystals are removed from the cathodes, they are washed, melted, and cast into ingots (8).

Ref.: Allison Butts and Charles D. Coxe, eds., *Silver: Economics, Metallurgy, and Use* (Princeton, New Jersey: D. Van Nostrand Co., Inc., 1967), pp. 57-94.

8 Ingot, 1978
Engelhard Minerals & Chemicals Corporation,
Iselin, New Jersey
W. 6¼″ (159 mm); WT. 100 oz (3100 gm)
Engelhard Minerals & Chemicals Corporation

Silver emerges from the modern refinery most often in the
form of ingots, or bars, which are guaranteed at a minimum
of 999 parts per thousand "fine," or pure. The silver crystals
(7) deposited in the electrolytic bath are melted and cast to
produce these ingots, which ordinarily weigh between 1,000
and 1,100 troy ounces; this example, produced by the Engelhard Minerals & Chemicals Corporation, weighs only 100
ounces. Twenty-six refineries in the United States produce
silver ingots, which they stamp with their identifying
maker's mark.

Refs.: Allison Butts and Charles D. Coxe, eds., *Silver: Economics, Metallurgy, and Use* (Princeton, New Jersey: D. Van Nostrand Co., Inc., 1967), p.
91. *Silver Refiners of the World and Their Identifying Ingot Marks* (Washington, D.C.: The Silver Institute, 1977).

9 Sheet Silver, 1978
Engelhard Minerals & Chemicals Corporation,
Iselin, New Jersey
W. 6″ (152 mm); WT. 2 oz, 15 dwt (85 gm)
Gift of Engelhard Minerals & Chemicals Corporation

In 1747, R. Campbell noted in *The London Tradesman* that
the London goldsmith's "Business required much more
Time and Labour formerly than at present; they were
obliged to beat their Metal from the Ingot into what Thickness they wanted; but now there are invented Flatting-
Mills, which reduce their Metal to what Thinness they require, at a very small Expence." By the late eighteenth century, labor-saving rolled sheet silver was widely used by
silversmiths in this country, including Paul Revere (**172**).
Most modern silversmiths begin work with a piece of sheet
silver purchased from a manufacturer, such as this piece
made by Engelhard Minerals & Chemicals Corporation. In
fact, the use of sheet silver is so widespread today that a
recent textbook by Oppi Untracht defines silversmithing as
"the art of raising or shaping sheet metals into forms by the
use of hammers, anvils, and other tools."

Silver's malleability, its ability to withstand rolling or
hammering without breaking or cracking, is second only to
that of gold and is a property for which silver has long been
noted. *Harper's New Monthly* reported in September 1868,
for example, that "in London once a grain of silver was
beaten out so thin that it covered ninety-eight square
inches." The creative possibilities allowed by this malleability make silver perfectly suited for the fashioning of
beautiful, useful objects in nearly any form the silversmith
chooses.

Refs.: R. Campbell, *The London Tradesman* (1747; reprint, Newton Abbot, England: David and Charles, 1969), p. 141. Oppi Untracht, *Metal
Techniques for Craftsmen* (Garden City, New York: Doubleday & Company, Inc., 1975), pp. 38-42, 240.

10 **Jesse Hart White and Two Children,** unknown artist
Daguerreotype, ca. 1850-1860
H. 5½″ (140 mm); W. 4 5/16″ (110 mm)
Gift of A. D. Brittingham   1977.42.1

Although the lens system necessary for photographic reproduction had been in common use in the *camera obscura*
since the middle of the eighteenth century, the ability to
create permanent images was not realized until the 1830s.
Photography was finally made possible through the discovery that images produced by the exposure of certain photo-
sensitive silver compounds to light could be made permanent through the action of various developing chemicals.
The daguerreotype, a photographic print on silver-plated
copper, was the earliest photographic process to be used
in the United States. Invented by Louis Jacques Mandé
Daguerre, who disclosed his discovery to the public in 1839,
daguerreotypes were first made in America by Samuel F. B.
Morse. Many American experimenters, including Morse,
John William Draper, Robert Cornelius, John Johnson, and
Alexander Simon Wolcott, perfected the process for use in
taking portraits. Because the plates required long periods of
exposure under bright lights or in blinding sunlight, it is
little wonder that many portraits are somewhat blurred.
Children, in particular, found it difficult to remain still for
several minutes.

In many ways the daguerreotype was responsible for
the democratization of the portrait. Photographic salons
were established in the large cities, while hundreds of itiner-
ant daguerreotypists toured the American countryside. A
daguerreotype of this size would have cost the sitter less than
two dollars including the case, and as a result people from all
walks of life found it economically feasible to have their
portraits made with the new process.

Ref.: Beaumont Newhall, *The Daguerreotype in America,* rev. ed. (New
York: Dover Publications, 1976), pp. 15-110.

12 **Silver-plated Retainer with Ball Bearings,**
Danbury, Connecticut, 1978
Barden Corporation
D. 5″ (127 mm)
Gift of the Barden Corporation   1978.54

The qualities of silver as a metal enable it to serve a wide variety of uses in science and industry, in addition to its role in photography and in the making of sterling and plated silverware. This bearing, with a silver-plated retainer, is representative of the myriad functions which silver serves in modern technology. These bearings are used on the main shafts of gas turbine engines such as those that drive Boeing 707's, 727's, and 747's and military aircraft. The silver, plated over high carbon steel, acts as a supplement to the oil lubrication system. Should the oil lubrication fail, the silver will serve to prevent wear or seizing of the bearing, allowing it to continue to function for at least a short time.

Ref.: Allison Butts and Charles D. Coxe, eds., *Silver: Economics, Metallurgy, and Use* (Princeton, New Jersey: D. Van Nostrand Company, Inc., 1967), pp. 446-454.

11 **Untitled,** Jerry N. Uelsmann (b. 1934)
Silver print photograph, 1967
H. 13⅜″ (340 mm); W. 9 1/16″ (230 mm)
Director's Discretionary Purchase Fund   1972.58.1

Photography is a medium which can be exploited to create rich and variable effects, and it has therefore become an important artistic vehicle. Photographic film consists of silver bromide grains locked in a gelatinous coating. The silver atoms in these compounds become activated when exposed to light, and as the film is developed they actually migrate within the gelatin to form the photographic image. During the developing process the photographer can manipulate these silver atoms to heighten contrasts and create special types of images.

Jerry Uelsmann is one of a number of artists exploring the possibilities inherent in the medium to produce highly expressive photographs. Uelsmann uses contrasting meanings played off against contrasting textures and the dramatic effects of light and dark to create striking, often surrealistic, images.

Refs.: Minor White, Peter Lorenz, and Richard Zakia, *The New Zone System Manual* (Dobbs Ferry, New York: Morgan Press Incorporated, 1976). John Szarkowski, *Mirrors and Windows: American Photography Since 1960* (Boston: New York Graphic Society, 1978), p. 23.

13 **Tankard,** Charleston, South Carolina, ca. 1720-1730
Lucas Stoutenburgh, Sr. (1691-1743)
H. 6¾″ (171 mm); WT. 24 oz, 19 dwt (774 gm)
Mabel Brady Garvan Collection   1930.1072

Because of its malleability, ductility, and shiny white color, silver is particularly well-suited as a medium for objects which are beautiful as well as useful. To make a tankard like this one in the traditional manner a silversmith would first melt scrap silver in a crucible and cast it into flat ingots. Variously shaped ingots could then be raised with a hammer into the top, body, and handle of the tankard. Silver must be worked cold, but after repeated hammer blows the crystal structure of the metal is broken down and stretched to its limits. Annealing, or heating the metal to a temperature of

about 1200° F, allows the crystals which make up the metal to reform so that the silver becomes malleable again. The process of annealing would be repeated many times during the raising of a tankard. Because of its ductility silver can be drawn through dies into wire for use as hinge pins or into flat moldings like that used around the base of this tankard. Other ornaments, such as the lion on the handle of this piece, were cast in sand molds and applied with silver solder.

The tankard shown here is a good example of the early silversmith's ability to use the attributes of the metal to create fine objects. Its maker, Lucas Stoutenburgh, Sr., was a man skilled in his craft. Although he spent most of his career in Charleston, South Carolina, it is believed that he learned to work silver from his father in New York. The wide proportions, flat top, cocoon-shaped thumbpiece, and cast handle terminal are features common in New York tankards and reflect Stoutenburgh's early training.

Refs.: Buhler and Hood, no. 976. E. Milby Burton, *South Carolina Silversmiths, 1690-1860* (Rutland, Vermont: The Charles E. Tuttle Company, 1968), pp. 178-179.

Coins and Medals

14a **Peru, Eight Reales or Spanish Dollar,** 1669, Potosí Mint
D. 1⅝″ (41 mm); WT. 393.3 gr (25.49 gm)
Numismatic Collection, Yale University

b **Mexico, Four Reales,** no date, ca. 1712-1714,
Mexico City Mint
D. 1 5/16″ (33 mm); WT. 206.4 gr (13.38 gm)
Numismatic Collection, Yale University

c **Mexico, Two Reales, Pillar Type,** 1742, Mexico City
Mint
D. 1 1/16″ (26 mm); WT. 103.8 gr (6.73 gm)
Numismatic Collection, Yale University

d **Utrecht, Rijksdaalder or Lion Dollar,** 1655
D. 1⅝″ (41 mm); WT. 420.3 gr (27.24 gm)
Numismatic Collection, Yale University; gift of
William H. Owen

e **France, Ecu Blanc,** 1711, Rennes Mint
D. 1 11/16″ (42 mm); WT. 473.1 gr (30.66 gm)
Numismatic Collection, Yale University; gift of
William H. Owen

f **Great Britain, Shilling,** 1708, London Mint
D. 1″ (25 mm); WT. 92.4 gr (5.99 gm)
Numismatic Collection, Yale University; gift of
William H. Owen

These irregular coins, *macuquinas* or cobs, cut from bar
silver and stamped with standard dies, were among the vast
issues of the silver-rich Spanish colonies of Mexico and Peru.
Such coins found their way into the British colonies primarily as the result of the brisk trade with the West Indies and the
Canary Islands. Spanish-American coins were the most
common coins circulating in the North American colonies
during the seventeenth and eighteenth centuries. Because of
the generally unfavorable balance of trade, however, most
hard money was reexported in payment for English goods
and most local trade was carried on by barter. By the end of
the seventeenth century, Massachusetts, New York, and
Virginia had all enacted laws establishing the eight reales,
or piece of eight, as one of their basic units of exchange.

a (obverse)　　　　b (obverse)　　　　c (obverse)　　　　d (obverse)

a (reverse)　　　　b (reverse)　　　　c (reverse)　　　　d (reverse)

In a world where wealth was based upon precious metals it is not surprising that Spanish treasure ships carrying gold and silver coins across the Atlantic were often preyed upon by marauding pirates and enemy privateers. Countless others went down because of bad weather or overloading. This particular eight reales was recovered recently from the waters surrounding the dry Tortugas. The Mexican cob four reales is from the wreck of the Spanish treasure fleet which sank off the coast of Florida on 31 July 1715.

During the colonial period numerous other silver and gold coins from Mexico, Spain, Holland, France, Brazil, Portugal, and England were used as money. Because of the confusion caused by worn coins and the common practice of clipping silver from the edges of coins, laws were passed which established values on the basis of weight rather than face value. Pillars, lion dollars, shillings, and French ecu are all referred to in contemporary documents, and some fine specimens are found embedded in tankard lids and set into the bowls of ladles as decoration. This latter practice suggests that these coins were valued for their design as well as their weight even in a society where hard money was scarce. Clipped and worn coins were often melted down by silversmiths as the raw material for making objects.

Refs.: Sylvester S. Crosby, *Early Coins of America and the Laws Governing Their Issue* (Boston: Published by the Author, 1875). Margaret G. Myers, *A Financial History of the United States* (New York: Columbia University Press, 1970), pp. 1-6. Bernard Bailyn, *The New England Merchants in the Seventeenth Century* (New York: Harper Torchbooks, 1964), pp. 182-189.

15a **Massachusetts, NE Shilling,** 1652
John Hull (1624-1683) and Robert Sanderson (1608-1693)
D. 1⅛″ (28 mm); WT. 69.3 gr (4.49 gm)
Mabel Brady Garvan Collection　1930.1356

b **Massachusetts, Willow Tree Shilling,** 1652–ca. 1660
John Hull (1624-1683) and Robert Sanderson (1608-1693)
D. 1¼″ (30 mm); WT. 70.2 gr (4.55 gm)
Mabel Brady Garvan Collection　1930.1357

c **Massachusetts, Oak Tree Six Pence,** 1660-1667
John Hull (1624-1683) and Robert Sanderson (1608-1693)
D. 13/16″ (21 mm); WT. 34.0 gr (2.20 gm)
Mabel Brady Garvan Collection　1930.1361

d **Massachusetts, Pine Tree Shilling,** 1667-1674
John Hull (1624-1683) and Robert Sanderson (1608-1693)
D. 1 5/16″ (33 mm); WT. 70.2 gr (4.55 gm)
Mabel Brady Garvan Collection　1930.1364

Because of the severe shortage of coins in the colony as well as the confusing diversity of foreign coins in circulation, the General Court of Massachusetts passed a law establishing a mint to coin silver money in 1652. John Hull and Robert Sanderson contracted as mintmasters, and the colony provided them with a building and all the necessary equipment for the new mint.

The first coins struck in America were pieces of silver stamped with the letters NE on one side and the value of the coin in Roman numerals on the other. The example shown here is a twelve pence or shilling piece; three pence and six pence pieces were also coined. Each was to be about 20 percent lighter in weight than the equivalent English coin but equal in fineness to sterling. Later in 1652 a law passed "for the prevention of washing or clipping of . . . money" also established the tree design with the following words: "henceforth all pieces of money coined . . . shall have a double Ring on either side, with the inscription Massachusetts, and a tree in the Center on one side, and New England and the yeere of our lord on the other side." Three such designs, first the willow tree, then the oak tree, and lastly the pine tree, were minted between 1652 and 1682. All of the coins except the two pence piece authorized in 1662 are dated 1652.

The coinage of money was a royal prerogative, and because the Massachusetts coinage was clearly illegal under English law the crown eventually put a stop to the practice. However, the coins continued in circulation and were still in use well into the nineteenth century.

16 (obverse)

Refs.: Sydney P. Noe, *The New England and Willow Tree Coinages of Massachusetts* (New York: The American Numismatic Society, 1943). _____, *The Oak Tree Coinage of Massachusetts* (New York: The American Numismatic Society, 1947). _____, *The Pine Tree Coinage of Massachusetts* (New York: The American Numismatic Society, 1952). Sylvester S. Crosby, *The Early Coins of America and the Laws Governing Their Issue* (Boston: Published by the Author, 1875), pp. 25-100.

16   **Libertas Americana Medal,** 1783, Struck in Paris
Designed by Augustin Dupré (1748-1833)
D. 1⅞" (47 mm): WT. 843.3 gr (54.65 gm)
Numismatic Collection, Yale University; gift of
C. Wyllys Betts

Commissioned by Benjamin Franklin during his years as Minister to France, the *Libertas Americana* medal commemorates the victories at Saratoga and Yorktown, and celebrates the grand American-French alliance which brought about the defeat of the British army and secured American independence. Medals were struck in bronze, copper, silver, and gold; the silver ones were presented to the President of the Continental Congress, the French ministers, and to the Grand Master of Malta. Special gold editions were given to Louis XVI and Marie-Antoinette.

Augustin Dupré, one of the foremost French medallists of his day and a personal friend of Franklin's, designed and executed the medals. The obverse shows the head of Liberty, her hair flowing freely in the breeze, with a *pileus*, or liberty cap, on a pole behind her. The reverse is an allegory of the American Revolution as conceived by Benjamin Franklin. An infant Hercules holding snakes by their throats represents the new United States in its triumph over the armies of Burgoyne and Cornwallis, while Minerva, holding the shield of France, protects the young nation from the snarling British leopard. The whole is surrounded by a Latin inscrip-

16 (reverse)

tion which reads "NON SINE DIIS ANIMOSUS INFANS" ("Not without the gods is the infant courageous").

The *Libertas Americana* medal is particularly important in the history of American numismatics because it helped to establish the basic iconography of American coinage. The head of Liberty provided the inspiration for the design of the first American cents and silver dollars.

Refs.: Hugh Honour, *The European Vision of America* (Cleveland, Ohio: The Cleveland Museum of Art, 1975), nos. 217-218. Vermeule, pp. 9-10. J. F. Loubat, *The Medallic History of the United States, 1776-1876* (New York: Published by the Author, 1880), pp. 86-92.

17 (obverse)   17 (reverse)

17 United States, Dollar, 1795, Philadelphia Mint
Design attributed to Robert Scot (w. ca. 1793-1824)
D. 1 9/16″ (39 mm); WT. 411.2 gr (26.73 gm)
Numismatic Collection, Yale University; courtesy
of Stack's, New York

In 1792 the United States adopted the bimetallic standard
and authorized the coinage of gold and silver at a fixed ratio
of 15 to 1, and by 1794 the first silver dollars were being
minted in Philadelphia. A simple maiden Liberty with flowing hair, reminiscent of the bust on Dupré's *Libertas
Americana* medal (16), is surrounded by fifteen stars repre-
senting the fifteen states of the Union. On the reverse is a
rather goose-like eagle, delicately framed by a wispy wreath.
One interesting feature of the coin is the inscription "HUN-
DRED CENTS ONE DOLLAR OR UNIT" in the outside rim, each
word separated by circles and stars. In its own time the coin
was criticized for "a want of that boldness of execution
which is necessary to durability and currency," and the striking of the coin is so subtle that perfectly preserved specimens
are rare. This coin and its successor, on which Liberty has
become a middle-aged matron, were probably both based
on the plaster casts of classical sculpture which were being
brought to America during the late eighteenth century. This
Greco-Roman symbolism would continue to be a trademark
of American coinage into the early twentieth century.

Refs.: Vermeule, pp. 28-30. United States Bureau of the Mint, *Catalogue of
Coins of the United States* (Washington, D.C.: United States Government
Printing Office, 1928), pp. 8-9. Theodore V. Buttrey, Jr., ed., *Coinage of the
Americas* (New York: The American Numismatic Society, 1973), pp. 114-
115.

18 Cincinnati Industrial Exposition, Prize Medal, 1870
Designed by Anthony Paquet (1814-1882); struck by
W. W. McGrew, Cincinnati, Ohio
D. 2½″ (62 mm); WT. 1677.1 gr (108.67 gm)
Numismatic Collection, Yale University

The nineteenth century was an age of fairs and exposi-
tions—suitable expressions of the period's pride in its
achievements and faith in future progress. The Cincinnati
Industrial Exposition of 1870 was one such fair, the first of
an annual series sponsored by the Ohio Mechanics Institute,
the Chamber of Commerce, and the Board of Trade. The
impressive show of inventions and products at the exposition naturally required some form of recognition for those
exhibits judged to be superior. "From the time fairs of a
public nature came in vogue, until of late, the giving of
premiums . . . had been regarded a necessity. . . . Following
time-honored precedents, the General Committee determined on a most liberal list of premiums. These, in artistic
merit and expense, were on a scale commensurate with the
magnitude and dignity of the exhibition."

This medal, awarded to Coffin and Standish for a steam
plow, is one of the 318 prizes awarded in 1870; the General
Committee presented 18 gold medals, 132 large silver medals (of which this is one), 76 small silver medals, and 92
diplomas at a total cost of $7,000.

The reverse of the medal bears an inscription of presentation to the winners. On the obverse, the importance of
commerce and industry is represented by high-relief allegorical figures in classical garb, surrounded by warehouses,
goods, tools, a bridge, and a steamboat, evidence of the
progress of the modern industrial world. Beneath the
figures, the medal bears the marks "Paquet" and "W. W.
McGrew. Cinn." Anthony C. Paquet (1814-1882) was a
medallist who was born in Hamburg and emigrated to
America in 1848. From 1857 to 1864 he served as assistant
engraver at the Philadelphia mint. William Wilson McGrew
is listed in *Williams' Cincinnati Directory* as a dealer in
watches and jewelry with a shop on West Fourth Street,
Cincinnati.

Refs.: *Report of the General Committee of the Cincinnati Industrial Exposition* (Cincinnati, Ohio, 1870). L. Forrer, *Biographical Dictionary of
Medallists* (London: Spink and Son, Ltd., 1904), p. 381.

19 (obverse)   19 (reverse)

18 (obverse)

18 (reverse)

19 United States, Trade Dollar, 1873, San Francisco Mint
Designed by William Barber (1807-1879)
D. 1½″ (39 mm); WT. 420.0 gr (27.22 gm)
Numismatic Collection, Yale University; courtesy of
Stack's, New York

In the nineteenth century the increase in America's commerce with the Far East created an unfavorable balance of trade for the United States. This difference was made up in silver, a metal more highly prized in the East than in the West. Because the Chinese and Japanese preferred silver in the form of the Mexican eight reales, American traders were forced to purchase Mexican coins at a premium over their bullion value in order to pay their Far Eastern creditors.

In 1873, at the urging of a number of California politicians and businessmen, Congress authorized the issuance of the trade dollar. Weighing 420 grains (the regular dollar weighed 412½ grains), the new coin contained three fourths of a grain more pure silver than its Mexican rival. It was felt that this heavier dollar would not only save American merchants the premium they paid for Mexican dollars but would also provide an outlet for the silver being mined in the American West.

Believed to be the design of Chief Engraver William Barber, the trade dollar shows Liberty seated among symbols of commerce on its obverse. On the reverse is the familiar eagle, a feature which prompted the Chinese to refer to the coin as the "precious goose," "precious duck," "flying hen," or "devil's head" dollar.

The act of 1873 which eliminated the standard silver dollar from the regular coinage simultaneously made the trade dollar legal tender in the United States in amounts up

20 (obverse) 20 (reverse)

21 (obverse) 21 (reverse)

to five dollars. Because of the falling price of silver, however, the new heavier coin created confusion and encouraged fraud; its status as legal tender was therefore revoked in 1876. The coin never achieved full acceptance in the Orient and by 1878 the trade dollar had been virtually discontinued. "America's only unwanted, unhonored coin," the trade dollar was never produced in large quantities; only thirty-six million were ever minted.

Ref.: John M. Willem, *The United States Trade Dollar: America's Only Unwanted, Unhonored Coin* (Racine, Wisconsin: Whitman Publishing, 1965).

20 **United States, Dollar,** 1878, Carson City Mint
Designed by George T. Morgan (1845-1925)
D. 1½″ (38 mm); WT. 412.5 gr (26.73 gm)
Numismatic Collection, Yale University, gift of
Stack's, New York

In 1873 the standard silver dollar was excluded from the coinage. Inasmuch as it was the only coin adhering to the 16 to 1 silver-gold ratio adopted in 1837, its elimination implied the effective adoption of the gold standard. Since it had been coined in small numbers, its absence from the new mintage attracted little attention. Shortly thereafter, however, the beginning of the long-term decline in the price of silver aroused the silver interests, who began referring to the removal of the silver dollar from the coinage as the "Crime of '73."

The Bland-Allison Act, passed over the veto of President Hayes in 1878, was a compromise measure resulting from the attempts of the silverites and silver mining interests to return to bimetallism. It required the purchase of from two to four million dollars worth of silver monthly at the market price to be coined into "standard silver dollars" of the old weight and legal tender status.

Under the Bland-Allison Act, the Sherman Silver Purchase Act of 1890, and subsequent measures, the Morgan dollar was coined until 1904. Reauthorized by the Pittman Act of 1918, its coinage was resumed for a short time in 1921.

The coin's designer, George T. Morgan, drew his inspiration for the head of Liberty from Greco-Roman statuary, and possibly, if legend is correct, from the profile of a young

Philadelphia schoolmistress named Anna Williams as well. The eagle on the reverse, although more naturalistic than some of its predecessors, caused the coin to be called the "buzzard dollar" in some quarters. The design of the new coin was generally well-received, but most people outside of the hard-money areas of the West and the South still found the coin itself inconveniently large and heavy for common use. Over 650,000,000 Morgan dollars were coined, but few saw active circulation. This particular specimen was struck at the Carson City mint in Nevada, very near the great Comstock lode.

Refs.: Vermeule, pp. 11, 74-77. Margaret G. Myers, *A Financial History of the United States* (New York: Columbia University Press, 1970), pp. 197-202. Theodore V. Buttrey, Jr., ed., *Coinage of the Americas* (New York: The American Numismatic Society, 1973), pp. 134-135.

21 **United States, Columbian Exposition Commemorative Half Dollar,** 1892, Philadelphia Mint
Designed by Charles E. Barber (1840-1917) and George T. Morgan (1845-1925)
D. 1 3/16″ (30 mm); WT. 192.9 gr (12.50 gm)
Numismatic Collection, Yale University; gift of Philip Neufeld

The Columbian half dollar of 1892 and 1893 was the first of the many commemorative coins produced as legal tender by the United States Mint. It marked the four hundredth anniversary of the discovery of America and was part of the great national celebration which centered around the exposition in Chicago. The World's Columbian Exposition represented a triumph for academic classicism in numismatics just as surely as it did in architecture, for the design of the Columbian half dollar, the obverse by the chief designer of the United States Mint, Charles E. Barber, and the reverse by George T. Morgan, is quite conservative and traditional.

There was a great interest in producing artistic coinage in 1892, and a correspondent of the *Boston Transcript* was moved to comment, "the money of a nation is expressive of its art culture. Therefore, lest posterity imagine the present generation to have been barbarous, it is desirable that our silver pieces should be as handsome as may be." Perhaps because of such high expectations, the Columbian half dollar received, at best, a half-hearted reception. The portrait of Columbus was criticized by contemporaries as looking more like Daniel Webster or Henry Ward Beecher, even though it was said to be based on a portrait of Columbus by Lorenzo Lotto—a portrait which had won a silver medal at the Columbian Historical Expositon in Madrid as the most authentic likeness of Columbus. The Columbian half dollar was followed in 1893 by a quarter dollar featuring Queen Isabella and acclaiming the role of women, and in 1900 by a silver dollar depicting Washington and Lafayette. Up to 1954 many commemorative half dollars were issued, celebrating events as diverse as the Battle of Antietam and the two hundred and fiftieth anniversary of the Cincinnati Music Center. The bicentennial coins of 1976 did not sell at a premium when issued and are therefore considered part of the regular coinage, although they are commemorative in nature.

Refs.: Vermeule, pp. 86-93. Don Taxay, *The U. S. Mint and Coinage* (New York: Arco, 1966), pp. 285-294.

22 (obverse)

22   "Bryan Dollar," 1896, Providence, Rhode Island
     Struck by the Gorham Manufacturing Company
     D. 2 1/16″ (52 mm); WT. 823.0 gr (53.33 gm)
     Numismatic Collection, Yale University

22 (reverse)

During the late nineteenth century complex monetary problems beset the nation. Declining farm prices and periods of depression associated with a scarcity of circulating money led many to advocate the free coinage of silver as an easy solution to the nation's economic ills.

A strange coalition of debt-ridden farmers, Greenbackers, other proinflation forces, and the large Western silver mining interests formed to give William Jennings Bryan the Democratic nomination for President in 1896. Bryan made the unlimited coinage of silver at the ratio of 16 to 1 a primary issue of the campaign. He and his followers saw "free silver" as the salvation of the common man. The sound-money Republicans, led by standard-bearer William McKinley, argued that the free coinage of silver at the old ratio would cause economic disruption and runaway inflation.

The "Bryan dollar" illustrated here is one of a number of satirical pieces made during the campaigns of 1896 and 1900. Its size, compared to that of a standard silver dollar on the reverse, dramatized the fact that the drastic fall in the price of silver since the 1870s had made the silver dollar a subsidiary coin whose intrinsic value by 1900 was less than forty-eight cents. These dollars were struck by a number of Eastern silver companies, including Gorham and Tiffany.

In 1900 Bryan again ran for President on a "free silver" platform and was decisively beaten by McKinley. Earlier that year Congress passed the Gold Standard Act, making the gold dollar the standard unit of value. This act together with Bryan's defeat made "free silver" a dead issue, and the United States formally joined the international movement toward a single gold standard.

Refs.: J. Earl Massey, *America's Money* (New York: Thomas Y. Crowell Company, 1968), pp. 192-193. Stanley L. Jones, *The Presidential Election of 1896* (Madison, Wisconsin: The University of Wisconsin Press, 1964), pp. 6-13.

23 (obverse)

23 (reverse)

23   **United States, Dollar,** 1934, Philadelphia Mint
Designed by Anthony De Francisci (1887-1965), 1921
D. 1½″ (39 mm); WT. 412.5 gr (26.73 gm)
Numismatic Collection, Yale University; gift of
Paul Atkins

Although the United States formally adopted the gold
standard in 1900, silver continued to be used for subsidiary
coinage including the dime, quarter dollar, and half dollar.
Attractive new designs for these denominations were introduced in 1916, and in 1921 Anthony De Francisci, an independent medallist, was commissioned to create a new design
for the silver dollar. The resulting Peace dollar owes much to
previous designs. The head depicted on the obverse is an
idealized portrait of the sculptor's wife in the guise of Liberty. With her streaming hair and crown of radiant sun-
beams she recalls Augustus Saint-Gaudens's design for the
ten-dollar gold piece (1907) but is also closely related to
earlier representations of Liberty. On the reverse a passive
eagle stands upon a mountain top labeled ''PEACE,'' looking
toward the rising sun.

Coined in increasingly smaller numbers, the Peace dollar was not minted after 1935. While the Eisenhower dollar,
first issued in 1971, was struck in a 40 percent silver composition for collectors as well as a copper-nickel composition
for circulation, the Peace dollar was the last standard silver
dollar of the United States of America.

Ref.: Vermeule, pp. 148-152.

Traditional Craft Practices

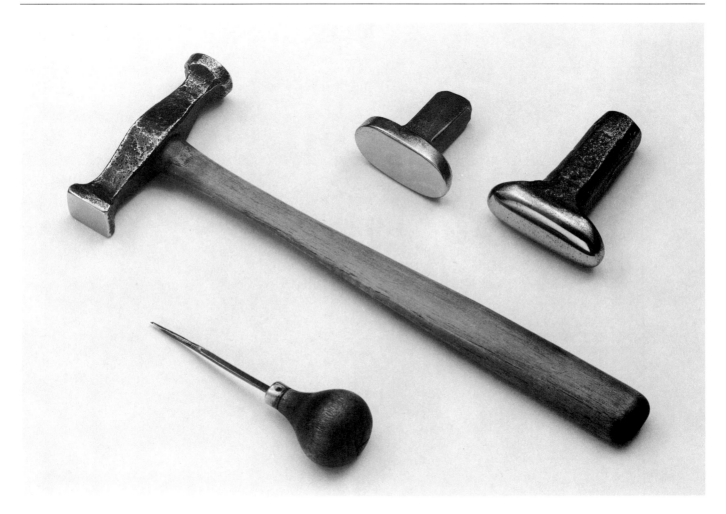

24 Planishing Hammer, Stakes, and Graver,
American, 1750-1900
L. hammer 10 1/16" (256 mm)
Gift of Mr. and Mrs. Joseph A. Link   1978.88A-D

The colonial silversmith used hammers to raise silver into hollow shapes and also to form flatware pieces. During the raising process the metal was compressed over a form called a stake. Stakes, like the two shown here, were held in place by a vice as the silversmith worked over them. Throughout his career, a craftsman usually developed many specialized tools for his own use and as a result accumulated a large number of hammers and stakes. Early inventories show that the average silversmith might own as many as one hundred hammers and nearly as many stakes. Modern firms continue to follow in this tradition; the shop of Gebelein Silversmiths in Boston maintains a large stock of hammers and stakes in its workroom for specialized uses.

By contrast, it appears that few silversmiths required more than one or two gravers, presumably because most did not use a great variety of lines in their engraved decorations. Furthermore, by the eighteenth century many silversmiths

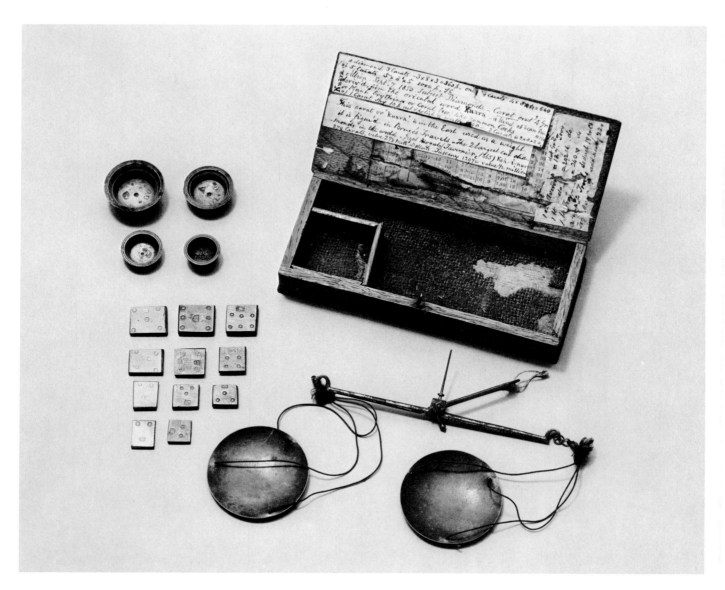

hired specialists to engrave their silver. The list of tools traditionally used by silversmiths is extensive, and the development of new techniques has increased the variety of equipment needed to set up a basic workshop.

Refs.: William de Matteo, *The Silversmith in Eighteenth-Century Williamsburg* (Williamsburg, Virginia: Colonial Williamsburg, 1956), pp. 21-31. Oppi Untracht, *Metal Techniques for Craftsmen* (Garden City, New York: Doubleday & Company, Inc., 1968), pp. 240-262, 422-447. Bernard Cuzner, *A Silversmith's Manual* (1935; reprint, London: N.A.G. Press Ltd., 1949).

25 **Silversmith's Scales,** England, ca. 1700-1750
   w. box 5¾" (146 mm)
   Gift of Sarah W. Cotting   1964.73

26 **Single Link of Gold Sleeve Buttons,** Boston,
   ca. 1710-1720
   Attributed to John Burt (1693-1746)
   D. 7/16" (11 mm)
   Mabel Brady Garvan Collection   1947.194

Most American silversmiths worked in gold as well as silver, and the titles goldsmith and silversmith were used interchangeably in early documents. Gold, rare in the colonies, was only used to fashion small pieces of jewelry such as this sleeve button (26) made by John Burt and engraved with the name of its owner.

Such objects were frequently weighed on small delicate scales (25). While the silversmith would use larger scales to weigh scrap silver and most finished pieces, scales like these were used to weigh the coins, precious stones, and bits of gold and silver which he handled in his daily business. According to family tradition this set of scales with brass weights belonged to Edward Winslow (1669-1753), one of the most important of Boston's early silversmiths. Like many of his fellow artisans, Winslow may have also imported this type of pocket scale to sell along with other small wares in his shop. On 4 July 1763 Daniel Parker offered for sale in the *Boston Evening Post* "scales & weights, small money ditto for the pocket, pennyweights and grains; [and] piles of brass weights," among other goods lately imported from London.

26

At a time when the value of money was reckoned strictly on the basis of its weight, scales of this type were a necessity, and no doubt silversmiths sold numerous sets to local merchants and tradesmen who used them regularly in their shops.

Refs.: Buhler and Hood, nos. 51, 107. Flynt and Fales, pp. 33-37. Rupert Gentle and Rachael Feild, *English Domestic Brass, 1680-1810, and the History of its Origins* (New York: E. P. Dutton & Co., Inc., 1975), p. 103, nos. 337, 340, 341.

27 **The Silversmith's Shop of William Homes, Jr.,**
    unknown artist
    Oil on canvas, ca. 1816-1822
    H. 12″ (305 mm); W. 10⅛″ (257 mm)
    Gift of Josephine Setze   1973.128

28 **Ladle,** Boston, ca. 1765-1775
    William Homes, Jr. (1742-1825)
    L. 14¼″ (362 mm); WT. 2 oz, 1 dwt (64 gm)
    Mabel Brady Garvan Collection   1931.334

This small painting by an unknown artist might very well be one of the earliest extant views of an American silversmith's shop, that of William Homes, Jr. (1742-1825) of Boston. In all likelihood, the scene depicted here represents a situation which only existed between 1816 and 1825. As Martha Gandy Fales discovered, William Homes, goldsmith, and John Homes, hardware, both at 63 Ann Street, and Cornelius B. Simmons, slop shop, at 62 Ann Street, were first listed as neighbors in the Boston directory of 1816. By 1825, William Homes had died, John Homes had moved to 27 Ann Street, and no C. B. Simmons is listed.

Homes seems to have a teapot and other ready-made goods on display in his front window, a feature also visible in an exterior view of the shop of William A. Williams which appeared in the *Alexandria Gazette and Advertiser* in 1823. Homes's workshop, where he made such goods as this ladle (28), was probably also located at this address, perhaps at the back of the house, to reduce the risk of fire from the forge, or in the basement.

Refs.: Buhler and Hood, no. 274. Fales, *Early American Silver,* pp. 195-198. Flynt and Fales, pp. 249-250.

29

30

29 **Porringer**, Boston, ca. 1720-1730
William Cowell, Sr. (1682-1736)
D. bowl 5¼″ (133 mm); WT. 7 OZ, 14 dwt (239 gm)
Mabel Brady Garvan Collection   1930.1253

30 **Porringer**, Boston, ca. 1730-1740
Rufus Greene (1707-1777)
D. bowl 5⅛″ (130 mm); WT. 7 OZ, 8 dwt (230 gm)
Mabel Brady Garvan Collection   1930.947

Traditionally, young men learned the art of silversmithing by serving an apprenticeship, usually between the ages of fourteen and twenty-one. In the early stages of his training, the apprentice was given simple tasks to complete, such as polishing finished pieces, helping to run the lathe, or drawing wire on the bench. By the time a young man had worked in a shop for several years he was ready to begin making whole objects by himself.

Apprentices learned both styles and techniques from their masters and it is not surprising that when they themselves became masters, they often adopted the handles, finials, and cast decorations which they had learned to make during their years of training. William Cowell, Sr., made several porringers with this distinctive handle piercing (**29**). Rufus Greene, a documented apprentice of Cowell's, was no doubt looking back to his master's work when he made this nearly identical porringer (**30**) about ten years later.

Refs.: Buhler and Hood, nos. 90, 170. Kathryn C. Buhler, *Colonial Silversmiths, Masters and Apprentices* (Boston: Museum of Fine Arts, 1956), p. 34.

31 **Coffee Pot**, Philadelphia, ca. 1780-1790
Joseph and Nathaniel Richardson (w. 1771-1791)
H. 11⅞″ (302 mm); WT. 32 OZ, 9 dwt (1006 gm)
Mabel Brady Garvan Collection   1930.1269

". . . the shop which my Sons Joseph and Nathaniel now Occupy . . . I will and direct them the Use of as heretofore, and . . . I give unto my said two Sons my Show Glass working Tools and Utensils of Trade equally to be divided between them. . . ."

Thus, upon the death of their father Joseph in 1784, Joseph Jr. and Nathaniel Richardson inherited the oldest goldsmith's shop in continuous operation in the city of Philadelphia. The family tradition in silversmithing had been founded by their grandfather Francis, and through the generations the Quaker Richardson family built a reputation for sound business sense and good craftsmanship. In the period from 1771 to 1791 (when Nathaniel retired from silversmithing) Joseph Jr. and Nathaniel Richardson worked together, and the objects which left their shop bore the I·NR mark of the partnership. One such object is this beautifully proportioned coffee pot, whose clean, elegant lines make it an outstanding example of Philadelphia silver. The fact that the initials of both Joseph and Nathaniel Richardson appear on this pot does not necessarily mean that the brothers actually worked together on its production. It was customary for the mark of the master, in this case the partnership of masters, to appear on each object which left a shop, no matter who actually made it.

Refs.: Buhler and Hood, no. 884. Fales, *Richardson*, pp. 164-197.

32   **Sugar Bowl,** Philadelphia, ca. 1790-1800
      John Germon (w. ca. 1782-1816)
      H. 10 9/16″ (267 mm); WT. 15 oz, 1 dwt (466 gm)
      Mabel Brady Garvan Collection   1930.1025c

In the eighteenth century, the existence of specialists led to what we recognize today as regional characteristics in silver, furniture, pewter, and other objects. This urn-shaped neo-classical sugar bowl by John Germon has a pierced scalloped band around its top and, as Charles F. Montgomery noted, such "pierced galleries are a regional hallmark of late eighteenth-century tea- and coffeepots and sugar bowls made in Philadelphia; Wilmington, Delaware; Baltimore; and Annapolis, Maryland. Banding for the galleries was probably made by a Philadelphia specialist in long strips and sold to silversmiths in the region." It has been suggested that this banding, a type of ornamentation found on Swedish silver of the same period, may have been produced by a Swedish-trained Philadelphia craftsman.

Refs.: Buhler and Hood, no. 899. Montgomery and Kane, p. 56. Kathryn C. Buhler, *American Silver* (Cleveland: The World Publishing Company, 1950), p. 58.

33   Tankard, New London, Connecticut, ca. 1735-1750
      Pygan Adams (1712-1776)
      H. 6⅝″ (168 mm); WT. 17 oz, 17 dwt (553 gm)
      Kevin G. Rafferty Memorial Fund   1966.54

The advertisements and account books of eighteenth-century craftsmen provide ample and repeated testimony to the fact that repair work constituted a large part of the silversmith's, pewterer's, or cabinetmaker's business. Often the silversmith would be confronted with an object such as this tankard, one of the few surviving pieces of hollow ware made by Pygan Adams, a prominent silversmith and citizen of New London. Without its lid and with a dented and cracked body expressive of the wear and tear of daily use, this tankard would be an obvious candidate for repair, an alternative which would have been less costly than fashioning a new object.

   This tankard, however, was never repaired. It was in its present condition when it entered the collection in 1966, and no attempt has been made to restore its battered body, which remains an evocative record of the vicissitudes of time.

Refs.: Buhler and Hood, no. 342. George Munson Curtis, *Early Silver of Connecticut and Its Makers* (Meriden, Connecticut: International Silver Company, 1913), pp. 72-73. Jennifer Goldsborough, *An Exhibition of New London Silver, 1700-1835* (New London, Connecticut: Lyman Allyn Museum, 1969), pp. 8-9.

34 Tankard, Boston, ca. 1690-1710
Jeremiah Dummer (1645-1718)
H. body 5⅛" (130 mm); WT. 23 oz, 10 dwt (729 gm)
Gift of Francis B. Trowbridge   1944.24

Repairs have been a common part of the silversmith's work since the seventeenth century, and many old objects show evidence of several alterations. With heavy use the handle of a tankard will begin to pull away from its body, and many surviving examples have been repaired and reinforced over the years. Solder marks inside the body and on the handle of this object indicate that the handle was refastened or possibly even replaced. Perhaps later in its long life this tankard lost its original cover and thumbpiece and looked much like the tankard by Pygan Adams (33) looks today. When first made in about 1700 a tankard of these proportions would have had a flat top (126). However, the silversmith who repaired this piece fitted it with a stepped, domed cover of the type popular about 1750. The alteration may have been made in the middle of the eighteenth century to bring an old piece up to date. It is also possible that the tankard was restored in the late nineteenth or early twentieth century by a silversmith who, instead of fashioning a new top for the piece, chose to use an old top which he found among his bits of scrap silver.

Refs.: Buhler and Hood, no. 18. Gerald W. R. Ward, ed., *The Eye of the Beholder: Fakes, Replicas, and Alterations in American Art* (New Haven: Yale University Art Gallery, 1977), p. 38.

35 Ladle, Lexington, Kentucky, ca. 1810-1830
Asa Blanchard (w. ca. 1808-1838)
L. 5½" (140 mm); WT. 16 dwt (25 gm)
Mabel Brady Garvan Collection   1931.1287

A large part of every silversmith's business was the making of small items. This was particularly true for craftsmen working in frontier towns and in rural areas where the market for silver wares was relatively small.

   This ladle was made by Asa Blanchard, one of Kentucky's earliest and best-known silversmiths, who worked in Lexington at the corner of Mill and Short streets from about 1808 until his death in 1838. Surviving bills and advertisements indicate that Blanchard made numerous small objects, including tablespoons, ladles, and silver-rimmed spectacles. This sauce ladle, with its long narrow handle, appears to be characteristic of his work in flatware. The piece was made from coin silver, that is, 900 parts silver to 100 parts copper, or of the fineness of the circulating coinage. According to Kentucky legend many families set aside coins especially for the purpose of having them converted into spoons, pitchers, and other objects, as may well have been the case here.

Refs.: Buhler and Hood, no. 987. Margaret M. Bridwell, "Kentucky Silversmiths Before 1850," *The Filson Club History Quarterly* 16, no. 2 (April 1942): 111-126. Henry H. Harned, "Ante-Bellum Kentucky Silver," *Antiques* 105, no. 4 (April 1974): 818-824. Noble W. Hiatt and Lucy F. Hiatt, *The Silversmiths of Kentucky, Together with Some Watchmakers and Jewelers, 1785-1850* (Louisville, Kentucky: The Standard Printing Company, 1954), pp. 13-17.

36 Shoe Buckle, Medford, Massachusetts, ca. 1780-1790
William Gowen (1749-1803)
L. (curved) 4¼" (108 mm); WT. 2 oz, 3 dwt (67 gm)
Mabel Brady Garvan Collection   1930.1110a

Shoe buckles were an important accessory to the costume of a fashionable gentleman in the eighteenth century. High-topped boots and high-heeled dress shoes were designed to fasten with buckles which were made, according to one's means, of steel, pewter, silver, or gold. Account books of silversmiths working in rural areas of New England indicate that a significant part of their business consisted of making

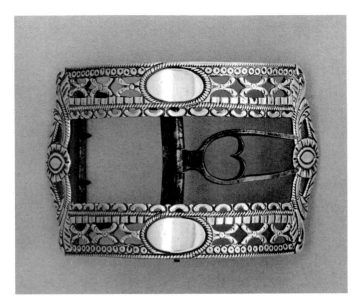

37 **Tobacco Box,** London, ca. 1681-1682
Engraved by John Coney (1656-1722), Boston, ca. 1701
L. 3 13/16″ (97 mm); WT. 4 oz, 17 dwt (150 gm)
Mabel Brady Garvan Collection   1935.235

small items of jewelry such as shoe buckles and knee buckles. Although the shoe buckle began to go out of style in England and Europe toward the end of the eighteenth century, American gentlemen continued to wear them into the nineteenth century, and silversmiths apparently found that such objects were in enough demand to warrant importing them in large numbers. Inventories show that many people who owned no pieces of hollow ware nevertheless owned small pieces of jewelry; because very few such pieces have survived the melting pot over the years, their importance in colonial life and in the work of the silversmith has often been overlooked.

This example was made by William Gowen, who worked in Medfield and Charlestown, Massachusetts, between 1780 and 1790. Its diamond-faceted face and oval medallions are characteristic of buckles made toward the end of the eighteenth century. Often buckles of similar design were also set with paste jewels.

Refs.: Buhler and Hood, no. 286. Ruth Turner Wilcox, *Five Centuries of American Costume* (New York: Charles Scribner's Sons, 1963), pp. 126-147. Fales, *Richardson*, pp. 147-148.

Silversmiths regularly imported small boxes, buttons, and buckles from England to sell in their shops. Some pieces would arrive plain so that the local silversmith could embellish them as his customers required.

This handsome tobacco box bears the worn mark of a London silversmith as well as the mark of John Coney of Boston. Coney probably engraved the Jeffries arms on the cover and the inscription "Donum RG 1701" for the purchaser and then marked the piece to indicate that it had been engraved in his shop. Coney also made boxes of this type himself, for his inventory mentions that he possessed a "tobacco box anvil."

It was not unusual for silversmiths and other craftsmen to sell objects they did not produce. John Coney would doubtless have had many small ready-made objects on hand in his display cases. At the time of his death his inventory shows that he had "Gold Earrings wth glass drops," "stone rings," "coral beads," a "toothpick case," and a "snuff box" in his shop, some of which may have been imported items.

Refs.: Buhler and Hood, no. 32. Hermann Frederick Clarke, *John Coney, Silversmith, 1655-1722* (Boston: Houghton Mifflin Company, 1932), facsimile of Coney's inventory printed between pp. 12-13.

38 Tankard, Boston, 1762
Paul Revere, II (1735-1818)
H. 8⅝" (219 mm); WT. 30 oz, 5 dwt (938 gm)
Mabel Brady Garvan Collection   1930.1196

Many silversmiths were skilled engravers, and the cleverest ones found it lucrative to engrave copper plates for printing in addition to their regular engraving on silver. Of the many American silversmith-engravers Nathaniel Hurd and Paul Revere are the best known.

Revere must have been particularly proud of his abilities as an engraver, for when John Singleton Copley painted Revere's portrait in the late 1760s, he showed the silversmith with his engraving tools as he was about to engrave a silver teapot. In addition to his hundreds of pieces of engraved silver, Revere also did at least seventy-two copper-plate engravings, the most famous of which is his version of "The Bloody Massacre" of 1770. Other engravings include paper money for the Province of Massachusetts, trade cards, bookplates, invitations, book illustrations, views of Boston Harbor and Harvard College, and numerous illustrations and political cartoons for the *Royal American Magazine*.

Revere's finest original designs are his ornamental compositions which incorporate the flourishes, shells, and swags of the rococo and which are clearly related to his work on silver. This tankard, made for Thomas Greene of Boston and his wife Martha, is embellished with a coat of arms similar to the one Revere used for the bookplate for David Greene (Fig. 30) and indicates the close relationship between Revere's work on silver and on copper. The source for the Greene coat of arms and many other heraldry designs used by Revere was probably John Guillim's *A Display of Heraldry* (41).

Refs.: Buhler and Hood, no. 240. Clarence S. Brigham, *Paul Revere's Engravings* (New York: Atheneum, 1969), pp. ix-xii, 3-9, 158-166. Montgomery and Kane, pp. 133-134.

Figure 30
Paul Revere (1735-1818)
Bookplate of David Greene
Line engraving (one of four known states), ca. 1760-1770
Bookplate Collection, Yale University Library

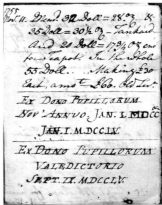

39   Tankard, Little Rest, Rhode Island, 1755
Samuel Casey (ca. 1724-ca. 1780)
H. 8⅛″ (206 mm); WT. 27 oz, 13 dwt (857 gm)
Mabel Brady Garvan Collection   1938.319

In some cases surviving documents help to provide a clearer picture of the relationship between a silversmith and one of his patrons. In 1755 Ezra Stiles, who would later become President of Yale College, resigned his position as tutor at the College to become pastor of the Second Congregational Church of Newport, Rhode Island. His students apparently presented him with a farewell gift of silver or money to be fashioned into a token of their esteem, and after he arrived in Newport, Stiles decided to convert the gift into this silver tankard. An entry in Stiles's account book shows that he calculated the amount of silver needed for the tankard and provided it to Samuel Casey, a silversmith of Exeter, Rhode Island. As was customary at the time, Stiles paid separately for the cost of fashioning the tankard, and Casey received an additional £30 old tenor for his labor; the silver for the tankard itself was worth about £75 old tenor. In his account book Stiles also sketched the way he wanted the engraving

to appear on the bottom of the tankard (Fig. 31). Patrons may often have had more instructions for the silversmith, perhaps even indicating the type of decoration desired.

Samuel Casey, the maker of this tankard, was one of Rhode Island's most accomplished, and most colorful, silversmiths. Probably trained in Boston, he worked in Exeter and Little Rest (later Kingston) between 1745 and 1770. In addition to his activities as a silversmith he apparently also spent many hours in his garret counterfeiting Spanish and Portuguese coins. He and his several accomplices were arrested in 1770 and Casey, known as "Silver Sam," was sentenced to death. On 3 November 1770, however, he and his friends were freed from jail by a mob of supporters and Casey fled from the colony. His wife petitioned for his pardon in 1779, but although the General Assembly acquitted him of his crimes he never returned to his home. Some sources say that he may have died fighting on the side of the King in the Revolution.

Refs.: Buhler and Hood, no. 482. William Davis Miller, *The Silversmiths of Little Rest* (Kingston, Rhode Island: Privately Printed, 1928), pp. 2-9. Kenneth Scott, *Counterfeiting in Colonial America* (New York: Oxford University Press, 1957), pp. 210-235.

40 **Punch Bowl,** New York, ca. 1760
   John Heath (Freeman 1761)
   D. lip 10⅛″ (257 mm); WT. 29 oz, 11 dwt (916 gm)
   John Marshall Phillips Collection   1953.10.3

Another object associated with an existing document is this
fine punch bowl made by John Heath of New York for Pierre
Van Cortlandt (1721-1814). Van Cortlandt was an important
New York political figure and master of Van Cortland
Manor at Croton-on-Hudson.

Heath's bill (Fig. 32) for both the punch bowl and a
sugar bowl or "Boox" (also in Yale's collection) indicates
the way in which the silversmith calculated the cost of a
finished object. It is interesting to note that while Van
Cortlandt paid nine shillings and fourpence (new tenor) per
ounce for the silver in the punch bowl, Heath's labor was
only worth three shillings and sixpence per ounce. Heath's
charge for fashioning the sugar bowl was a flat rate of £2, a
cost of only two shillings and ninepence per ounce.

Engraving the lavish coat of arms on the bowl and a
small crest on the sugar bowl must have been a time-consuming job for Heath, judging from the fact that the cost of
these embellishments was one half the price for fashioning
the sugar bowl. The coat of arms is indicative of Heath's
skill as an engraver. Scrolls and leafage cover an entire side
of the bowl, giving richness and rococo flair to an otherwise
plain surface. Very little is known of Heath, although a
number of pieces by his hand survive. He became a freeman
of New York in 1761 and probably worked there until about
1770.

Refs.: Buhler and Hood, no. 724. Martha Gandy Fales, *American Silver in
the Henry Francis du Pont Winterthur Museum* (Winterthur, Delaware:
The Henry Francis du Pont Winterthur Museum, 1958), nos. 46, 120.

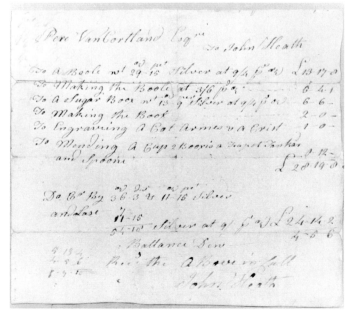

Figure 32
Original bill from John Heath to
Peter Van Cortlandt.
Yale University Art Gallery
1953.10.4a.

Figure 33
John Singleton Copley (1737-1815)
Portrait of Nathaniel Hurd
Oil on canvas, ca. 1765
The Cleveland Museum of Art; gift
of the John Huntington Art and
Polytechnic Trust

41   **A Display of Heraldry,** John Guillim (1565-1621)
London: Printed by T. W., 1724, sixth edition
Gift of Florence M. Montgomery

John Guillim's *A Display of Heraldry* was one of the design
sources most frequently used by American colonial silversmiths when engraving coats of arms on silver for their
customers. The hundreds of patterns illustrated and described by Guillim were freely adopted and modified by
Americans, who were not bothered by the fact that they had
no legitimate sanction to use them. Paul Revere, for example, chose a design from Guillim when engraving a heraldic
device for the Greene family on a tankard (**38**) in this exhibition. The various mantlings shown in Guillim were also an
important source of inspiration for American silversmith-
engravers. First published in 1611, this book had gone
through five editions and substantial revisions by 1724,
when the sixth edition (seen here) was published. A copy of
this edition can be seen in John Singleton Copley's *Portrait
of Nathaniel Hurd* (Fig. 33), painted about 1765. The book
was in common use throughout the eighteenth century, although the use of heraldic devices declined after the Revolution.

Refs.: Fales, *Early American Silver,* pp. 235-244. Charles K. Bolton, *Bolton's American Armory* (Boston: The F. W. Faxon Co., 1927).

42

43

42 Two-handled Cup, London, 1705-1706
John Gibbons (w. ca. 1700-1744)
H. 5 3/16″ (132 mm); WT. 13 oz, 3 dwt (408 gm)
Gift of Mrs. James B. Neale as part of a collection
of silver presented as a memorial to James B. Neale
1948.156

43 Two-handled Cup, Boston, ca. 1710-1720
William Cowell, Sr. (1682-1736)
H. 4 3/16″ (106 mm); WT. 8 oz, 4 dwt (254 gm)
Mabel Brady Garvan Collection 1944.72

Styles in American silver closely followed English taste, and
American silversmiths relied in large part upon imported
English objects for their knowledge of the latest fashion.
When William Cowell, Sr., of Boston made this two-handled
cup (**43**) in about 1710-1720 he may well have been looking
at an English example very much like this one by John
Gibbons of London (**42**). Although Cowell's cup is also
quite definitely related to a cup made by Jeremiah Dummer,
who may have been Cowell's master, its height and the addition of the smaller gadrooned band near the lip indicate
that Cowell was aware of more up-to-date English examples
of the form. Cowell is known to have made at least five other
similar gadrooned cups, three of which are owned by
churches in Massachusetts and Connecticut.

Although Cowell seems to have made a large number
of silver objects, apparently that business alone was not
enough to afford him a comfortable living. In 1709 he petitioned to "Sell (Strong Drinck) as Inholder," and when he
died in 1736 he was listed as a innholder, although his inventory indicates that he still continued to work in silver.

Refs.: Buhler and Hood, no. 88. Fales, *Early American Silver*, pp. 115-132.
Kathryn C. Buhler, *Massachusetts Silver in the Frank L. and Louise C.*
Harrington Collection (Worcester, Massachusetts: Privately Printed,
1965), pp. 35-38.

44 **Creamware Pitcher,** Liverpool, England, ca. 1800
H. 8⅞″ (225 mm)
Mabel Brady Garvan Collection   1931.1880

45 **Pitcher,** Boston, ca. 1805
Paul Revere, II (1735-1818)
H. 6 5/16″ (160 mm); WT. 17 oz, 8 dwt (539 gm)
Mabel Brady Garvan Collection   1930.1223

Silversmiths often used ceramic forms as models when creating objects in silver, and the relationship between objects made in different materials at about the same time is quite close. The use of a specific ceramic form as a design source for silver is particularly evident in the case of Paul Revere's famous pitcher (**45**), which is copied directly from popular English creamware pitchers (**44**) imported into this country in great numbers in the early nineteenth century.

Only twelve of Revere's pitchers have survived to the present day. The form, however, is frequently reproduced, and today "Revere pitchers" rank second in popularity only to copies of Revere's "Liberty Bowl."

Refs.: Buhler and Hood, no. 264. Montgomery and Kane, p. 212.

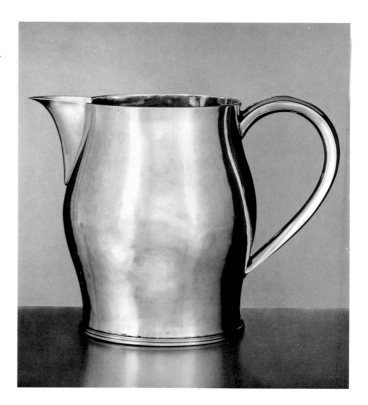

46 left, 47 right

46 Tea Caddy, London, 1750-1751
John Payne (ca. 1720—ca. 1799)
H. 5″ (127 mm); WT. 7 oz, 16 dwt (242 gm)
Mabel Brady Garvan Collection   1936.161b

47 Tea Caddy, New York, ca. 1805-1820
John W. Forbes (1781—ca. 1838)
H. 5″ (127 mm); WT. 7 oz, 6 dwt (226 gm)
Mabel Brady Garvan Collection   1936.161a

Imported English objects were an important design source for early American silversmiths (42-43). Frequently, English objects in the latest style were copied directly in this country to provide patrons with the most fashionable objects or to fill out a set or complete a pair. When John Forbes made this tea caddy (47), however, he was not producing an object in the latest style, but rather copying an English model that was over half a century old. The rococo tea caddy (46) which Forbes duplicated with only slight changes in the chased decoration had long been out of style; but the rococo style in silver, noted for its all-over repoussé and chasing, was revived in the third decade of the nineteenth century by such firms as Samuel Kirk and Sons. Thus Forbes's caddy can be viewed as foreshadowing the rococo revival, in addition to being an important example of the influence of English design. The copy is so close to the original that the two caddies were long thought to be a pair until Payne's marks were discovered hidden in the repoussé of the earlier piece.

Refs.: Buhler and Hood, no. 756. Fales, *Early American Silver,* pp. 115-132.

Mass Production and Craft Revival

Mechanization
Industrialization
Silver-plating
Arts and Crafts Revival
Contemporary Artist-Craftsmen

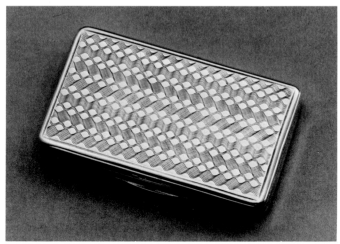

48   Snuff Box, American, ca. 1848
w. 3 1/16″ (92 mm); wt. 1 oz, 18 dwt (59 gm)
Yale University Archives   U1965.10.2

In the nineteenth century, the making of silver objects evolved from a craft to an industry. Labor-saving techniques such as drop stamping, spinning, and machine engraving augmented traditional methods of handcraftsmanship.

This small unmarked snuff box bears two kinds of typical nineteenth-century ornament. On the back, the opti-

cal effects of engine turning, an immensely popular form of machine engraving, give depth to the surface of the silver and produce what one early observer called "the wonderful imitations of the delicate tracery with which the nimble fingers of Jack Frost decorate our windows." The inscription on the lid is surrounded by engraved floral panels suggestive of printed title pages in contemporary books. "Presented to Eli A. Yale, by his fellow Clerks as a token of Esteem, September 1848," this box originally belonged to a collateral descendant of the benefactor who gave his name to Yale College.

Ref.: "The Americans at Work: Among the Silver-Platers," *Appletons' Journal* 5, no. 31 (December 1878): 489.

49   Water Pitcher, Providence, Rhode Island, 1876
Gorham and Company
H. 8¾″ (222 mm); wt. 27 oz, 19 dwt (866 gm)
Marie-Antoinette Slade Fund   1973.146

Water pitchers of this design, sometimes accompanied by matching goblets, were produced in several sizes by Gorham in the early 1870s. The body of the pitcher was formed of two parts, each produced by a machine process known as spinning, a technique which replaced earlier methods of hand-raising. The upper part of the body was then hand-chased in a design incorporating various Renaissance motifs, including winged dragons, medallions, and lush acanthus foliage. Below this frieze is an applied roll-stamped band, which masks the seam between the two spun parts of the body. This band is in a pattern used by Gorham on other objects as well (**184**), and reflects the standardization of design found in even the high-quality productions of the period. The design of this band was surely inspired by patterns found in popular design books of the period such as Owen Jones's *The Grammar of Ornament* (1856), which was available to the Gorham designers in the company library assembled by the president of the company, Edward Holbrook.

Refs.: Owen Jones, *The Grammar of Ornament* (1856; reprint, New York: Van Nostrand Reinhold Co., 1972), pl. LXVII, no. 37; pl. LXXXII, no. 34. "Have You Seen the Gorham Factory?" *The Jewelers' Circular and Horological Review* 23, no. 7 (16 September 1891): 31.

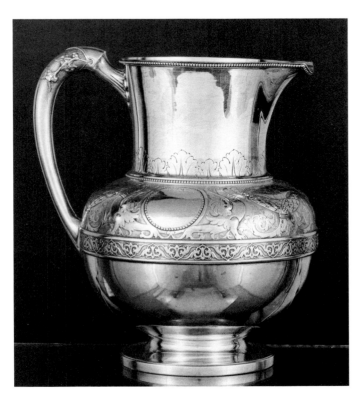

50   **Silver-plated Teapot,** Taunton, Massachusetts, 1872
Reed & Barton; retailed by Starr and Marcus,
New York
H. 9 15/16″ (252 mm)
Gift of the David H. Clement family in memory of
Charles F. Montgomery   1978.66

In the middle of the nineteenth century, American manufacturers began experimenting with electroplating, a process developed in England earlier in the century. By electroplating silver onto a base metal, objects with the appearance of sterling silver could be cheaply produced and widely marketed.

Standard production silver-plated tea sets of the 1870s are frequently characterized by angular handles, tall splayed feet, and varied eclectic ornament, loosely related if related at all. This teapot is a typical example, replete with cast mask feet and heavy, mechanical ornament. Its design was patented on 21 May 1872 by William Parkin for Reed & Barton; the Patent Office drawing shows a central panel conveniently left blank for the engraver, an indication of the lack of concern for the integration of ornament with design prevalent in this period. On this teapot, the blank space has been filled with rather stiff blossoms, below a date of 1872. Although the piece was made by Reed & Barton, their mark on the bottom has been effaced and replaced by the mark of Starr and Marcus, New York retailers. Originally part of a seven-piece tea and coffee service, this pot was purchased as a wedding gift for Florence (Wick) Chambers of Cleveland, Ohio.

Ref.: Dorothy T. and H. Ivan Rainwater, *American Silverplate* (Nashville, Tennessee: Thomas Nelson, Inc.; Hanover, Pennsylvania: Everybodys Press, 1968), pp. 104-106.

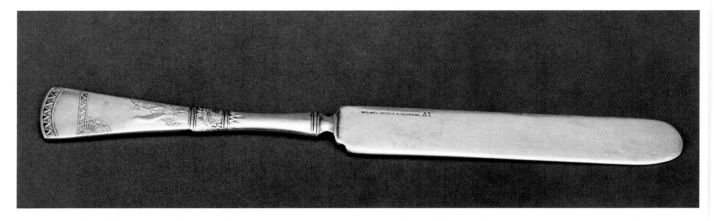

51 Silver-plated Butter Knife, Waterbury, Connecticut,
ca. 1870-1885
Holmes, Booth, and Haydens
L. 7" (178 mm)
Gift of Alexander O. Vietor, B.A. 1936   1974.22.4

This silver-plated butter knife in the "Japanese" pattern has
different decoration on the front and back of its handle, a
form of ornamentation made possible through the use of
two-part shaped dies and machine stamping. As Noel D.
Turner explains, "the machine, with the aid of handwork at
the finishing point, could turn out thousands like the one
model, once the dies had been completed. It was just as easy
to produce heavily decorated patterns as it was to manufacture the plain and simple ones."

Holmes, Booth, and Haydens began operation in Waterbury as a brass rolling company, and after a boom in the
brass business during the Civil War expanded their operation to include the mass manufacture of electroplated
nickel-silver.

Ref.: Turner, pp. 28-29, 33-35, 139.

Figure 34
Page from the 1891 sales catalogue
of Simpson, Hall, Miller, and Com-
pany illustrating the tilting water
set (52).
Historical Library, International
Silver Company, Meriden,
Connecticut.

52 Silver-plated Tilting Water Set, Wallingford,
Connecticut, ca. 1891
Simpson, Hall, Miller, and Company
H. stand 23¾" (603 mm)
Millicent Todd Bingham Fund   1978.57A-C

Pitchers for ice water, double- or even triple-walled for
insulation, were first patented in the 1850s, and reached the
height of their popularity in the 1880s. Reed & Barton's
1885 catalogue, for example, offered ice water pitchers in
fifty-one different styles.

This silver-plated "Tilting Water Set" made by Simpson, Hall, Miller, and Company was one of three closely
related versions illustrated in their 1891 catalogue (Fig. 34).
The pitcher is fitted with a multicolored porcelain sleeve and
is designed to rest on a supporting framework to facilitate
pouring. The set originally had two gold-lined goblets, now
missing, in addition to the extant slop bowl. The entire set
sold for $56.00.

The decoration of the set might best be described as
exuberant and eclectic. A band of Egyptian sphinxes,
camels, pyramids, and palm trees in low relief form a border
on the pitcher, stand, and slop bowl; seminude female
figures adorn each side of the stand; fish figure prominently
on the handle and the spout; birds and flowers are hand-
painted on the porcelain sleeve; floral decoration abounds;
and the whole is presided over by the head of a goddess. It all
adds up to a pattern known in its own time as "Denizen."

By 1900 these sets had largely gone out of fashion.
Perhaps they were too cumbersome (the pitcher of this set
weighs thirteen pounds when filled with water) or too difficult to keep clean. The coming of mechanical refrigeration
in the early twentieth century helped to make them obsolete.
This highly ornate set in good condition, a rare survival, is a
reminder of a way of life far removed from our own which
existed less than a century ago.

Refs.: E. P. Hogan, "The Old Fashioned Ice Pitcher," *Spinning Wheel* 31,
no. 4 (June 1975): 8-12. Dorothy T. and H. Ivan Rainwater, *American Silverplate* (Nashville, Tennessee: Thomas Nelson, Inc.; Hanover, Pennsylvania: Everybodys Press, 1968), pp. 248-263.

53 Pitcher and Tray, Providence, Rhode Island, ca. 1900
Designed by William C. Codman (1839-1921)
Gorham Manufacturing Company
H. pitcher 9¼″ (235 mm); WT. both 61 oz, 3 dwt
(1896 gm)
Gift of Mrs. Samuel Schwartz   1978.48.1-.2

The two facets of silversmithing, design and craft, became
increasingly separated during the nineteenth century. Large
numbers of objects were designed to include the same machine-produced parts, and individual craftsmanship was on
the wane.

About 1895 Edward Holbrook, president of Gorham
and a connoisseur and collector of the arts, and his English-
trained chief designer, William C. Codman, conceived
the idea of producing a line of handcrafted silver in the
"modern" taste. Each piece was to be "the work of a man's
hands, unaided by machinery of any kind," and silversmiths
were provided with full-scale patterns and drawings of the
pieces they were to make. Although every designer was
apparently an artisan with a thorough knowledge of metal-
working, not every silversmith played a part in the design
process.

Designs were meant to be naturalistic, and it is therefore not surprising that the water lily and the lily pad were
favorite motifs. According to a review of a special exhibition
of the Martelé (after the French *Martelé* or "hammered")
line held in New York in 1897, a pitcher similar to this one,
described as "a water pitcher . . . with water lilies and ferns
brought out upon its body with quaint effect of suggestion,"
was among the objects on display. In spite of such previews
for members of the trade, Martelé pieces were apparently
not available to customers until 1899. Handcrafted work
enjoyed great popularity in Chicago around the turn of the
century, and it is significant that this tray bears the retailer's
mark of Spaulding and Company, Chicago.

Refs.: John S. Holbrook, *Silver for the Dining Room, Selected Periods*
(Cambridge: Printed for the Gorham Company by the University Press,
1912), pp. 112-119. Charlotte Moffit, "New Designs in Silver," *The House
Beautiful* 7, no. 1 (December 1899): 55-58. "Rare and Unique Exhibit of
Works in Hand Wrought Silver," *The Jewelers' Circular and Horological
Review* 35, no. 16 (17 November 1897): 16-17.

Detail of mark on Sugar Bowl

54 Hot Beverage Set, Boston, 1906
Karl F. Leinonen (1866–1957)
H. pot 8 1/16″ (205 mm); WT. pot 13 oz, 17 dwt (429 gm)
Gift of Mrs. Alfred E. Bissell and Mrs. Edward
Leisenring in memory of Alfred Elliott Bissell, B.A. 1925
1978.64A-D

Reacting against the uninspired mechanical productions of
the late nineteenth century, proponents of the Arts and
Crafts movement advocated a return to handwork and in-
sisted "upon the necessity of sobriety and restraint, of ordered arrangement, of due regard for the relation between
the form of an object and its use, and of harmony and fitness
in the decoration put upon it." The purity and simplicity of
form, the hammered surface, and the high quality of handcraftsmanship of this set express in three-dimensions the
reforming spirit of the style.

Karl F. Leinonen, born in Finland in 1866, was already a
trained silversmith when he came to this country in 1893. In
1901 he was appointed by Arthur Astor Carey, president of
the Boston Society of Arts and Crafts, the first organization
of its kind in America, to supervise the silversmithing operations of the Society's new Handicraft Shop. Leinonen held
this position for over thirty years, working side by side with
other members of the Shop, including at various times
George C. Gebelein (76), Frederick J. R. Gyllenberg, Seth
Ek, Adolphe Kunkler, C. R. Forssen, and others.

As J. Herbert Gebelein discovered, this hot beverage
set, inscribed "L.G.D. from A.A.C. and the children July
1905," was a gift to Louise G. Dietrick, governess of the
Hillside School in Waltham, Massachusetts, from Arthur
Astor Carey. Two of the four pieces are dated 1906, however, indicating that the set was not completed until that
year. Each piece bears the H anvil S mark of the Handicraft
Shop in addition to Leinonen's simple L mark.

Refs.: Allen H. Eaton, *Handicrafts of New England* (New York: Harper
and Brothers, 1949). pp. 238-239, 281-294. Dorothy T. Rainwater, *Encyclopedia of American Silver Manufacturers* (New York: Crown Publishers,
Inc., 1975), p. 95.

55 **Sugar Bowl,** Boston, ca. 1760-1775
Zachariah Brigden (1734-1787)
H. 6⅜″ (162 mm); WT. 10 oz, 16 dwt (334 gm)
Mabel Brady Garvan Collection   1930.1228

56 **Sugar Bowl,** Gardner, Massachusetts, 1927
Herman W. Glendenning (b. 1906) of Arthur J. Stone
Associates
H. 6 1/16″ (154 mm); WT. 14 oz, 14 dwt (456 gm)
Bequest of Peter J. Meyer   1975.48a

At the turn of the twentieth century, the Arts and Crafts
movement combined with a revival of interest in the colonial
period to stimulate a renewed concern with both the craft
process and colonial style in American silver. One of the men
who carried the old craft traditions into the twentieth century was Arthur J. Stone. Born in England, Stone emigrated
to New Hampshire in 1884, and in 1901 he opened a shop
for the production of handwrought silver in Gardner, Massachusetts. It was in this shop that the sugar bowl (56)
displayed here was made, hammered up by hand into an
inverted pyriform shape reminiscent of mid-eighteenth-
century sugar bowls such as this one by Zachariah Brigden
of Boston (55). Herman W. Glendenning, the craftsman in
Stone's shop who made this bowl and whose initial letter G
appears underneath the Stone mark on the bottom of the
bowl, adapted colonial models somewhat, yet he remained
basically faithful to colonial design and method. After Stone
sold his shop in 1937, Glendenning worked for George
Erickson until 1971, when he established his own shop in
Gardner.

Refs.: Gerald W. R. Ward, ed., *The Eye of the Beholder: Fakes, Replicas,
and Alterations in American Art* (New Haven: Yale University Art Gallery,
1977), p. 68. Herman W. Glendenning, "Arthur J. Stone, Master Craftsman," *Silver* 6, no. 5 (September-October 1973): 27-28. _____, "Glendenning–Sterling Handwrought," *Silver* 7, no. 3 (May-June 1974): 17-19.

57 **Coffee Pot,** Oslo, Norway, 1965
Robert W. Ebendorf (b. 1938)
H. 7 15/16″ (202 mm); WT. 22 oz, 18 dwt (710 gm)
American Arts Purchase Fund   1978.81

Today's silversmith is usually a teacher as well as an artist. In
recent years metalsmithing has become an integral part of
the curricula of many American colleges, universities, and
art schools, a fact which accounts for the large number of
artists now working in the field. Liberated from the caprices
of the marketplace, the metalsmith can experiment freely
with new forms and techniques, and as a result much important creative work is currently being done in gold and silver.
    Robert W. Ebendorf, the maker of this coffee pot, is
currently Professor of Art at the State University of New
York at New Paltz. Born in Topeka, Kansas, he received his
artistic training at the University of Kansas and the University of Oslo, Norway. Returning to Norway under a Ful-

bright grant in 1965, Ebendorf created this coffee pot while studying and teaching at the State School for Applied Arts in Oslo. Although simple and clean in outline, it has a strongly architectural form which continually changes as it is viewed from different angles, like that of a modern day skyscraper. Ebendorf arrived at this design in response to a particular challenge: to make a pouring vessel which could be used easily by left-handed as well as right-handed people. His resolution of this problem and the strength of the resulting object are testimony to the fine design sensibilities and concern for functionalism which characterize the best contemporary works in hollow ware.

Ref.: *Precious Metals: The American Tradition in Gold and Silver* (Miami, Florida: Lowe Art Museum, University of Miami, 1976), pp. 12-13, 28.

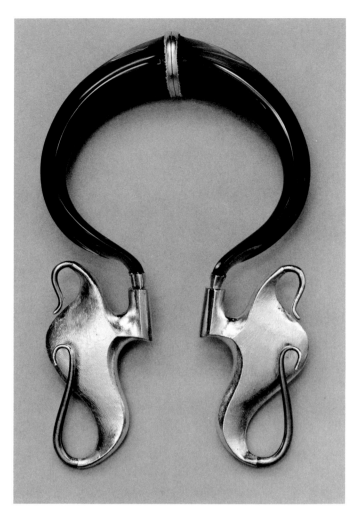

58 Torque #33D, Philadelphia, 1973
Stanley Lechtzin (b. 1936)
L. 12″ (305 mm); WT. 12 oz, 9 dwt (386 gm)
American Arts Purchase Fund   1978.86

Electroforming is one of the many important new techniques which have opened up fresh creative possibilities for the metalsmith in recent years. Similar to electroplating, electroforming is the process of chemically depositing precious metals onto less expensive materials. By lengthening the time in the plating bath, it is possible to create thick deposits which become forms able to stand independently after the base material is removed.

Stanley Lechtzin, who pioneered the use of this technique, has been teaching at the Tyler School of Art at Temple University since 1963. In that same year, he began experimenting with the industrial process of electroforming in an effort to adapt it to studio conditions. Interested in creating lightweight yet massive forms which could be worn as jewelry, he soon discovered that many variable effects could be produced with the technique. Lechtzin's torques, named for the metal collars or neck chains worn by ancient Gauls, Germans, and Britons, are notable for a boldness which makes each piece a successful sculptural form as well as an object of personal adornment. Many metalsmiths working today use acrylics and other materials to further lighten their jewelry and provide interesting textural contrasts. This torque, for example, combines a purple acrylic collar with parcel-gilt forms.

Refs.: *Philadelphia: Three Centuries of American Art* (Philadelphia: Philadelphia Museum of Art, 1976), pp. 614-615. Oppi Untracht, *Metal Techniques for Craftsmen* (Garden City, New York: Doubleday and Company, Inc., 1968), pp. 379-391.

59 Teapot, Taunton, Massachusetts, 1978
Designed by John A. Prip (b. 1922), 1958
Reed & Barton
H. 7¾″ (197 mm); WT. 20 oz, 17 dwt (646 gm)
American Arts Purchase Fund   1978.79

Much of the silver produced by large manufacturers today is in traditional styles and patterns which have changed remarkably little in this century. Graham Hughes suggests that machinery has been the "brake" which has slowed the evolution of silver design; the cost of introducing new styles has become prohibitive "because of the small size of the luxury market." In short, Hughes claims, "machine-made silver remains constant because so few people want it." Furthermore, the trend toward conservatism is accelerated because in designing for a large company, the designer must often address himself to a client who will not find highly individualistic works acceptable.

Although its clean lines, hard edges, and lack of ornament clearly identify it as "modern," and therefore an exception to the various revival patterns which are still the most frequently produced styles, this teapot in the "Diamond" pattern has been in production for twenty years. Designed by Prip in 1958, it is still being produced by Reed & Barton today. Trained as a silversmith in Denmark, Prip now teaches at the Rhode Island School of Design. His hand-crafted work in silver and other metals is considerably different from this teapot. In common with the work of other modern metalsmiths, many of his objects are (in his own words) "sort of an excuse for sculptural form," and consciously strive to be works of art.

Refs.: Graham Hughes, *Modern Silver* (New York: Crown Publishers, Inc., 1967), p. 129. Ronald Hayes Pearson, "John Prip," *Craft Horizons* 33, no. 1 (February 1973): 20-25, 73. Hugh J. Gourley, III, *The New England Silversmith* (Providence, Rhode Island: Museum of Art, Rhode Island School of Design, 1965), no. 153.

60   **Agate Necklace,** Taunton, Massachusetts, 1977
       Designed by Mary Ann Scherr (b. 1921), 1976
       Reed & Barton
       L. 9 1/16″ (230 mm); WT. inc. agate 9 oz, 17 dwt
       (305 gm)
       Gift of Reed & Barton   1978.53

"Contemporary in concept, and created for today's woman and the multitude of lives she leads," Reed & Barton's Signature V Collection, introduced in 1977, is part of a trend toward collaboration between creative artists working in silver and large manufacturing concerns. The collection consists of twenty pieces designed by Glenda Arentzen, Ronald Hayes Pearson, Arline Fisch, Mary Ann Scherr, and Lynda Watson. Each piece bears the mark of the designer as well as the manufacturer, and the integrity of the artist's design is respected in every detail. Mass production, however, presents problems to the silversmith which are not normally encountered in studio work; designs must be simple enough to be produced successfully by machine without sacrifice of detail, and must adhere to the requirements of standardized materials and machinery. Mary Ann Scherr has actually capitalized on these restrictions in this sleek body-conforming design which effectively contrasts soft curves and the smoky surface of polished agate with the hard edges of the sectional neckbar.

Mary Ann Scherr was educated at the Cleveland Institute of Art, the University of Akron, and Kent State University, and is currently Associate Professor of Jewelry and Metals in the School of Art, Kent State University. In recent years she has worked closely with scientists and manufacturers on the development of body-monitoring jewelry, innovative pieces designed to monitor air quality and heart function while serving in the traditional role of personal adornment. One of these designs, a smoke monitoring necklace, is scheduled for production by Reed & Barton within the next few years.

Refs.: *A Collection of Fine Jewelry, Signature V* (Taunton, Massachusetts: Reed & Barton, undated promotional pamphlet). Annalee Gold, "Crafts in Industry, Five Jewelers Join Skills with Reed & Barton," *Craft Horizons* 37, no. 4 (August 1977): 10-15.

Silver and Society

61-64 Top Row, left to right
65-67 Bottom Row, left to right

61 **Two-handled Cup,** Boston, ca. 1720-1740
Andrew Tyler (1692-1741)
H. 4 13/16″ (122 mm); WT. 7 oz, 14 dwt (239 gm)
Mabel Brady Garvan Collection   1930.1339

62 **Two-handled Cup,** Boston, ca. 1713
John Edwards (1671-1746)
H. 5¾″ (146 mm); WT. 8 oz, 18 dwt (276 gm)
Mabel Brady Garvan Collection   1930.1336

63 **Two-handled Cup,** Boston, ca. 1745
William Cowell, Jr. (1713-1761)
H. 4¾″ (121 mm); WT. 7 oz, 11 dwt (234 gm)
Mabel Brady Garvan Collection   1930.1340

64 **Two-handled Cup,** Boston, ca. 1747
Jacob Hurd (1703-1758)
H. 4¾″ (121 mm); WT. 7 oz, 7 dwt (228 gm)
Mabel Brady Garvan Collection   1930.1341

65 **Two-handled Cup,** Boston, ca. 1724
John Burt (1693-1746)
H. 5⅞″ (149 mm); WT. 8 oz, 8 dwt (260 gm)
Mabel Brady Garvan Collection   1930.1337a

66 **Two-handled Cup,** Boston, ca. 1724
John Burt (1693-1746)
H. 5⅞″ (149 mm); WT. 8 oz, 3 dwt (253 gm)
Mabel Brady Garvan Collection   1930.1337b

67 **Two-handled Cup,** Boston, ca. 1788
Benjamin Pierpont (1730-1797)
H. 6″ (152 mm); WT. 8 oz, 8 dwt (260 gm)
Mabel Brady Garvan Collection   1930.1338d

Because of its association with endurance and purity, silver has traditionally played an important role in the religious ritual of most faiths. Much of the surviving early American religious silver was used in Protestant churches in the administration of the sacraments, particularly that of communion. As Anthony N. B. Garvan has observed, the form and number of objects used in the communion service varies considerably according to the denomination and specific practices of a given church.

In seeking a return to the simplicity of the primitive church, the Puritans did not reject silver vessels but only Roman Catholic forms. Domestic forms such as standing cups and beakers replaced the elaborate chalices associated with popish practices. In the early Congregational churches of New England, communion was often served at a small table, with communicants drinking from individual vessels in a manner imitative of the Last Supper. Toward the end of the seventeenth century, full communion was gradually extended from a small group of the elect to the general congregation. This change brought about the need for vessels which could be passed among communicants seated in the pews. Hence we find a steady increase in the number of beakers and two-handled cups fashioned for church use throughout the eighteenth century.

Although founded in 1670, the First Congregational Church of Hatfield, Massachusetts, purchased its earliest surviving silver cup (**62**) with Daniel White's bequest of 1713. Made by John Edwards of Boston, this two-handled cup with its straight gadrooning is stylish for a church piece. Purchased specifically for church use, it indicates the preference of the church deacons for a two-handled vessel. This preference persisted over the next seventy-five years, and all of the ten surviving pieces originally owned by the church are nearly identical in form. Seven of these pieces (**61-67**) now belong to Yale.

Refs.: Buhler and Hood, nos. 65, 105, 109, 159, 180, 227. E. Alfred Jones, *The Old Silver of American Churches* (Letchworth, England: Privately Printed for the Colonial Dames of America, 1913), pp. xix-lxxxvij, 210-212, pl. LXXIII. Anthony N.B. Garvan et al., "American Church Silver: A Statistical Study," in *Spanish, French, and English Traditions in the Colonial Silver of North America* (Winterthur, Delaware: The Henry Francis du Pont Winterthur Museum, 1969), pp. 73-109.

68 **Communion Service**, Philadelphia, ca. 1815-1830
Christian Wiltberger (1769-1851)
H. flagon 12″ (305 mm); WT. flagon 68 oz (2108 gm)
Mabel Brady Garvan Collection   1932.57a-e

This communion service was probably made for St. John's Church, Philadelphia, shortly after its founding in 1816. In the Episcopal Church the priest traditionally filled the chalices from the flagon and served the wine to communicants at the altar rail. The serving of the bread differed slightly from church to church, and the inclusion of three plates in this set may indicate that the members of this church received small pieces of bread rather than the more customary wafers.

Christian Wiltberger was a member of St. Paul's Episcopal Church, Philadelphia, although his two daughters were married in St. John's Church in 1819 and 1820. The forms of the vessels which he made for St. John's show a conscious rejection of the prevailing neoclassical style which, with its pagan associations, may have been consid-

ered inappropriate for an Episcopal church. The double-bellied flagon is unusual in American church silver but closely related to tankards made in New York and Philadelphia during the rococo period. Wiltberger himself fashioned a plain cylindrical flagon for St. James' Church, Philadelphia, in about 1795. John David, Wiltberger's Philadelphia neighbor, made a slightly smaller double-bellied flagon for St. Peter's Church, Lewes, Delaware, in 1773.

Refs.: Buhler and Hood, no. 874. E. Alfred Jones, *The Old Silver of American Churches* (Letchworth, England: Privately Printed for the Colonial Dames of America, 1913), pp. 242-243, 372-373, pl. LXXXII. Norris Stanley Barratt, *Outline of the History of Old St. Paul's Church, Philadelphia, Pennsylvania* (Lancaster, Pennsylvania: The Colonial Society of Pennsylvania, 1917), pp. 204, 226, 280. Thomas B. Lloyd, "The Wiltberger Communion Set at Yale," seminar paper, Yale University, 1978.

Figure 35
Unknown Artist
Commodore Edward Tyng
(1683-1755)
Oil on canvas, ca. 1725-1750
Mabel Brady Garvan Collection
1930.52

69   **Two-handled Covered Cup,** Boston, 1744
       Jacob Hurd (1703-1758)
       H. 15 1/16″ (383 mm); WT. 96 oz, 5 dwt (2984 gm)
       Mabel Brady Garvan Collection   1932.48

The presentation of silver objects has long been considered an appropriate means of expressing gratitude. On 26 June 1774 a group of grateful Boston merchants unanimously voted "that the thanks of the Town be given to Capt. Edward Tyng" (Fig. 35) for his part in the first American naval engagement of King George's War. As a result this cup was presented to him with an inscription appropriately surrounded by a cartouche comprising guns, swords, and other arms: "To EDWARD TYNG Esqr. Commander of ye SNOW Prince of Orange As an Acknowledgement of his good Service done the TRADE in Taking ye First French Privateer on this Coast the 24th of June 1744 This Plate is presented BY Several of Ye Merchts. in Boston New England."

At the time of its presentation the cup was used to hold "Bishop," a sweet drink made of wine, oranges or lemons, and sugar mixed with mulled and spiced port. The cup was a worthy means of expressing the civic pride of Boston, for it is surely one of the masterpieces of Queen Anne silver. Bold, almost haughty, it stands firmly balanced as its two curving handles sweep outward to reach a width almost equal to its height. Despite its large size, the Tyng cup is graceful in bearing, without a trace of the awkwardness of related examples.

Interestingly, the military history of Captain Tyng's cup does not end with King George's War, for it was stolen by colonial soldiers from Tyng's son, a Loyalist, during the Revolution. A contemporary account explains, "They have this day carried off Mr. Tyng's Bishop, a piece of plate said to be worth 500 pounds old Tenor, and his laced hat, but they say they have only taken these things as pawns to make the owner behave better." The cup was later restored to Tyng's mother-in-law by order of the Provincial Congress.

Refs.: Buhler and Hood, no. 157. John Marshall Phillips, "Mr. Tyng's Bishop," *Bulletin of the Associates in Fine Arts at Yale University* 4, no. 3 (1932): 148-149. Phillips, *American Silver*, p. 72.

69 *See Frontispiece*

70 **Punch Bowl,** New Haven, Connecticut, 1745
Cornelius Kierstede (1675-1757)
D. lip 7½″ (190 mm); WT. 11 oz, 17 dwt (368 gm)
Bequest of Miss Helen S. Darling, in memory of
Thomas Darling   1913.688

In the eighteenth century students often presented their tutors with silver objects as an expression of appreciation and affection. While Yale owns few such pieces today, Harvard University has an extensive collection of tutorial plate and many other examples survive in public and private collections.

The Yale class of 1746 presented this bowl to their tutor Thomas Darling (1720-1789) upon his retirement in 1745 with the inscribed tribute: "Domino THOMAE: DARLING Tutori: Dignissimo: hos: Damus Cyathos: aeterni: Pigniis:

Amoris Classis: sua 1745." Later engraving indicates that it passed from father to son until it came to Yale as a gift from the sister of its last owner.

The bowl was made by Cornelius Kierstede, who began his career as a silversmith in New York. In 1724 he came to Connecticut to oversee his interests in a copper mine, and settled in New Haven until his death in 1757. In spite of its date of 1745, this bowl has the floral decoration within panels characteristic of two-handled cups made in New York in the late seventeenth century by Kierstede and others. It has been called "the most ornamental piece of silver produced in Connecticut" in the early period.

Refs.: Buhler and Hood, no. 329. Phillips, *American Silver,* p. 75, pl. 18a. Peter Bohan and Philip Hammerslough, *Early Connecticut Silver, 1700-1840* (Middletown, Connecticut: Wesleyan University Press, 1970), pp. 12-13, 30. John N. Pearce, "New York's Two-Handled Paneled Silver Bowls," *Antiques* 80, no. 4 (October 1961): 341-345.

71 **Medal,** New York, 1764
Daniel Christian Fueter (w. ca. 1754–ca. 1776)
D. 2⅛″ (54 mm); WT. 1 oz, 15 dwt (54 gm)
Mabel Brady Garvan Collection   1932.85

The custom of presenting silver medals to high-ranking
Indian chiefs as a gesture of peace and good will was widely
practiced by representatives of the crown in colonial
America. This medal by Daniel Christian Fueter was given
by Sir William Johnson (1715-1774), Superintendent of Indian Affairs for the northern colonies, to the Indians who
had pledged allegiance to the English after the suppression
of Pontiac's Rebellion in 1763. A bust of George III decorates the front (not shown), while on the back a seated
Indian and Englishman peacefully share a pipe beneath the
motto "HAPPY WHILE UNITED." With each medal Johnson
presented a printed certificate, filled in with the name, tribe,
and specific service of the recipient, and bearing an inscription which read in part: "Whereas I have received repeated
proofs of your Attachment to his Britannic Majestys Interests, and Zeal for his Service upon sundry occasions . . . I do
therefore give you this public Testimonial thereof as a Proof
of his Majesty's Esteem & Approbation." His ability to
establish cordial relations with the Iroquois tribes in the
Mohawk Valley earned Johnson his baronetcy, and his liberal dispensation of medals and other emoluments helped
him maintain the vital support of the Indian allies.

Indian medals continued to be issued by the United
States government after the Revolution and throughout the
nineteenth century.

Refs.: Buhler and Hood, no. 719. Francis P. Prucha, *Indian Peace Medals in
American History* (Lincoln, Nebraska: University of Nebraska Press,
1971), p. 4. R.W.G. Vail, "Sir William Johnson's Indian Testimonial," *The
New-York Historical Society Quarterly* 30, no. 4 (October 1946): 209-214.

72 **Arm Band,** Bangor, Maine, ca. 1810-1820
Zebulon Smith (1786-1865)
H. 5 1/16″ (129 mm); WT. 4 oz, 18 dwt (151 gm)
Mabel Brady Garvan Collection   1934.360

Large numbers of silver ornaments were habitually presented to Indians as a preface to peace negotiations during
the colonial period. This custom continued well into the
early years of the new republic, and numerous examples of
armbands engraved with the Great Seal of the United States
were made by Joseph Richardson and Joseph Richardson,
Jr., of Philadelphia for presentation to the Indians of
Pennsylvania.

This simple yet bold armband by Zebulon Smith was
probably among a group of pieces presented to the Penob-
scot Indians of Maine in the early nineteenth century.

Refs.: Buhler and Hood, no. 512. Fales, *Richardson*, pp. 38, 140-141,
159-161. Francis P. Prucha, *Indian Peace Medals in American History*
(Lincoln, Nebraska: The University of Nebraska Press, 1971), pp. 3-11.

73 **Covered Two-handled Urn,** Philadelphia, 1830
Thomas Fletcher and Sidney Gardiner (w. 1814-1838)
H. 21″ (533 mm); WT. 65 oz, 16 dwt (2042 gm)
Gift of Joseph B. Brenauer   1942.245

The Philadelphia firm of Thomas Fletcher (1787-1866) and
Sidney Gardiner was renowned for the large presentation
pieces it made to order for military heroes, civic leaders,

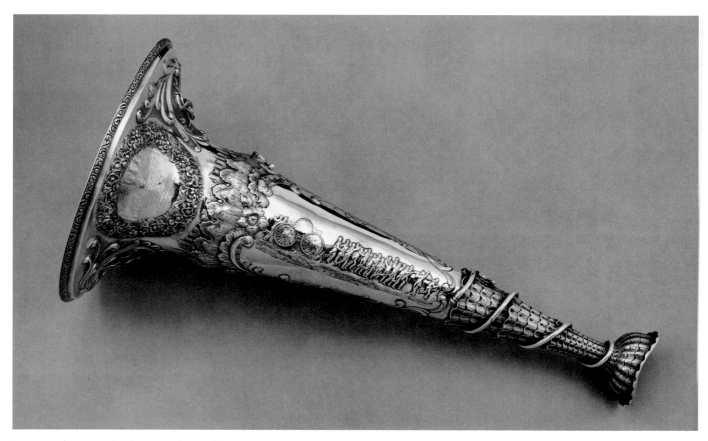

business men, and other worthies of the era. This monumental urn was "Presented by the Proprietors of the Chesapeake and Delaware Canal to JAMES C. FISHER ESQ. in testimony of his faithful and useful Services as President of the Company June 7, 1830." Canals played a relatively brief yet highly important part in the transportation revolution and the subsequent opening of the American West in the nineteenth century. Fisher's contribution to the success of the Chesapeake and Delaware Canal was thus as important a public service in its own time as Captain Tyng's capture of a French privateer in 1744 (69). Indicative of the concerns of the new nation also are related presentation pieces made by Fletcher and Gardiner for the managers of the Schuylkill Navigation Company and for Dewitt Clinton in recognition of his support of the Erie Canal. In common with the Schuylkill and Clinton pieces, this urn is resplendent with Greek Revival and other ornament, including egg-and-dart moldings, acanthus leaves, and anthemions. A river god, or perhaps Neptune, presides over the whole. Much of the decoration, particularly the handles in the form of twisted vines and the grape-leaf borders, is derived from an ancient classical object known as the Warwick vase, excavated in Italy in 1771 and later owned by the Duke of Warwick.

Refs.: Buhler and Hood, no. 928. *Nineteenth-Century America*, no. 51. Elizabeth I. Wood, "Thomas Fletcher, A Philadelphia Entrepreneur of Presentation Silver," in Milo B. Naeve, ed., *Winterthur Portfolio III* (Winterthur, Delaware: The Henry Francis du Pont Winterthur Museum, 1967), pp. 136-171.

74 Fireman's Trumpet, New York (?), ca. 1852
L. 21⅝" (549 mm); WT. 34 oz, 10 dwt (1070 gm)
Mabel Brady Garvan Collection   1934.371

This magnificent silver representation of a fireman's speaking trumpet was presented to James R. Mount, foreman of New York City's Atlantic Hose Company Number 14, for his heroic rescue of four people trapped in a burning building. The *New York Tribune* of 18 March 1852 described the rescue: "By rapid progress of the flames, all retreat for the inmates of the house was entirely cut off; . . . . A ladder was instantly procured from an adjoining paint shop, by . . . which two men made their escape. The ladder falling short by several feet . . . the women were still afraid to venture down. At this critical moment, James Mount, . . . at the risk of his life, rushed up the ladder four times, and succeeded in saving two women and two children, bringing them down in his arms." Twelve citizens formed a committee to honor Mount's deed with a suitable memorial. Probably commissioned from a New York silversmith, this horn vividly displays the creative imagination and technical skill of its unknown maker. The actual scene of the fire is recreated in bold repoussé on the sides of the horn, while sheets of water encircled by a fire hose cascade from the mouthpiece. The wreathed inscription near the mouth of the horn is surrounded by rococo leafage and depictions of contemporary fire-fighting equipment as well as a figure of Neptune, the Roman god of the sea.

Ref.: Buhler and Hood, no. 1014.

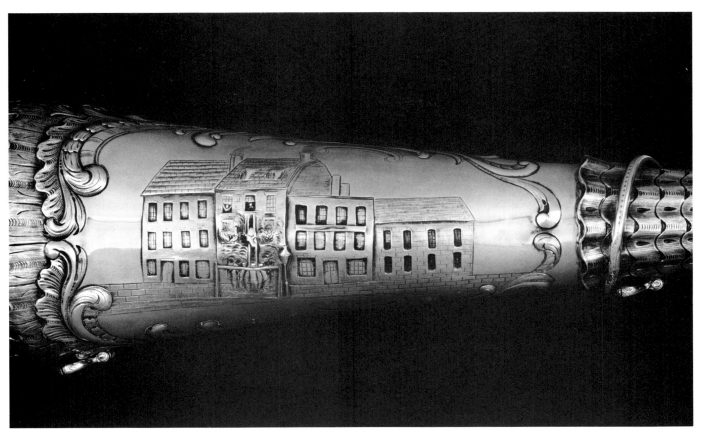

Detail of Fireman's Trumpet

Figure 36
The victorious Yale crew of 1876.
University Archives, Yale University.

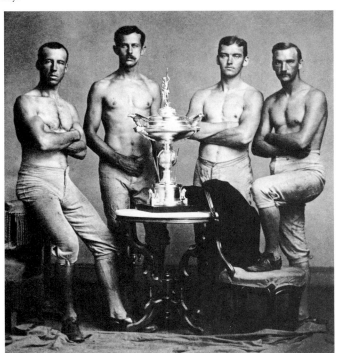

75 Loving Cup, American, ca. 1876
H. 30½″ (775 mm); WT. 171 OZ (5301 gm)
Department of Athletics, Yale University

"At the signal Yale started off first. . . . At the bend of the river Yale and Columbia were on even terms but Cambridge pulled hard and overlapped Columbia. Yale was only a quarter of a length ahead, but as the bridge was sighted Yale gained a length and steered over towards the eastern shore. . . . Cambridge now unfortunately steered past the flag buoys and got into the weeds. . . . Columbia, the second boat, did so, too. . . . [The captain of the Cambridge crew] suddenly fell back in a fainting condition, and was immediately taken on board the press boat. The race from now to the finish was a tight one between Yale and Columbia, but Yale passed the winning post [first]. . . ."

Thus Yale won the college division of the 1876 Centennial Regatta in Philadelphia (Fig. 36), reportedly earning "the hearty congratulations of not only every graduate of Yale, but of every man with a drop of American blood in his veins." The trophy which Yale also won suitably reflected the bounding optimism which typified the post-Civil War era and the patriotic self-confidence which highlighted the fair.

75

It is magnificent in size, eclectic in ornament, and suffused with symbolic significance. A contemporary writer explained its features: "the prize . . . comprises a tureen of magnificent design, the upper part being embellished with the heads of eagles. The tureen rests on a shank consisting of a silver globe, flanked by four oars. The globe rests on two columns for side supports, and a representation of old Independence bell for the centre support. The bell has on it the United States coat of arms, and the columns the coats of arms of England and Ireland. On the lid of the tureen is a figure of Victory."

In its use of symbolic figures, the cup is reminiscent of the medal awarded at the Cincinnati Industrial Exhibition (18), while in its design and its contrasting use of matte and highly polished finishes, the trophy is related to other contemporary presentation silver. The cup was donated by George W. Childs, publisher of the Philadelphia *Public Ledger*. It seems appropriate that this self-made man, representative of a new class of successful businessmen and himself an amateur yachtsman, should have provided a silver prize which in its exuberance celebrates the spirit of an era.

Refs.: *New Haven Evening Register*, 2 September 1876. *New York Herald*, 30 August 1876. *Nineteenth-Century America*, no. 181. James Dabney McCabe, *Illustrated History of the Centennial Exhibition* (Philadelphia: National Publishing Co., 1876), pp. 675-676.

76   Inkstand, Boston, 1928-1929
      George C. Gebelein (1878-1945)
      H. 7⅞" (202 mm); WT. 40 oz, 4 dwt (1246 gm)
      Gift of Edwina Mead Gagge   1976.19a-d

Since the beginning of the twentieth century, many presentation pieces have been made as exact reproductions of early objects with important historical associations. In 1928 and 1929 Francis P. Garvan of New York commissioned George Christian Gebelein to produce thirty reproductions of the famous inkstand by Philip Syng, Jr. (1703-1789) which was made in 1752 and used by the signers of the Declaration of Independence and the Constitution. This particular inkstand is inscribed to Larkin G. Mead, a friend of Garvan's and a fellow-member of the Chemical Foundation, an organization established following World War I to foster American independence in the field of chemical research and production.

Gebelein was an important figure in the Boston Arts and Crafts movement. Born in Bavaria in 1878, he came to the United States with his family when he was only six months old. Gebelein learned the silversmith's craft as an apprentice in the Boston firm of Goodnow and Jenks, and later worked as a member of the Handicraft Shop of the Boston Arts and Crafts Society. In 1909 he established his own shop at 79 Chestnut Street, Boston. Gebelein collected and sold antique silver and specialized in making creative pieces in the colonial revival style. A true proponent of the Arts and Crafts aesthetic, he believed in the importance of handcraftsmanship and the purity of line and form he found in American objects produced during the late eighteenth century.

Refs.: Margaretha Gebelein Leighton, *George Christian Gebelein, Boston Silversmith, 1878-1945* (Boston: Privately Printed, 1976), pp. 12-55, 74. Allen H. Eaton, *Handicrafts of New England* (New York: Harper & Brothers Publishers, 1949), pp. 238-239.

77 **Cupboard,** Eastern Massachusetts, 1670-1710; restored ca. 1890
Oak, pine, maple
H. 63⅛″ (1603 mm)
Mabel Brady Garvan Collection 1930.2778

78 **Two-handled Covered Cup,** London, 1683-1684
Unidentified maker's mark, IA
H. 5⅝″ (143 mm); WT. 14 oz, 10 dwt (450 gm)
Gift of Mrs. James B. Neale as part of a collection of silver presented as a memorial to James B. Neale
1948.193

79 **Standing Cup,** London, 1631-1632
Unidentified maker's mark, IT
H. 7½″ (190 mm); WT. 12 oz, 7 dwt (383 gm)
Mabel Brady Garvan Collection 1936.138

80 **Tankard,** Boston, ca. 1690-1700
Jeremiah Dummer (1645-1718)
H. 8¼″ (210 mm); WT. 45 oz, 1 dwt (1397 gm)
Mabel Brady Garvan Collection 1934.358

81 **Pewter Dish,** Boston, ca. 1684-1729
John Dolbeare (w. ca. 1664-1740)
D. 16 9/16″ (421 mm)
Mabel Brady Garvan Collection 1973.70

82 **Broad-brimmed Pewter Dish,** England, ca. 1660
D. 18¾″ (476 mm)
Gift of Mrs. James C. Greenway 1942.127

83 **Cup,** Boston, ca. 1705-1715
Attributed to Edward Webb (1666-1718)
H. 2¾″ (70 mm); WT. 2 oz, 14 dwt (83 gm)
Mabel Brady Garvan Collection 1930.1013

84 **Porringer,** Boston, ca. 1700-1710
John Edwards (1671-1746)
D. bowl 4 15/16″ (125 mm); WT. 6 oz, 1 dwt (188 gm)
Mabel Brady Garvan Collection 1932.66

The practice of displaying silver in the home as decoration and as an ostentatious indication of one's wealth held sway for centuries. The custom can be traced back to Roman times, when the family's eating and drinking silver, together with the family heirlooms, was grouped and exhibited on special tables.

Following English practice, the cupboard served this same function of displaying the family plate in seventeenth-century America. The cupboard was usually the most up-to-date, most important, and most expensive piece of furniture in the seventeenth-century house. A comedy of 1611 by George Chapman indicated the range of objects one might expect to find on a cupboard: "And so for the feast, you have your court cupboards planted with flagons, cans, cups, beakers, bowls, goblets, basins and ewers." Thus embellished with silver, pewter, and expensive ceramics arrayed on a "cubboard cloth," the arrangement formed what William Fitzhugh of Virginia referred to in 1688 as "an handsome cupboard of plate."

English as well as New England silver and pewter is displayed on this eastern Massachusetts cupboard of the late seventeenth century. A cupboard so decorated would have existed only in the homes of the very well-to-do in the seventeenth century, where, as E. McClung Fleming has summarized, it would have "connoted wealth, sophistication, luxury, business success, possibly to the Puritan even election to salvation."

This cupboard, which was heavily restored in the late nineteenth century, originally belonged to Henry F. G. Waters, an early Salem collector. A photograph of about 1896 exists showing the cupboard in Waters's home, with glass, ceramics, and other objects appropriately displayed on top.

Refs.: Buhler and Hood, nos. 11, 42, 63, 542. E. McClung Fleming, "Artifact Study: A Proposed Model," in Ian M. G. Quimby, ed., *Winterthur Portfolio 9* (Charlottesville, Virginia: The University Press of Virginia, 1974), p. 169. Gerald W. R. Ward, ed., *The Eye of the Beholder: Fakes, Replicas, and Alterations in American Art* (New Haven: Yale University Art Gallery, 1977), p. 36.

85 **Tea Table**, Pennsylvania, 1755-1795
Cherry
H. 28¼″ (718 mm)
Bequest of Olive Louise Dann   1962.31.23

86 **Sugar Bowl**, Philadelphia, ca. 1765-1780
Joseph Richardson (1711-1784)
H. 6¼″ (159 mm); WT. 13 oz, 7 dwt (414 gm)
Mabel Brady Garvan Collection   1930.1287

87 **Sugar Scissors**, American, ca. 1750-1775
Unidentified maker's mark, G.C./W.C.
L. 4 15/16″ (125 mm); WT. 1 oz, 3 dwt (36 gm)
Gift of Mr. and Mrs. F. B. Schell, Jr., B.A. 1918
1972.128.12

88 **Creampot**, Philadelphia, ca. 1740-1760
Joseph Richardson (1711-1784)
H. 4 9/16″ (116 mm); WT. 4 oz, 8 dwt (137 gm)
Mabel Brady Garvan Collection   1947.352

89 **Salver**, Philadelphia, ca. 1750-1760
Joseph Richardson (1711-1784)
D. 7″ (178 mm); WT. 9 oz, 7 dwt (290 gm)
Mabel Brady Garvan Collection   1930.1296

90 **Six Teaspoons**, Philadelphia, ca. 1750-1760
Philip Syng, Jr. (1703-1789)
L. 5¼″ (133 mm); WT. each 9 dwt (14 gm)
Mabel Brady Garvan Collection   1930.3329a-f

91 **Teapot**, Philadelphia, ca. 1755-1765
William Hollingshead (w. ca. 1754-1785)
H. 6⅜″ (162 mm); WT. 19 oz, 17 dwt (615 gm)
Mabel Brady Garvan Collection   1934.337

92 **Chinese Export Porcelain Teacup and Saucer**,
ca. 1750
D. saucer 4 11/16″ (119 mm)
Bequest of Edith Malvina K. Wetmore   1966.81.15a-b

The earliest European references to tea indicate that it was originally esteemed for its reputed medicinal properties. When introduced into England in the seventeenth century, tea was served only in the coffeehouses where gentlemen were accustomed to gather for friendly conversation. By late in the century, however, tea-drinking had become a domestic entertainment and was enjoyed by men and women alike. This change meant that suddenly every hostess required the proper equipment for serving the expensive new beverage, and the ownership of an extensive tea service became an important symbol of one's social position.

The same fashions were carefully followed in the colonies, and by the middle of the eighteenth century, Americans were consuming vast amounts of tea. The first teapots, cups, saucers, creampots, and sugar bowls were ceramic pieces imported from England and the Orient. As early as 1690 American silversmiths copied these forms in silver at the request of affluent patrons. Silver lent importance to the new custom, as well as serving as a display of the host's wealth. In addition, a new specialized piece of furniture, the tea table, came into use about 1720, and great attention was lavished on its decoration. The example seen here is of the "pie-crust" type popular in Pennsylvania and Connecticut during the Chippendale period. The pieces of a tea service were usually acquired by their owners over a period of time, whereas later tea pieces were made in large matching sets. Scissor-type tongs for sugar, a footed creampot, a "double-bellied" sugar bowl and teapot, teaspoons, a porcelain teacup and saucer, and a salver grace this elegant table of about 1760-1770. The salver was used as a tray to catch the drips as the tea was poured, and may have served as a holder for used spoons.

In the eighteenth century tea-drinking was an important social ritual. When Moreau de Saint-Méry visited Philadelphia in 1798 he described the ceremony as practiced in that city: "Tea is served in the evening as in the morning. . . . The whole family is united at tea, to which friends, acquaintances and even strangers are invited. . . . Evening tea is a boring and monotonous ceremony. The mistress of the house serves it and passes it around, and as long as a person has not turned his cup upside down and placed his spoon upon it, just so often will he be brought another cup. You hear a thousand true and false accounts of Frenchmen

who, in their ignorance of this peculiar custom, have been so inundated by tea that they have suffered intensely."

The tea table was brought well into the center of the room and the hostess, who was usually the mistress of the house or one of her marriageable daughters, sat before the table and filled the teacups. The company assembled in a setting like this one may have consisted of the immediate family alone or a large party of guests gathered about the table or clustered in groups throughout the room. Cakes, nuts, fruits, and pastries were often served, depending upon the formality of the occasion. Conversation was social as well as serious, and no doubt much earnest courting took place at these gatherings.

Refs.: Buhler and Hood, nos. 828, 833, 834, 845, 862. Rodris Roth, "Tea Drinking in Eighteenth-Century America: Its Etiquette and Equipage," *United States National Museum Bulletin 225, Contributions from the Museum of History and Technology* (Washington, D.C.: Smithsonian Institution, 1961), pp. 62-91. J. M. Scott, *The Great Tea Venture* (New York: E. P. Dutton & Co., Inc., 1965), pp. 5, 16-17, 112-116, 151-158. Mederic Louis Elie Moreau de Saint-Méry, *Moreau de St. Méry's American Journey,* trans. and ed. Kenneth Roberts and Anna M. Roberts (Garden City, New York: Doubleday & Company, Inc., 1947), p. 266.

93 **Centerpiece,** New York, ca. 1880-1891
    Tiffany & Company
    D. bowl 14 3/16″ (360 mm); WT. 44 oz, 16 dwt (1389 gm)
    Gift of Fenton Brown   1975.125.1

94 **Silver Service,** New York, 1892-1895
    Tiffany & Company
    H. tea kettle on stand 13½″ (343 mm); WT. tea kettle on
    stand 92 oz, 6 dwt (2861 gm)
    Anonymous loan

95 **Silver-deposit Crystal Stemware,** Stourbridge,
    England, 1905-1910
    Attributed to Thomas Webb and Son
    H. goblet 6⅛″ (156 mm)
    Gift of John D. Diamond, B.A. 1958   1972.136

96 **Silver-deposit Porcelain,** Staffordshire, England,
    1905-1920
    Cauldon, Ltd.; retailed by Higgins and Sieter,
    New York
    D. plate 10 1/16″ (256 mm)
    Gift of John D. Diamond, B.A. 1958   1972.136

97 **Pair of Candlesticks,** London, 1762-1763
    William Cafe (w. ca. 1757-1802)
    H. 8 3/16″ (208 mm); WT. 15 oz, 9 dwt (479 gm)
    Bequest of Olive Louise Dann   1962.31.54a-b

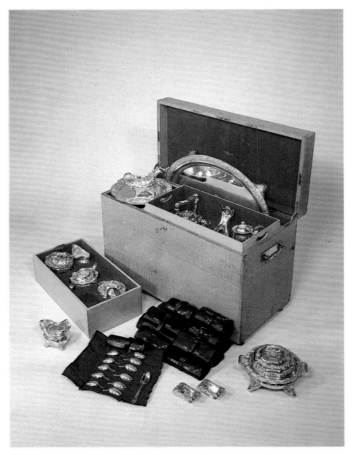

Figure 37
Oak chest containing the Tiffany &
Company silver service (94).

"The people who enter a modern dining-room find a picture
before them, which is the result of painstaking thought,
taste, and experience, and, like all works of art, worthy of
study." Thus one arbiter of manners stresses the importance
of the properly outfitted dining room, "which should be
fresh, well aired, filled with flowers, [and] made bright with
glass and silver" for the benefit of the guests and betterment
of all, since "all that is unpleasant lowers the pulse and
retards digestion. All that is cheerful invigorates the pulse
and helps the human being to live a more brave and useful
life." With such a heavy responsibility on her hands, it is no
wonder that the hostess of the 1890s was concerned with the
smallest details of the crisp white damask linen, the proper
silver for each course, and the correct arrangement of glasses
for water and wine. Of all this, however, the silver was perhaps the most important. Tiffany introduced flatware in the
"Chrysanthemum" pattern in 1880. Its immediate success
led to imitation within a few years by several other silver
companies and to the expansion of the Tiffany line to hollow
ware pieces. By the 1890s, "Chrysanthemum" tableware
was the dream of every young bride, for it achieved the
heavy, lavish, ornate effect then desirable.

This table is set for the first two courses, bouillon and
fish, and the flatware is complemented by salts, a vegetable
dish, sauceboat, ladle, and tray, all from a set (94) given to
members of the Leisenring family in installments at Christmas time between 1892 and 1895. The china (96), made in
England but sold in New York, is by Cauldon, and the

stemware (95) by Thomas Webb and Sons; both have silver
rims and the monogram D for the Diamond family, the
original owners. The tea and coffee service, also part of the
same set, probably would have remained on the sideboard
during the meal. In the center of the table is a shallow
centerpiece (93) filled with an arrangement of flowers, restrained and low enough for the diners to converse over it
comfortably. This centerpiece is flanked by eighteenth-
century English candlesticks (97), the sort of heirlooms that
writers of the late nineteenth century urged hostesses to
bring out of exile and display proudly.

After the meal, the silver could be packed away and
stored in a box specially made for the purpose (Fig. 37):
"Nowadays [1892] the silver chest is getting weighty. Silver
and silver-gilt dishes, banished for some years, are now
reasserting their preeminent fitness for the dinner table."

Refs.: *A Scene of Adornment* (Rochester, New York: Margaret Woodbury
Strong Museum, 1975), pp. 76-77. M.E.W. Sherwood, *The Art of Enter-
taining* (New York: Dodd, Mead and Co., 1892). Mrs. John Sherwood,
Manners and Social Usages (New York: Harper and Brothers, 1884).
Almon C. Varney, *Our Homes and their Adornment* (Detroit: J. C. Chilton
and Co., 1883).

98 Child's Toys, London (?), ca. 1680-1690
    H. tankard 2⅜" (60 mm)
    Mabel Brady Garvan Collection   1938.309, 1935.228,
    1930.1004, 1935.226a-b, 1935.227a-b

These silver child's toys originally belonged to Bethiah
Shrimpton (1681-1713) of Boston, who stated in her will that
"her Sister Hunt's children should have her Silver Baby
things." Their subsequent line of descent is engraved on the
caudle cup, which has survived along with a tankard, a
caster, a pair of candlesticks, a box snuffers, and a snuffer
tray. Another caudle cup, a plate, and a matching caster

from the same set are now at the Museum of Fine Arts,
Boston.

Miniature silver made in the seventeenth century by
John Coney and John Edwards has survived, and it is possible that the Shrimpton toys are of American manufacture.
The marks on all the Shrimpton pieces have been obliterated
or are illegible, but it is probable that they were made in
London, where several silversmiths made a specialty of such
work in the late seventeenth century.

Refs.: Buhler and Hood, no. 544. Alice Winchester, "Silver Toys," *Antiques*
37, no. 6 (June 1940): 285-287. John D. Kernan, "American Miniature
Silver," *Antiques* 80, no. 6 (December 1961): 567-569.

99   **Child's Set,** Providence, Rhode Island, ca. 1905
Gorham Manufacturing Company
D. plate 7 9/16" (192 mm); WT. both 14 oz, 14 dwt
(456 gm)
Gift of Mrs. Harvey K. Smith   1971.99.5a-b

By the middle of the nineteenth century, "children's sets"
were popular as gifts for young children. The major manufacturing companies issued sets throughout the last half of
the century in both sterling and silverplate in a wide variety
of designs such as "Little Miss Muffet," "This Little Pig Went
to Market," and "Ring Around the Rosey." By 1878, the
Gorham Manufacturing Company made "For Children:
Cups, napkin rings, bowls, porringers, pap boats, cup sets,
plates, knife, fork and spoon, Christening sets, rattles, [and]
whistles." This plate and gilt-lined bowl, decorated in the
"Noah's Ark" pattern, was given to Harvey Kennedy Smith
and inscribed with his birth date.

Ref.: McClinton, pp. 255-262.

100 **Mustard Pot,** New York, ca. 1705-1715
Peter Van Dyck (1684-1751)
H. 5⅛" (130 mm); WT. 4 oz, 18 dwt (152 gm)
Mabel Brady Garvan Collection   1930.1332

By 1700, despite being under English rule since 1664, New
York was only beginning to undergo a process of angliciza-
tion. This delightful egg-shaped mustard pot, the only surviving American example of its kind, is evidence of the
lingering Dutch influence in the early eighteenth century.
Closely based on Dutch prototypes, it is indicative of the
special importance placed by the Dutch on family meals
accompanied by numerous articles of table silver. A "mustard pot and spoon" were included in the inventory of the
New York merchant Pieter Jacobse Marius, along with a
silver tankard, silver salt cellars, beakers, sweetmeat spoons,
tumblers, cups with two ears, an "old-fashioned" salver, a
mug with cover, and a baby's chafing dish.

Refs.: Buhler and Hood, no. 589. Michael Kammen, *Colonial New York*
(New York: Charles Scribner's Sons, 1975). Maud Esther Dilliard, *An
Album of New Netherland* (New York: Bramhall House, 1963), pp. 101-
102.

101 Dish Cross, New York, ca. 1765-1775
Myer Myers (1723-1795)
L. 10 13/16″ (275 mm); WT. 11 oz, 4 dwt (347 gm)
John Marshall Phillips Collection   1960.22

The adjustable dish cross, with four legs pivoting around a center circle designed to hold a spirit lamp, was an elegant way to keep plates or bowls warm while simultaneously protecting the surface of the table. This example by Myer Myers has pierced shell supports for dishes, a motif repeated in its feet, and is a fine example of the rococo style. In common with other forms of Myers silver, this dish cross is a rare form in American silver and, like his candlesticks (163), is closely related to English work.

Refs.: Buhler and Hood, no. 660. G. Bernard Hughes, "Keeping Georgian Food Hot," *Country Life* 144 (26 December 1968): 1702-1703.

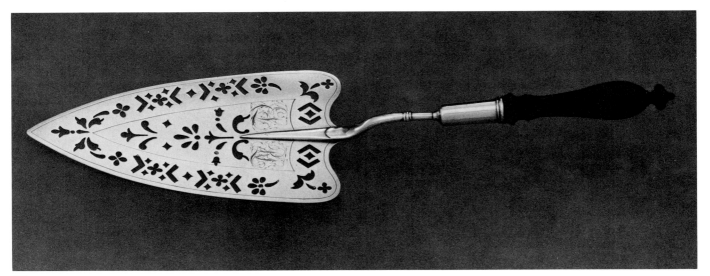

102 Fish Slice, Philadelphia, ca. 1790
Joseph and Nathaniel Richardson (w. 1771-1791)
L. 12 11/16″ (322 mm); WT. 3 oz, 19 dwt (122 gm)
Mabel Brady Garvan Collection 1930.1283

In the middle of the eighteenth century, silver began to be used for a wider variety of accessories having to do with the serving, seasoning, and eating of food, a trend which accelerated in the nineteenth century. One new specialty item was the fish slice (sometimes called a trowel or spade), which began to be popular in England in the 1770s. This heart-shaped slice, made near the end of Joseph and Nathaniel Richardson's partnership, is an early example of the form in American silver.

Refs.: Buhler and Hood, no. 880. Clayton, p. 135.

103 Strainer, Boston, ca. 1740-1750
Paul Revere, I (1702-1754)
L. 10 15/16″ (278 mm); WT. 4 oz, 14 dwt (146 gm)
Mabel Brady Garvan Collection 1930.1218

Punch, introduced to New England in the seventeenth century, remained popular throughout the colonial period. By the middle of the eighteenth century, silver punch bowls, ladles, and strainers were among the most fashionable articles of table silver used in entertaining. Although recipes varied according to region, date, and individual taste, punch usually contained a mixture of five ingredients: water, sugar, spices, lemon or other fruit juice, and spirits, often rum. Strainers were used when adding the spices and fruit juice; one 1860 recipe noted "the finer the strainer is, the better the punch." Alice Morse Earle suggested that punch bowls "were passed from hand to hand and drunk from without intervening glasses," and one drunken merchant can be clearly seen so imbibing in John Greenwood's *Sea Captains Carousing in Surinam* (ca. 1752-1758) at The St. Louis Art Museum. Dr. Hamilton also "put about the bowl" on more than one occasion during his 1744 trip along the East coast. However, the existence of large punch bowls, which are difficult to pass when full, and accompanying ladles suggests that this communal sharing was not the only method of drinking, especially in mixed company or at fashionable gatherings.

This strainer, an early example of the form, is attributed to the elder Paul Revere, although it bears a mark used by both father and son. A number of similar strainers by contemporary Boston silversmiths are known.

104

105

Refs.: Buhler and Hood, no. 134. John Hull Brown, *Early American Beverages* (Rutland, Vermont: Charles E. Tuttle Company, 1966), pp. 18-19, 74-75. Alice Morse Earle, *Customs and Fashions in Old New England* (1893; reprint, Rutland, Vermont: Charles E. Tuttle Company, 1973), pp. 176-177. Carl Bridenbaugh, ed., *Gentleman's Progress: The Itinerarium of Dr. Alexander Hamilton, 1744* (Chapel Hill, North Carolina: University of North Carolina Press, 1948).

104 **Grape Shears,** Taunton, Massachusetts, ca. 1885
Reed & Barton
L. 7" (178 mm); WT. 3 oz, 18 dwt (121 gm)
Gift of Mrs. Harvey K. Smith   1971.99.6

Grapes, "the wholesomest and most grateful of fruits," were a much prized dessert during the Victorian era. The writer of *Host and Guest,* published in 1864, reminded his readers that "grapes have all the effect of the Cheltenham waters. 'They open the body,' says old Lemery, physician to Louis XIV, 'create an appetite, are very nourishing, and qualify the sharp humour of the heart. They agree with every age and constitution. . . .'"

It is no surprise that the popularity of grapes combined with the Victorian propensity for specialization of utensils led to the frequent use of grape shears, special scissors whose sole function was to snip clusters of grapes from a generous bunch. The decoration of this pair of shears suitably reflects its purpose, for the handles are entwined with vining grape, a ubiquitous motif in Victorian silver.

Ref.: A. V. Kirwan, *Host and Guest* (London: Bell and Daldy, 1864), p. 225.

105 **Bread Fork,** Providence, Rhode Island, 1895
Gorham Manufacturing Company
L. 6⅜" (162 mm); WT. 1 oz, 2 dwt (34 gm)
Gift of Louis J. Camuti   1974.120.4

In the second half of the nineteenth century, the forms of specialized flatware produced by the major manufacturers proliferated to an extraordinary degree. For example, between 1850 and 1900 over forty varieties of forks alone were available, including asparagus, beef, strawberry, cake, chow chow, dessert, fish, fruit, ice cream, lemon, lettuce, lobster, mango, melon, olive, oyster, pastry, pickle, pie, salad, sardine, spinach, terrapin, toast, tomato, and vegetable forks. Knives and spoons were made in comparable species, and great numbers of scoops, servers, ladles, tongs, and other accoutrements were also available. Part of this trend, the bread fork was introduced about 1880. This florid, trident-shaped example was made by the Gorham Company in 1895, and was available with a matching bread knife.

Refs.: Turner, pp. 175-185, 405-407. McClinton, p. 91.

106 Sugar Spoon, Providence, Rhode Island, ca. 1892
Gorham Manufacturing Company; retailed by Daniel
Low and Company, Salem, Massachusetts
L. 5 15/16″ (151 mm); WT. 19 dwt (30 gm)
Yale University Art Gallery   1940.846.1

The phenomenon of souvenir spoon collecting began in the
late nineteenth century and continues with full vigor today.
Literally thousands of varieties commemorating people,
places, and events have been produced over the years. The
Salem "Witch" spoons, issued in two patterns in the early
1890s, are usually considered to be the spoons which caught
the American imagination and started the craze.

This sugar spoon is in the second, more elaborate pattern issued in 1892. It was manufactured by the Gorham
Company and marketed by Daniel Low and Company of
Salem, Massachusetts, who stamped their name on the
spoon near the Gorham trademark. The design of the spoon
has been attributed to Seth Low, Daniel's son and a partner
in the business. Capitalizing on the famous witchcraft trials
of 1692, Low incorporated in his design "all the features
connected with the witchcraft delusion: the place and the
date, the cat, the broom, the rope, the witch pins, the new
moon and, surmounting all, the witch." The witch design,
patented in 1891, was also used on other types of spoons and
on numerous small articles sold by Daniel Low.

Refs.: Dorothy T. Rainwater and Donna H. Felger, *American Spoons,
Souvenir and Historical* (Camden, New Jersey: Thomas Nelson and Sons;
Hanover, Pennsylvania: Everybodys Press, 1968), pp. 16, 361, 400. Larry
Freeman, *Victorian Silver* (Watkins Glen, New York: Century House,
1967), pp. 211-213.

107 Gold Locket and Beads, Southampton, New York,
ca. 1775-1790
Elias Pelletreau (1726-1810)
L. beads 12⅛″ (308 mm); WT. 11 dwt (17 gm)
John Marshall Phillips Collection   1956.10.3

Eighteenth-century silversmiths worked with gold as well as
silver, and among the most common items they produced in
gold were objects of personal adornment, such as buttons,
buckles, and beads. More than half the yearly work re-

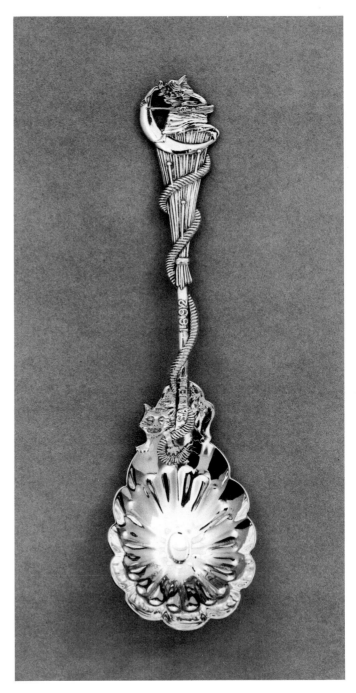

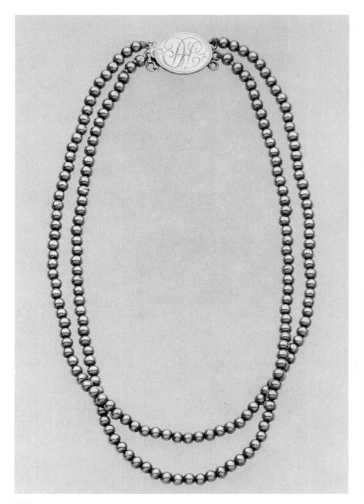

107

108

corded in the account books of Elias Pelletreau, a silversmith in Southampton, New York, was jewelry production. One such item would have been this double string of gold beads and locket engraved with the initials "H P," possibly made for his sister Hannah (the beads descended in the goldsmith's family).

As a young man Pelletreau no doubt learned the art of bead-making during his apprenticeship with Simeon Soumain, for beads were a frequently ordered item and their manufacture was simple yet tedious, as Daniel Burnap's account of 1779 testifies. Starting with a thin flat sheet of gold, the silversmith would "Then cut it out & punch out the centers, and then half hollow them, and then anneal them and hollow them up, & rub them down, and then cramp them, and then charge them, & then solder them, & then boil them out, & then file them up, & then polish them, & then anneal them, & then color them, & then boil them out in clean water, & then burnish them, and then open the holes to a suitable bigness & they are compleated. . . ."

Refs.: Buhler and Hood, no. 672. Penrose R. Hoopes, *Shop Records of Daniel Burnap, Clockmaker* (Hartford, Connecticut: The Connecticut Historical Society, 1958), p. 117. Dean F. Failey, "Elias Pelletreau, Long Island Silversmith" (M.A. dissertation, University of Delaware, 1971), pp. 51-52. Dean F. Failey, *Long Island Is My Nation* (Setauket, New York: Society for the Preservation of Long Island Antiquities, 1976), p. 143.

108 **Pendant with Chains,** Guilford, Connecticut, ca. 1756
Samuel Parmelee (1737-1807)
L. each chain 10⅞" (276 mm); WT. 15 dwt (23 gm)
Gift of Miss Emily Chauncy   1946.117

Although many American silversmiths are known to have referred to themselves as jewelers, very little marked eighteenth-century jewelry survives. In his day books, Joseph Richardson recorded making lockets, chains, rings, and beads in both silver and gold, and inventories of other silversmiths indicate similar activity. Like much early American jewelry, this pendant with chains may have been made as a mourning piece. Engraved with a face reminiscent of gravestone carvings and surrounded by clouds and leafage, it is inscribed with the name of Anne Cushing and the date 1756. Its maker, Samuel Parmelee of Guilford, Connecticut, also made a baptismal basin and a beaker for the First Congregational Church of Guilford, but the bulk of his surviving work indicates that he primarily produced small pieces such as rings, snuff boxes, and spoons.

Refs.: Buhler and Hood, no. 371. Philip Hammerslough, "A Master-Craftsman of Early Guilford," *Connecticut Historical Society Bulletin* 19, no. 4 (October 1954): 123-128. Fales, *Richardson*, pp. 142-149.

109 Lady's Pin, Newark, New Jersey, 1901-1910
Unger Brothers
W. 2″ (51 mm); WT. 9 dwt (14 gm)
American Arts Purchase Fund   1973.25.4

A description of the jeweler's trade in the middle of the eighteenth century noted that "a new Fashion takes as much with the Ladies in Jewels as any thing else: He that can furnish them oftenest with the newest Whim has the best Chance for their Custom." What was true then applies with equal force to the nineteenth and twentieth centuries. For example, Unger Brothers, along with other firms, including William B. Kerr and Company, attempted to meet the fancy for silver jewelry in the early years of this century by mass-producing large numbers of pins, brooches, clasps, pendants, and other small decorative objects. Many of these objects, such as this small pin by Unger Brothers in the art nouveau style, were machine-stamped in imitation repoussé and probably hand-finished. This jewelry would seem to have been produced primarily for a growing middle-class clientele; in the 1890s, women of high fashion, such as the fictional Mrs. Gereth in William James's *The Spoils of Poynton* (1897), regarded the sort of woman who would be seen wearing silver jewelry with condescension.

Refs.: R. Campbell, *The London Tradesman* (1747; reprint, Newton Abbot, England: David & Charles, 1969), p. 143. Charlotte Gere, *American and European Jewelry, 1830-1914* (New York: Crown Publishers, Inc., 1975), pp. 75-76, 197, 225.

110 Masonic Medal, American, ca. 1800
L. 2 5/16″ (59 mm); WT. 4 dwt (6 gm)
Mabel Brady Garvan Collection   1930.4886

The making of small silver seals, medals, and badges formed part of the silversmith's trade during the eighteenth and nineteenth centuries. Awards of merit for scholarship and Masonic medals, such as this example, were among the forms most frequently made.

This unmarked medal, or jewel as it is more properly called, has the name I. BAILEY engraved on the back and was probably commisioned as a personal jewel and engraved according to Bailey's instructions. The front is engraved with over twenty Masonic symbols, each of them carrying moral overtones symbolic of the Mason's guiding principles and beliefs. For example, the beehive represents industry, the key stands for silence and secrecy, and the level symbolizes equality. The "all-seeing eye," a symbol of watchfulness and of the Supreme Being, can be seen just under the loop. These personal jewels, worn at meetings, were particularly popular from about 1775 to 1820. Larger, more impressive Masonic mark jewels, each in the form of a specific symbol, were also made for the officers of each lodge. Many silversmiths were themselves Masons, including Paul Revere, Philip Syng, Jr., Robert Fairchild, Thomas Shields, and Myer Myers, among others whose work is in this exhibition.

Refs.: Buhler and Hood, no. 1042. Barbara Franco, *Masonic Symbols in American Decorative Arts* (Lexington, Massachusetts: Scottish Rite Masonic Museum of Our National Heritage, 1976). McClinton, pp. 203-215.

111 Hunting Sword, New York, ca. 1765-1775
Ephraim Brasher (1744-1810)
L. 32½″ (826 mm)
Mabel Brady Garvan Collection   1930.1432

"To a greater degree than any other weapon, [the silver-hilted sword] represented the elegance and importance of a privileged class. . . . But this decorative badge of authority, despite its soft luster and delicate lines, was as deadly as it was beautiful and served as well on the battlefields as in the ballroom." This comment by the early sword collector Philip Mendicus applies with full force to this splendid hunting sword made for Petrus Wynkoop (1744-1818) and probably carried by him in the Revolutionary War in his capacity as ensign of the First Regiment of Ulster County. Complete with its leather scabbard, this sword has a blade of German steel, an ivory grip stained green, and a rare dog's head pommel with what are said to be amethyst eyes, in addition to its silver mounts made by Ephraim Brasher.

Refs.: Buhler and Hood, no. 693. Philip Mendicus, "American Silver-Hilted Swords," *Antiques* 46, no. 5 (November 1944): 264-266 and 46, no. 6 (December 1944): 342-344. Hermann Warner Williams, Jr., "American Silver-Hilted Swords," *Antiques* 67, no. 6 (June 1955): 510-513. Harold L. Peterson, *The American Sword, 1775-1945* (Philadelphia: Ray Riling Arms Books Co., 1973). John K. Lattimer, "Sword Hilts by Early American Silversmiths," *Antiques* 87, no. 2 (February 1965): 196-199.

112 Leather Belt with Conchas, Arizona, ca. 1880-1900
Navajo
L. 46″ (1168 mm)
The William P. Sargent Indian Collection, Peabody Museum of Natural History, Yale University

Native American silversmiths made silver jewelry to the virtual exclusion of other forms of silver objects. Unlike the Indians of South and Central America, the natives of North America did not have ready access to precious metals from their own mines. It was not until Europeans introduced silver into North America that the native tribes began fashioning silver, usually obtained from coins, into decorative objects. Iroquois, Seminole, Delaware, and many other Eastern tribes made small silver cape ornaments and pins perhaps as early as the eighteenth century. In the nineteenth

century, the Plains Indians worked in silver and also in "German" or nickel silver (an alloy of tin, copper, and nickel which contains no silver at all). Plains silverwork consisted mainly of round plaques used for hair ornaments and to decorate belts and bridles.

Although the Navajo were not the first native Americans to work in silver, they have been perhaps the most creative artists in this medium. The Navajo first learned to work silver from Mexican *plateros* working in the Southwest some time during the last half of the nineteenth century. At first they made simple designs decorated with small punches and awls, and seldom worked with solder. The *concha* (Spanish for "shell") form, influenced by Plains and Mexican silverwork, was originally round but soon developed into the well-known oval. The earliest *concha* belts consist of several round or oval *conchas* strung onto thin leather thongs. The *conchas* are notched in the center so that the leather can pass through. At first these leather belts were simply tied around the waist, but later, as the Navajo developed skill in casting, they were fastened by elaborate cast buckles such as the one on this belt and the one pictured in Figure 38.

Refs.: John Adair, *The Navajo and Pueblo Silversmiths* (Norman, Oklahoma: University of Oklahoma Press, 1944), pp. 3-54. Carl Rosnek and Joseph Stacey, *Skystone and Silver: The Collector's Book of Southwest Indian Jewelry* (Englewood Cliffs, New Jersey: Prentice-Hall, Inc., 1976), pp. 14-40. Margery Bedinger, *Indian Silver, Navajo and Pueblo Jewelers* (Albuquerque, New Mexico: University of New Mexico Press, 1973), pp. 58-68.

Figure 38
Slender Maker of Silver, Navajo silversmith, ca. 1885.
Museum of New Mexico; Ben Wittick collection.

113 **Man's Pouch,** Arizona, ca. 1880-1910
Navajo
L. 30″ (762 mm)
The William P. Sargent Indian Collection, Peabody
Museum of Natural History, Yale University

From the earliest period of Navajo silversmithing, possibly
as early as 1850, Indian smiths made silver buttons "by first
making a rounded or conical mold in wood . . . and hammering the coin until it fit into the mold." Buttons were also
sometimes made from coins, unaltered except for small
loops soldered to one side. Although buttons were primarily
used to decorate women's clothing, they were also important embellishments on men's pouches, leggings, and moc-
casins.

The pouch was used to carry tobacco and small neces-
sities and was an indispensable article of the Navajo man's
attire. Carried on the hip, the pouch hung from a leather
strap worn over the opposite shoulder. Early writers were
impressed by these "sashes, to run across the breast and
shoulder" which were lavishly decorated with silver. The
Navajo made these pouches exclusively for their own use
and apparently never produced anything like them for the
tourist trade. This pouch was probably purchased as "dead"
or unclaimed pawn from a local trader. Pouches were not
generally worn after 1900, although older members of the
tribe continued to wear them as late as the early 1940s.

Refs.: Margery Bedinger, *Indian Silver, Navajo and Pueblo Jewelers* (Al-
buquerque, New Mexico: University of New Mexico Press, 1973), pp.
28-31. Carl Rosnek and Joseph Stacey, *Skystone and Silver: The Collector's
Book of Southwest Indian Jewelry* (Englewood Cliffs, New Jersey:
Prentice-Hall, Inc., 1976), pp. 27, 33, 39-40, 49-57. John Adair, *The
Navajo and Pueblo Silversmiths* (Norman, Oklahoma: University of
Oklahoma Press, 1944), pp. 45-53.

114 **Leather Belt with Conchas,** Arizona, ca. 1910-1920
Navajo
L. 47¼″ (1200 mm)
The William P. Sargent Indian Collection, Peabody
Museum of Natural History, Yale University

Silver *conchas* were probably first set with turquoise between 1890 and 1900. Elaborate belts such as this one with
its repoussé and fine stamped decoration began to be made
shortly thereafter. By the 1920s the first crude dies had been
replaced largely by commercially produced stamps which
were readily available from white traders, although the best
smiths continued to make their own designs as well. It was at
this time that the Navajo first began to produce jewelry for
the tourist trade, and many Indians became full-time silversmiths.

This belt, however, lacks the excessive decoration of
trade jewelry, and was probably owned by a Navajo. Turquoise occurs in many color variations and often it was
impossible for a smith to obtain enough turquoise of uniform color to complete an entire belt. In addition, stones
sometimes turn color after long exposure to air, which may
also account for the varying color of the turquoise in this
belt. According to an old Navajo tradition, if a turquoise on
a piece of jewelry given to one's mate turned color it meant
that the owner had been unfaithful.

Refs.: John Adair, *The Navajo and Pueblo Silversmiths* (Norman, Oklahoma: University of Oklahoma Press, 1944), pp. 9-54. Carl Rosnek and
Joseph Stacey, *Skystone and Silver: The Collector's Book of Southwest
Indian Jewelry* (Englewood Cliffs, New Jersey: Prentice-Hall, Inc., 1976),
pp. 45-57.

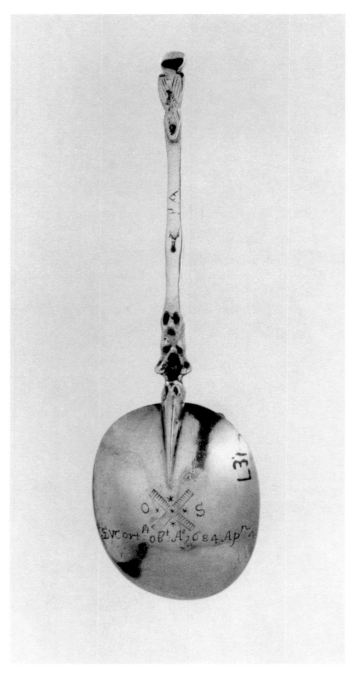

115 Spoon, New York, 1684
Cornelius van der Burch (ca. 1653-1699)
L. 6⅜″ (162 mm); WT. 1 oz, 5 dwt (39 gm)
Mabel Brady Garvan Collection   1936.215

Spoons such as this were often given to friends at funerals as a token by which to remember the deceased, a common custom in the seventeenth and eighteenth centuries. One of two funeral spoons by Cornelius van der Burch in the Yale collection, this example was a gift to a pallbearer at the funeral of Olof Stevense Van Cortlandt, who died in 1684. In contrast to general practice, in which spoons were hammered from a single piece of silver, these New York spoons were made in two parts; a cast handle, in this case terminating with an owl sejant (an owl in a sitting position, symbolizing death), was attached to a hammered round bowl. Although the custom of presenting funeral spoons was known in England, it was most widely practiced in America among the colonial Dutch of New York. New Englanders seem to have favored gloves, scarves, and mourning rings (116) as funeral tokens.

Refs.: Buhler and Hood, no. 552. Albert Scher, "Two Hoof Spoons," *Antiques* 114, no. 3 (September 1978): 567-569.

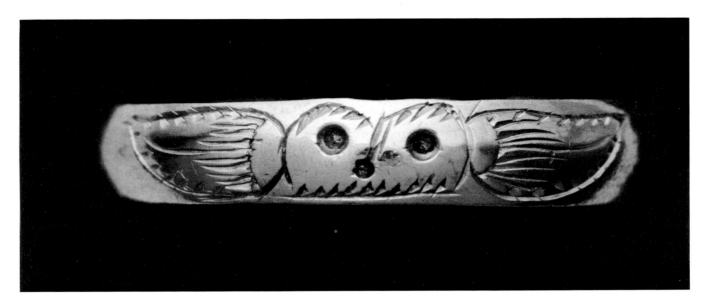

116 Gold Mourning Ring, Salem, Massachusetts, ca. 1736
    Jeffrey Lang (1707-1758)
    D. ¾″ (19 mm)
    Mabel Brady Garvan Collection   1934.344

After the death in 1684 of the wealthy Captain George Corwin of Salem, his estate was billed by Jeremiah Dummer and John Coney for a total of sixty gold mourning rings, which had been presented to the minister and to Corwin's friends at his funeral. This practice, well established in the seventeenth century, continued through the eighteenth century and well into the nineteenth. Gloves and scarves were also presented at funerals, and the combined cost of these gifts, in addition to the food and drink customarily provided, made these occasions very costly. The Massachusetts legislature made several attempts in the eighteenth century to control "the extraordinary Expence at Funerals."

This mourning ring, unusual in having a maker's mark, is engraved "E. Kitchen. obt 25. Octr. 1736. AE 3," and was made for the funeral of the young son of Edward and Freke Kitchen of Salem. Its winged death's head is a grim and severe reminder of mortality. All three of Jeffrey Lang's sons became silversmiths and made mourning rings in this early, plain style.

Refs.: Buhler and Hood, no. 172. Curwen Papers, Essex Institute, Salem, Massachusetts. Martha Gandy Fales, "The Early American Way of Death," *Essex Institute Historical Collections* 100, no. 2 (April 1964): 75-84. David E. Stannard, *The Puritan Way of Death* (New York: Oxford University Press, 1977), chap. 5. Peter J. Bohan, *American Gold, 1700-1860* (New Haven: Yale University Art Gallery, 1963), pp. 18-23.

A Gallery of American Silver

117 **Spoon**, Boston, ca. 1670-1680
Jeremiah Dummer (1645-1718)
L. 7 5/16″ (186 mm); WT. 1 oz, 15 dwt (54 gm)
Mabel Brady Garvan Collection   1938.300

118 **Spoon**, New York, ca. 1680-1690
Attributed to Gerrit Onckelbag (ca. 1670-1732)
L. 6 9/16″ (167 mm); WT. 1 oz, 13 dwt (51 gm)
Mabel Brady Garvan Collection   1936.211

119 **Spoon**, Boston, ca. 1690-1700
John Coney (1656-1722)
L. 7 3/8″ (187 mm); WT. 1 oz, 16 dwt (56 gm)
Mabel Brady Garvan Collection   1936.420

120 **Spoon**, Boston, ca. 1720-1730
John Burt (1693-1746)
L. 7 5/8″ (194 mm); WT. 1 oz, 9 dwt (45 gm)
Mabel Brady Garvan Collection   1930.1298

121 **Dessert Spoon**, Philadelphia, ca. 1785-1795
Richard Humphreys (adv. 1771-1796)
L. 7 3/8″ (187 mm); WT. 1 oz, 6 dwt (40 gm)
Mabel Brady Garvan Collection   1932.71a

122 **Tablespoon**, Watersford or Buffalo, New York,
ca. 1820-1830
George Hedge (w. ca. 1819-1848)
L. 9 1/8″ (232 mm); WT. 1 oz, 12 dwt (50 gm)
Mabel Brady Garvan Collection   1936.273a

123 **Dessert Spoon**, Providence, Rhode Island, ca. 1930
(design patented 1895)
Gorham Manufacturing Company
L. 6 15/16″ (176 mm); WT. 1 oz, 12 dwt (50 gm)
Gift of Miss Olive Louise Dann to the Yale University
Art Gallery Associates

124 **Teaspoon**, Providence, Rhode Island, ca. 1902
Designed by William C. Codman (1839-1921)
Gorham Manufacturing Company
L. 5 13/16″ (148 mm); WT. 1 oz (31 gm)
Gift of Dr. Louis J. Camuti   1974.120.3f

125 **Teaspoon**, Meriden, Connecticut, 1978
Designed by Ronald Hayes Pearson (b. 1924), 1959
International Silver Company
L. 6 1/4″ (159 mm); WT. 1 oz, 5 dwt (39 gm)
Gift of the International Silver Company   1978.61

Spoons have always been the most commonly produced silver item in America. Early inventories indicate that if an estate contained but one object of silver it was likely to be a spoon. However, neither their frequency of manufacture nor their utilitarian nature exempted spoons from the vagaries of style; like everything else, spoons changed over time. The earliest spoons made in America are of a type called slip-end or slipped-in-the-stalk, since the stem appears to have been sliced off at an angle as a gardener cuts a plant stalk. An example by Jeremiah Dummer (117) exhibits the fig-shaped bowl common to this type of spoon, which dates back to fifteenth-century England. In New York, spoons with cast handles, such as this one by Gerrit Onckelbag (118), were popular in the late seventeenth century and were often given to pallbearers at funerals. Here an oval hammered bowl has been attached to a handle cast in the form of a caryatid with foliage below. At the end of the seventeenth century in New England, decoration of the baroque style became popular for spoons and the back of a spoon bowl was often hammered into a swage to give it floral decoration in relief. Since spoons were placed face down on the table, this attention to the decoration of the back of the bowl is understandable. The spoon by John Coney (119) is of this type; a trifid end handle with an elaborately decorated front stems out from an oval bowl with a rattail drop and floral relief on the back. In the eighteenth century, spoons of the spatulate design such as this one by John Burt (120) were popular. The spoon has an oval bowl with a rattail and an upturned, ribbed handle. By the late eighteenth century, spoon handles had begun to turn backward. The spoon by Richard Humphreys (121) has bright-cut engraving characteristic of the neoclas-

117-125 left to right

117-125 left to right

sical style. In the nineteenth century, spoons with fiddle handles and pointed oval bowls were in fashion. Cast floral ornament was occasionally added to the handle of the spoon, as in this example by George Hedge (**122**). Later in the century a profusion of varied patterns were machine-produced by commercial silver companies. Many of these patterns were in the rococo taste, such as the "Chantilly" pattern patented by Gorham in 1895 (**123**). This pattern continues to be manufactured today. Another spoon produced by Gorham (**124**) is in the art nouveau style. Called "Patrician," this pattern was patented in 1902, when Gorham was under the artistic direction of William C. Codman. More recently, modern companies have produced patterns whose designs are the result of international competition. Such is the case with the "Vision" spoon (**125**), designed by Ronald Hayes Pearson in 1959 and put into production by International Silver in 1961. After twenty years, it still appears modern.

Refs.: Buhler and Hood, nos. 7, 25, 111, 573, 796, 878. Fales, *Early American Silver*, pp. 56-62. *Designed for Silver* (New York: International Silver Company, 1960), pp. 42-43. Turner, pp. 99-100.

126 Tankard, Boston, ca. 1685-1695
John Coney (1656-1722)
H. 7⅛" (181 mm); WT. 30 oz, 13 dwt (950 gm)
Mabel Brady Garvan Collection   1931.323

127 Tankard, Boston, ca. 1705-1715
John Dixwell (1680-1725)
H. 7 3/16" (183 mm); WT. 29 oz, 3 dwt (904 gm)
Mabel Brady Garvan Collection   1930.1346

128 Tankard, Boston, ca. 1745
John Burt (1693-1746)
H. 8¼" (210 mm); WT. 25 oz, 4 dwt (781 gm)
Mabel Brady Garvan Collection   1930.1195

129 Tankard, Boston, ca. 1787-1790
Joseph Foster (1760-1839)
H. 8¾" (222 mm); WT. 23 oz, 18 dwt (741 gm)
Mabel Brady Garvan Collection   1930.1302

130 Tankard, New York, ca. 1695-1705
Cornelius Kierstede (1675-1757)
H. 7¾" (197 mm); WT. 43 oz, 2 dwt (1336 gm)
Mabel Brady Garvan Collection   1934.356

131 Tankard, New York, ca. 1700-1710
Jan Van Nieu Kirke (w. ca. 1708-1715)
H. 7⅛" (181 mm); WT. 38 oz, 9 dwt (1192 gm)
Mabel Brady Garvan Collection   1936.145

132 Tankard, New York, ca. 1725-1740
Philip Goelet (ca. 1701-1748)
H. 6 3/16" (157 mm); WT. 25 oz, 3 dwt (780 gm)
Mabel Brady Garvan Collection   1930.1038

133 Tankard, New York, ca. 1750-1760
Myer Myers (1723-1795)
H. 7⅞" (200 mm); WT. 38 oz, 9 dwt (1192 gm)
Mabel Brady Garvan Collection   1930.1021

126

127

128

129

130

131

132

133

The diverging development of a form over the years in two distinct geographical areas can be traced in this series of tankards from Boston and New York. The tankard was an especially popular drinking vessel and ceremonial object in the colonies. Early Boston tankards, such as the one by John Coney (126), remain relatively true to English prototypes. Coney's commodious tankard is broad and low in proportion and is topped by a flat stepped cover with a serrated flange. It has a double spiral thumbpiece, a shield-shaped handle terminal, and an applied molded baseband and lip. The engraved ornament on the piece is limited and restrained. The spare, simple ornament and the harmony of proportions exhibited by this tankard make it an outstanding example of the seventeenth-century New England form.

Slightly later in date is a tankard by John Dixwell (127). This piece, following the trend of the eighteenth century, is taller and more vertical in its proportions than the earlier tankard. The stepped lid has swollen into a dome, and the mask-and-dolphin thumbpiece, a familiar feature of Boston tankards, has appeared.

As time progressed, Boston tankards developed an even stronger vertical emphasis. The tankard by John Burt (128) tapers more strongly from bottom to top than the earlier examples, the dome has become higher and more complex, the overhanging serrated flange has disappeared, and a bell-shaped finial has been added to the dome to give a further note of verticality. To balance these new proportions, the baseband has become splayed and much heavier and a mid-band has been added. A scrolled thumbpiece replaces the mask and dolphin.

As the eighteenth century drew to a close, the popularity of the tankard form declined, but one further step in its evolution can be seen in a tankard made by Joseph Foster (129) before the form became obsolete. Here the dome is higher than ever before and is topped by a tall flame finial in the rococo taste. The midband rides higher on the body, and above this midband on the front of the tankard is an inscription surrounded by an engraved oval and swags in the new neoclassical taste. Thus, the most up-to-date ornament is added to a transmuted but venerable form.

Although New York tankards of the seventeenth century also adhere to the English form, local silversmiths, often of Dutch ancestry, added ornament which was purely Dutch to the broad-bodied, flat-topped tankard. The tankard made by Cornelius Kierstede (130) has been elaborated with a band of stamped leaves above the wide molded baseband. The baseband itself is enriched with meander wire, a feature sometimes found on hinge-plates of Boston tankards (127) but used more freely in New York. The Kierstede tankard is further embellished with the fine, rich engraving typical of New York silver. The thumbpiece is of the corkscrew type common in New York, no doubt a result of craft specialization. A local silversmith probably made cast thumbpieces and sold them to his colleagues.

Another tankard with abundant Dutch ornament was made by Jan Van Nieu Kirke (131). Many features found in the Kierstede example reappear in this tankard, but the lion couchant has been replaced by a female mask with pendant fruit and swags, perhaps signifying fertility. On the cover of the tankard is a scrolled foliate design with punched circles and stars surrounding the initials R B C, for Robert Benson and Cornelia Roos, who were married in 1708. The terminal is of the type often associated with marriage tankards— clasped hands flanked by caryatids with a ram's head below.

The domed cover so popular in Boston never became a significant feature of New York tankards. Instead, a move to greater simplicity marks the development of the form in New York. Thus the tankard by Philip Goelet (132) retains its flat lid, but the stamped decoration, meander wire, and lavish engraving have disappeared. On the cover the cipher PFC appears with a floral device, and on the front above the baseband rests a crane, the crest of the Crane family of Elizabeth, New Jersey.

In late New York tankards, the eighteenth-century preference for vertical emphasis finally becomes evident, although not so strongly as in Boston tankards. The tankard by Myer Myers (133) is taller in its proportions than earlier New York tankards, but it lacks the domed cover and mid-band found in Boston examples. This tankard is simple and plain, with only an oval disk for a terminal. The only engraving is on the cover along the serrations of the flange and in the center, where the rococo-style cipher J EH is engraved in a circle.

Refs.: Buhler and Hood, nos. 26, 79, 114, 295, 578, 626, 637, 654. Montgomery and Kane, pp. 50-65.

134 Dram Cup, Boston, ca. 1650-1660
Robert Sanderson (1608-1693) and John Hull
(1624-1683)
D. bowl 2⅞″ (73 mm); WT. 1 oz, 8 dwt (43 gm)
Mabel Brady Garvan Collection   1949.78

John Marshall Phillips suggested that this small dram cup
was the earliest known piece of American silver to have
survived. According to family tradition, it was part of the
wedding silver given to Ruth Brewster, a descendant of Elder
Brewster who married John Pickett of New London in 1651.
It is presumably her maiden initials which are engraved on
the side of the shallow bowl. There is as yet no firm docu-
mentary evidence to support a date of 1651 for this piece,
however, and objects were occasionally engraved with the
owner's maiden initials after her marriage. Whatever its
precise year of manufacture, this dram cup has major importance as an example of the earliest style of silver made in this
country.

The cup is embellished with flat-chased ornament including stylized fleur-de-lis in each of four panels on its body,
and a Tudor rose on the bottom of the bowl. Two other dram
cups by Hull and Sanderson are known; they have the same
form and wire handles as this piece, but lack its chased
decoration.

Both Robert Sanderson and John Hull were born in
England and came to the Massachusetts Bay Colony in the
1630s. They are generally thought to have begun working
together in 1652, when Hull was appointed master of the
Massachusetts mint and chose Sanderson as his partner.
This dram cup is one of four pieces at Yale made during their
partnership and marked by both men.

Refs.: Buhler and Hood, no. 1. Kathryn C. Buhler, *American Silver, 1655-
1825, in the Museum of Fine Arts, Boston,* 2 vols. (Greenwich, Connecticut: New York Graphic Society, 1972), I, 1-9.

135 Covered Caudle Cup, Boston, ca. 1679-1685
John Coney (1656-1722)
H. 6 11/16″ (170 mm); WT. 31 oz, 11 dwt (978 gm)
Mabel Brady Garvan Collection   1932.46

With its wide proportions and fine cast caryatid handles, this
cup is a prime example of the seventeenth-century style in
American silver. Although English cups with covers of this
type were common about 1660, this is the earliest surviving
covered caudle cup made in the colonies and the only one of
this particular form. Because the gourd-shaped body has no
molding at its rim, the cover fits down over the body slightly.
This minimizes the break between the cup and its cover,
creating a continuously smooth surface. The flattened reel
handle allows the top, when turned over, to serve as a small
stand. The coat of arms, somewhat awkward in conception,
fills the plain surface with what Graham Hood has called
"splendid assurance."

Cups of this type were probably used domestically in
the service of beer and caudle, a drink made of hot spiced
gruel mixed with wine or ale, and are also found among the
communion plate of many New England Congregational
churches. This particular cup belonged to Isaac Addington
of Boston and is inscribed "Ex dono IL." It is believed that
this inscription indicates that Addington took the inheri-
tance of twenty pounds which he received in 1679 from his
uncle, Governor John Leverett, and had it transformed into
this splendid caudle cup. When John Coney made the cup he
was only twenty-three and had probably just opened his
own shop.

Refs.: Buhler and Hood, no. 22. Francis Hill Bigelow, *Historic Silver of the
Colonies and Its Makers* (New York: The Macmillan Company, 1917), pp.
104-127. Charles Oman, *Caroline Silver, 1625-1688* (London: Faber and
Faber, 1970), p. 40, pls. 12, 13B.

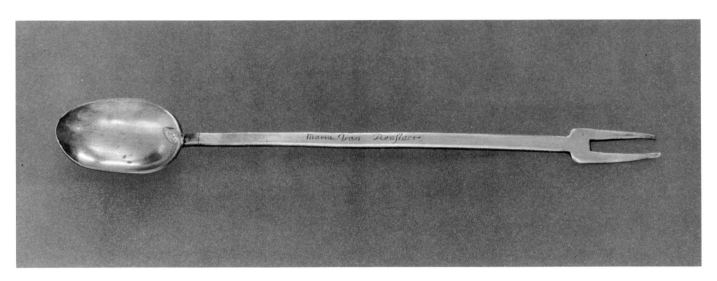

136 Beaker, New York, ca. 1680-1690
Attributed to Jurian Blanck, Jr. (ca. 1645-1714)
H. 6⅝″ (168 mm); WT. 11 oz, 3 dwt (346 gm)
Mabel Brady Garvan Collection   1930.1034

The beaker, a common seventeenth-century form, was used
for both ecclesiastical and domestic purposes. The interlaced strapwork, floral pendants, and delightful birds engraved on this example are characteristic of seventeenth-
century New York silver, as is the applied foliate band on its
base. Such motifs were probably derived from decorated
borders found in printed books of the period.

This beaker, engraved A^VG F, was presumably part of the
household furnishings of a Dutch-American family in New
York; it is closely related to other beakers by the same maker
created for the First Reformed Protestant Dutch Church in
Brooklyn and the First Reformed Church of Kingston, New
York. For years all of these beakers, each with an IB mark,
were attributed to Jacob Boelen. It was not until 1940 that
Helen Burr Smith reassigned them to Jurian Blanck, Jr.,
basing her conclusion on a number of facts discovered
through genealogical research, primarily the close family
relationship between Blanck and the donor of the Brooklyn
church beakers.

Refs.: Buhler and Hood, no. 548. Helen Burr Smith, "Unidentified Silver
Mark Believed Jurian Blanck's," *The New York Sun*, 5 October 1940.

137 Sucket Fork, New York, ca. 1680-1690
Jesse Kip (1660-1722)
L. 6⅛″ (156 mm); WT. 9 dwt (14 gm)
Mabel Brady Garvan Collection   1930.1041

This dual-purpose utensil was designed for the eating of
suckets, which were fruits, perhaps plums or grapes, preserved in sugar and served either candied or in syrup. Although these sweetmeats were popular in the seventeenth
century, the fashion was relatively short-lived and few
American sucket forks have survived. This example is one of
a pair made by Jesse Kip of New York. Its mate, also engraved with the name of "Maria Van Renslaer," is at the
Museum of the City of New York.

Silver in the New York style marked with the initials
"IK" had been known for many years before John Marshall
Phillips correctly linked the "IK" mark with the name of
Jesse Kip.

Refs.: Buhler and Hood, no. 559. George B. Cutten, "Sucket Forks," *Antiques* 57, no. 6 (June 1950): 440-441. John Marshall Phillips, "Identifying
the Mysterious IK," *Antiques* 44, no. 1 (July 1943): 19-21.

138 Candlestick, Boston, ca. 1680-1690
Jeremiah Dummer (1645-1718)
H. 10 13/16" (275 mm); WT. 25 oz, 4 dwt (781 gm)
Mabel Brady Garvan Collection 1953.22.1

Notable for its integration of horizontal and vertical elements and its bold simplicity, this piece and its mate are the only extant cluster-column candlesticks made by an American silversmith. Although the precise origin of the form has yet to be discovered, it is believed that the cluster-column design was adapted from traditional architectural motifs. Many silver, pewter, brass, and ceramic candlesticks of this type were made in England, Holland, and France during the seventeenth century, and doubtless many examples were imported into the colonies. When Dummer produced these candlesticks, he probably had a specific European model in mind. Engraved on the base are the arms of the original owners and their descendants.

Jeremiah Dummer, one of the first American-born silversmiths, grew up in Newbury, Massachusetts, and was apprenticed to John Hull and Robert Sanderson. Like Hull before him, Dummer engaged in shipping ventures and held several public offices in addition to his work as a silversmith. He was apparently a man of broad tastes for he gave his sons William and Jeremiah unusually cosmopolitan educations. Both served as colonial commissioners in England; William became Lieutenant Governor of Massachusetts, and Jeremiah, Jr., earned a doctorate in theology from the University of Utrecht, thus becoming the first Harvard graduate to receive an advanced academic degree.

An invalid in his later years, Dummer was probably forced to give up his activities as a silversmith in about 1715. The *Boston News Letter* of 2 June 1718 gave notice of his death and burial, commenting that he had "served his country faithfully" and been known to all as a "Just, Virtuous, and Pious man."

Refs.: Buhler and Hood, no. 9. Graham Hood, *American Silver: A History of Style, 1650-1900* (New York: Praeger Publishers, 1971), pp. 28-29, 40-45. Hermann Frederick Clarke and Henry Wilder Foote, *Jeremiah Dummer, Colonial Craftsman and Merchant, 1645-1718* (Boston: Houghton Mifflin Company, 1935), pp. 14-51, 92-93. Marc Simpson, "Tracing the Possibility of Dutch Influence in Boston Silver of the Seventeenth Century," seminar paper, Yale University, 1978.

139 Patch Box, Boston, ca. 1680-1690
William Rouse (1639-1705)
D. 1 15/16" (49 mm); WT. 1 oz, 5 dwt (39 gm)
John Marshall Phillips Collection, the gift of his nephews, Donald and Marshall Phillips 1955.10.2

While patches served the practical purpose of masking the scars so often left by the ravages of smallpox in the seventeenth and eighteenth centuries, they also appealed to the vanity of both men and women. Henry Glapthorpe, in his play *The Lady's Priviledge* (1640), hints at another important use for patches: "If it be a lover's part you are to act, take a black spot or two. I can furnish you; 'twill make your

face more amorous, and appear more gracious in your mistress' eyes." The vanity of patching was a frequent source of humor among the writers of the eighteenth century. The fictitious diary of Clarinda, published in *The Spectator* in 1712, contains the following entry: "Saturday . . . *From Eight to Nine*. Shifted a patch for Half an Hour before I could determine it. Fixed it above my left eye." Yet another significance of patching was satirized by Joseph Addison, who after a night at the theater reported in *The Spectator* that the ladies "were *Patched* differently; the Faces, on one Hand, being Spotted on the Right Side of the Forehead, and those upon the other on the left," according to whether the lady was of Tory sympathy or Whig.

This tiny box for holding patches was made by William Rouse, probably for Lydia Foster of Boston, whose initials are engraved on the bottom. The masterfully engraved sunflower on the cover is much like flowers found in embroidery of the period, an illustration of the natural interaction between crafts.

Refs.: Buhler and Hood, no. 6. Henry Glapthorpe, *The Lady's Priviledge* (1640; reprint, London: Hurst, Robinson and Co., 1825), p. 19.

Detail of Cover

140 Covered Skillet, Boston, ca. 1690-1700
William Rouse (1639-1705)
H. 4⅝″ (117 mm); WT. 18 oz (558 gm)
Gift of Mr. and Mrs. Donald W. Henry   1976.127

Covered skillets were used to serve hot food at the table in the seventeenth century. Several English examples in silver survive, but this skillet by William Rouse is one of a very few American examples of this exceedingly rare form. (Skillets by Hull and Sanderson and by Jan Van Nieu Kirke have also been reported.) The skillet consists of a deep bowl with a hollow scroll handle; it is raised on three feet similar to the brackets found on New England standing salts of around 1700. The cover, necessary for keeping the food warm, is decorated with floral engraving radiating out from a reel-shaped handle on which the arms of Foster are inscribed. The Foster arms are repeated on the front of the skillet's body, here surrounded by a florid acanthus cartouche executed with the excellence associated with Rouse's engraving. The family of Colonel John Foster of Boston seems to have been among Rouse's regular customers; of about a dozen known works by Rouse, four were made for the Foster family.

Refs.: Graham Hood, "A New Form in American Seventeenth-Century Silver," *Antiques* 94, no. 6 (December 1968): 879-881. Edward Wenham, *Domestic Silver of Great Britain and Ireland* (New York: Oxford University Press, 1931), pp. 61-62.

141 Two-handled Bowl, Boston, ca. 1690-1700
Jeremiah Dummer (1645-1718)
D. lip 6⅞″ (175 mm); WT. 17 oz, 10 dwt (542 gm)
Mabel Brady Garvan Collection   1940.55

This drinking bowl by Jeremiah Dummer of Boston is a curiosity in American silver. Closely related to contemporary Portuguese bowls, it is unique in this country. There has been much speculation about how a Boston silversmith came to be acquainted with the form. Dummer is known to have joined in at least one shipping venture with Robert Rogers and John Kelley, "English Merch^{ts} at Oporto in Portugal," and this connection suggests that he may have imported bowls of this type. John Marshall Phillips felt that the Spanish, Portuguese, and other foreign silver which arrived in Boston as a result of piracy and privateering may also have served as Dummer's inspiration.

During the Spanish period (1580-1640) the Portuguese maintained a distinctive style in the decorative arts which was plain and austere in comparison with prevailing Spanish styles. After the restoration of the Portuguese monarchy in 1640, renewed trade with India and the Orient influenced Portuguese design, and embossed floral and naturalistic motifs were assimilated into the national style.

Two-handled bowls with lobed rims and embossed floral designs and cast scroll handles are among the most characteristic of Portuguese forms. Dummer's bowl differs in that it is more nearly square in outline, devotes more space to the floral decoration, and has more lobes than the typical Portuguese example. In addition, Dummer's chased design is more free-flowing and may well be related to English embroidery designs of the period, although the open tulip motif is common in Portuguese work. The cast snake's head handles and square proportions also recall similar features in English pieces of the late seventeenth century.

Refs.: Buhler and Hood, no. 10. Hermann Frederick Clarke and Henry Wilder Foote, *Jeremiah Dummer, Colonial Craftsman and Merchant, 1645-1718* (Boston: Houghton Mifflin Company, 1935), pp. 28-29, 78-79. John Marshall Phillips, *Early American Silver Selected from The Mabel Brady Garvan Collection, Yale University* (New Haven: Yale University Art Gallery, 1960). *Les Trésors de L'Orfèvrerie du Portugal* (Paris: Musée des Arts Décoratifs, 1954), pp. 17-18, 44, nos. 110-112. Charles Oman and José Rosas, Jr., "Portuguese Influence Upon English Silver," *Apollo* 51, no. 304 (June 1950): 162-164.

142 **Two-handled Bowl,** New York, ca. 1690-1700
Bartholomew Le Roux (ca. 1663-1713)
D. bowl 8 15/16″ (227 mm); WT. 26 oz, 16 dwt (831 gm)
Mabel Brady Garvan Collection   1930.1043

This large two-handled bowl with paneled decoration and caryatid handles, although the only known example of its precise type, is related to a group of at least eighteen other New York bowls of the late seventeenth century. After a study of their origins, John N. Pearce concluded that "the general concept and the specific vocabulary of the New York bowls were taken from north European—and particularly Dutch—examples of approximately the same period as the earliest from New York," and that they are ultimately derived from the "work of the Italian masters of the high Renaissance."

Presumably made for Joseph and Sarah Wardel of Monmouth County, New Jersey, who were married in 1696, this bowl is engraved with the names of their daughter Sarah and seven subsequent descendants, all named Sarah, down to "Sarah McCalmont Lewisson great great great great great granddaughter of Joseph and Sarah Wardel Boston 1904." Although some have complained that this later engraving disfigures the plain surfaces and rhythmic movement of the lobed bowl, it makes the object an evocative and powerful document of the symbolic importance attached to silver objects throughout American history.

Refs.: Buhler and Hood, no. 564. John N. Pearce, "New York's Two-Handled Paneled Silver Bowls," *Antiques* 80, no. 4 (October 1961): 341-345.

143 Two-handled Covered Cup, New York, ca. 1690-1700
Gerrit Onckelbag (ca. 1670-1732)
H. 5¾″ (146 mm); WT. 23 oz, 5 dwt (721 gm)
Mabel Brady Garvan Collection   1936.135

Judith Bayard was baptized in the Dutch Church, New
York, on 13 December 1696, and as a token of that christening she probably received this two-handled covered cup
engraved with her initials, I.B., and with the arms of her
family. Judith's godparents were her maternal grandmother,
Gertrude Schuyler Van Cortlandt, and her paternal grand-
parents, Colonel Nicholas Bayard, secretary of New Netherlands and later of English New York, and his wife Judith
Varleth. It was customary for a godmother to give a piece
of plate to her godchild, and it seems likely that Judith Varleth Bayard might have commissioned a cup from Gerrit
Onckelbag, whose grounds in Princes Street were bounded
by "a passage belonging to Col. Nicholas Bayard." The gift
was all the more appropriate since the baptism occurred
soon after the Dutch children's festival of St. Nicholas.

The Onckelbag cup, with its cast handles and boldly
chased acanthus decoration around the base, is very similar
to English covered cups. In America this type of cup seems to
have been made only in New York. Of the three known
surviving examples, two are by Onckelbag (the other
Onckelbag cup is in the Heritage Foundation Collection)
and one is by Jurian Blanck, Jr. (Winterthur Museum). The
scrolled brackets on the cover of the cup double as feet when
the cover is inverted to serve as a dish or as a stand for the
cup.

Refs.: Buhler and Hood, no. 571. John Marshall Phillips, "Additions to the
Garvan Collection of Silver," *Bulletin of the Associates in Fine Arts at Yale
University* 8, no. 1 (June 1937): 6-7. "A Newly Discovered Masterpiece of
New York Silver," *Antiques* 30, no. 6 (December 1936): 284-285. Edward
Wenham, *Domestic Silver of Great Britain and Ireland* (New York: Oxford
University Press, 1931), pl. 12. Douglas Ash, *How to Identify English Silver
Drinking Vessels, 600-1830* (London: G. Bell and Sons, Ltd., 1964), fig.
16b.

144 Caster, New York, ca. 1705-1715
Peter Van Dyck (1684-1751)
H. 7½" (190 mm); WT. 12 oz, 1 dwt (374 gm)
Mabel Brady Garvan Collection   1942.350

This large sugar caster was made by Peter Van Dyck for
Myndert and Rachel (Cuyler) Schuyler and bears their engraved arms above the midband. Myndert Schuyler (1672-
1755), a member of the prominent Schuyler family of New
York, was appointed Mayor of Albany in 1719 and again in
1721. The caster remained in the hands of his descendants
until it came in 1942 to the Yale University Art Gallery,
where it is one of a dozen pieces made by Peter Van Dyck in
the collection.

　　The cover of this early caster is finely and beautifully
pierced in a floral pattern, and is surmounted by a ball finial
not unlike that on Van Dyck's mustard pot (100). Van Dyck
used so-called "bayonet" fasteners to attach the cover to the
base; they can be seen beneath the gadrooned flange of the
cover. Gadrooning is also used on the foot, unifying the
piece. It has been suggested that this caster was originally the
largest of a set of three, filled out by two smaller casters used
for spices. William Fitzhugh of Virginia ordered "a Sett of
Castors that is to say for Sugar, Pepper and Mustard about
24 or 25 oz." from London in 1689.

Refs.: Buhler and Hood, no. 588. "The Editor's Attic," *Antiques* 51, no. 6
(June 1947): 398. "Letters of William Fitzhugh," *The Virginia Magazine of
History and Biography* 2, no. 4 (April 1895): 377.

145 Porringer, New York, ca. 1710-1725
Peter Van Inburgh (1689-1740)
D. bowl 5⅛″ (130 mm); WT. 8 oz, 18 dwt (275 gm)
Mabel Brady Garvan Collection   1931.142

The intricate and lacy linear complexity of the fretwork in the cast handle of this porringer is in the tradition of baroque decoration, and marks the piece as an example of a type of New York porringer made in the early eighteenth century. The presence of a puzzling inscription, "1668. wunn.att.hanpsted.plaines.march 25," would seem, however, to refute so late a date. The porringer is probably of the early eighteenth century, remade from an earlier trophy whose inscription was preserved by Van Inburgh. The initials, F ˢ M, may be those of Maria Salisbury and her husband Francis, whose father, Sylvester, may have won the original trophy at the New Market course at Hempstead Plains, Long Island. This race course was described in 1670 by Daniel Dunton: "Towards the Middle of the island lyeth a plain 16 miles long and 4 broad where you will find neither stick nor stone to hinder the horses heels or endanger them in their races, and once a year, the best horses in the land are brought hither to try their swiftness, and the swiftest rewarded with a silver cup." The practice of presenting silver racing trophies was a common one in seventeenth-century England. The custom was adopted by colonial Americans and continues to this day.

Refs.: Buhler and Hood, no. 616. Phillips, *American Silver*, p. 50. Mrs. Russell Hastings, "The New York Mark PVIB," *Antiques* 24, no. 1 (July 1933): 6-9.

146 Monteith Bowl, Boston, ca. 1700-1710
John Coney (1656-1722)
D. lip 10¾″ (273 mm); WT. 50 oz, 4 dwt (1556 gm)
Mabel Brady Garvan Collection   1948.148

Characterized by massive outlines and a diversity of elaborate chased and cast ornaments, the baroque style, with its
undulating lines and contrasting surfaces, is perhaps the
most striking of all styles in early silver.

This monteith made by John Coney of Boston is truly
one of the masterpieces of this style in American silver. His
design was probably inspired by similar English objects
brought to Massachusetts by the new royal officials ap-

pointed under the commonwealth and royal charter toward
the end of the seventeenth century. The workmanship and
design show that Coney adopted the style with ease and was
capable of bringing it to perfection. The cast lion's head
masks holding the handles on either side of the bowl are
particularly well rendered, and the flutes of the body give the
piece a beautiful shimmering quality. The bowl, which still
shows minute traces of its original gilding, is engraved with
the arms of John Colman, a prominent seventeenth-century
Boston merchant.

Not only was the style of this bowl new when it was
fashioned but the form itself would have been new to Coney.
Contemporary accounts of the monteith form indicate that

it was "a vessel or bason notched at the brims to let drinking vessels hang there by the foot, so that the body or drinking place might hang into the water to cool them." The earliest English example known is dated 1684-1685.

As accomplished and refined as English monteiths, this piece created great public excitement when it was discovered to bear the mark of an American silversmith. Many experts felt that its exquisite workmanship was cause for a reappraisal of the work of the colonial silversmiths. Interest in the object was so keen that its auction in 1937 was broadcast on radio. It sold for the then-record price of $30,000.

Refs.: Buhler and Hood, no. 31. *A Silver Monteith by John Coney* (New York: American Art Association-Anderson Galleries, Inc., 1937). Jessie McNab, "Monteiths: English, American, Continental," *Antiques* 82, no. 2 (August 1962): 156-159. E. Alfred Jones, "Monteith Bowls," *Antiques* 37, no. 1 (January 1940): 22-25. "Prowlings," *Boston Evening Transcript*, 10 April 1937.

147 Trencher Salt, New York, ca. 1700-1708
Jacobus van der Spiegel (1668-1708)
D. base 3⅞" (98 mm); WT. 2 oz, 15 dwt (85 gm)
Mabel Brady Garvan Collection   1936.146a

This diminutive trencher salt is elaborated with spiral gadrooned borders at both the top and bottom of its body. These borders, which serve to refract the light and provide a shimmering surface full of movement, are characteristic of the baroque style. The initials on this example may be those of Helena Willets (1680-1715) of Flushing, Long Island.

By about 1700, small trencher salts such as these, designed to be used by an individual at his or her place at the table, began to replace the great, communal standing salts of medieval times. This evolution from a communal form to an individualistic, personalized object may reflect in a small way the vast changes that were taking place in America at this time, changes which placed greater emphasis on the individual and his place in society.

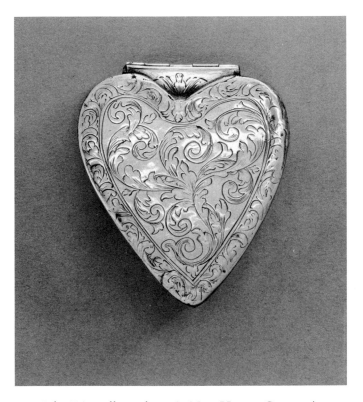

Refs.: Buhler and Hood, no. 569. Fales, *Early American Silver*, p. 65. James Deetz, *In Small Things Forgotten* (Garden City, New York: Anchor Books, 1977), pp. 39-43 and *passim*.

148 Snuff Box, Boston, ca. 1705-1725
John Dixwell (1680-1725)
L. 2 5/16" (59 mm); WT. 1 oz, 1 dwt (33 gm)
Mabel Brady Garvan Collection   1930.1323

In the eighteenth century, snuff boxes were fashionable accessories for women as well as men, and special feminine forms were developed. This small heart-shaped box may well have been a token of affection given by an admiring suitor to a fashionable young girl. The ornamental engraving, consisting of scrolled acanthus leafage reminiscent of the mantling found in heraldry designs, was probably adapted from a book like Guillim's *Display of Heraldry* (41) or from imported boxes.

John Dixwell was born in New Haven, Connecticut, the son of the well-known regicide judge of the same name. Young John was probably trained in Boston, for we know that he had been working there for several years before he traveled to England in 1710 to settle his father's estate. He returned to Boston and worked there until his death in 1725.

Refs.: Buhler and Hood, no. 78. Clare Le Corbeiller, *European and American Snuff Boxes, 1730-1830* (New York: The Viking Press, 1966), pp. 8-14, 49-50. Flynt and Fales, p. 203.

149 Chocolate Pot, Boston, ca. 1700-1710
Edward Winslow (1669-1753)
H. 9 9/16″ (243 mm); WT. 29 oz, 10 dwt (915 gm)
Mabel Brady Garvan Collection   1944.71

Edward Winslow's surviving work includes many of the
great masterpieces of the early baroque style made in the
colonies. Although extant bills show that he was active as a
goldsmith as late as 1736, it appears that his duties as Sheriff
of Suffolk County (1728-1743) and Judge of the Inferior
Court of Common Pleas (1743-1753) demanded much of his
time. When he died at age eighty-four, the goldsmith's tools
in Winslow's "Working Room" were valued at only four
pounds.

Chocolate became popular in America during the late
seventeenth century and is frequently mentioned in contemporary documents. Special pots for chocolate were made
with removable finials which allowed the insertion of a
wooden stick for stirring. This example (which unfortunately has a later spout, set slightly above the location of the
original) displays the skillful balance between smooth and
ornamented surfaces which characterizes Winslow's work
and the best silver of this period. A nearly identical chocolate
pot by Winslow at the Metropolitan Museum of Art retains
its original spout.

Refs.: Buhler and Hood, no. 49. Phillips, *American Silver,* pp. 57-58.
Kathryn C. Buhler, *American Silver, 1655-1825, in the Museum of Fine
Arts, Boston,* 2 vols. (Greenwich, Connecticut: New York Graphic Society,
1972), I, 79.

150 Mug, Albany, New York, ca. 1700-1710
Koenraet Ten Eyck (1678-1753)
H. 3½″ (89 mm); WT. 8 oz, 1 dwt (250 gm)
Mabel Brady Garvan Collection   1930.1059

This straight-sided mug, nearly as wide at the top as at the
bottom, is an early example of the form in American silver.
Its applied, molded baseband is embellished with a strip of
meander or spiral wire, and this decorative combination is
repeated on the midband encircling the mug. The only other
decoration is a long beaded rattail on the strap handle.

Although probably apprenticed in New York, Koenraet
Ten Eyck lived most of his life in Albany, where he was followed in the silversmithing trade by his sons Jacob (1705-
1793) and Barent (1714-1795). One of Koenraet's account
books has survived, and the transactions recorded in its
pages indicate that Ten Eyck, like many other early American craftsmen, was a merchant in addition to practicing his
chosen trade.

Refs.: Buhler and Hood, no. 583. Norman S. Rice, *Albany Silver, 1652-
1825* (Albany, New York: Albany Institute of History and Art, 1964), pp. 3,
16, 67. George B. Cutten, "The Ten Eyck Silversmiths," *Antiques* 42, no. 6
(December 1942): 299-303.

151 Salver, Boston, ca. 1700-1715
Thomas Savage (1664-1749)
D. 8½″ (216 mm); WT. 11 oz, 9 dwt (355 gm)
Gift of the Misses Edith and Maude Wetmore
1951.33.1

Defined in *Cocker's English Dictionary* (1704) as "a silver plate to hold glasses or sweetmeats," salvers of the early eighteenth century were flat dishes set on pedestal supports. The graceful spiral gadrooning of this example is a stylistic attribute adapted by English silversmiths from Dutch design sources. This type of ornament was used frequently in the elaboration of the many forms made in silver during the baroque period.

Thomas Savage worked both as a silversmith and tavernkeeper during his career and trained two of his sons in the goldsmith's art. In 1705 he went to Bermuda to carry on his trade, but returned to Boston in 1714.

Refs.: Buhler and Hood, no. 41. Flynt and Fales, p. 320. Kathryn C. Buhler, *Colonial Silversmiths, Masters and Apprentices* (Boston: Museum of Fine Arts, 1956), pp. 26-27, nos. 130, 131.

152 **Teapot,** New York, ca. 1720-1735
Peter Van Dyck (1684-1751)
H. 7⅛″ (181 mm); WT. 21 oz, 18 dwt (679 gm)
Mabel Brady Garvan Collection   1935.230

Characterized by balanced, symmetrical forms which rely on line and form rather than ornament for their visual impact, the Queen Anne style was popular in the colonies from about 1715 to 1750. Geometric forms, smooth surfaces, superb proportions, and the subtle interplay of reverse curves distinguish objects in this graceful style.

Known as an "Eight Square Tea-Pot" in its own time, this octagonal teapot by Peter Van Dyck assures his reputa-

tion as a master of the Queen Anne style and is one of the most beautiful objects in all of American silver. It exceeds in quality of line and proportion its Dutch and English prototypes. Although other New York silversmiths are known to have made octagonal teapots, this is apparently the only example to survive.

Unfortunately, this teapot has no known family history. It was in the hands of a London dealer in 1933 and was purchased by Mr. Garvan for Yale two years later.

Refs.: Buhler and Hood, no. 595. Mrs. Russell Hastings, "Peter Van Dyck of New York, Goldsmith, 1684-1750," *Antiques* 31, no 6 (May 1937): 236-239 and 31, no. 6 (June 1937): 302-305.

153 Teapot, Boston, ca. 1735-1745
Jacob Hurd (1703-1758)
H. 5⅛" (130 mm); WT. 15 oz, 6 dwt (474 gm)
Mabel Brady Garvan Collection   1930.1350

Globular or apple-shaped teapots were particularly popular in Boston and other New England towns, where they superseded the pear-shaped type of pot. Probably derived from contemporary English and Oriental ceramic teapots, this form began to be produced in American silver during the second quarter of the eighteenth century.

R. Campbell, author of *The London Tradesman* (1747), stated that the goldsmith "ought to be a good Designer, and have a good taste in Sculpture." As can be seen from this and other examples of his work, Jacob Hurd was truly a sculptor in silver as well as a master of the art of engraving. The graceful lift of the body of this teapot is accentuated by its high-set S-shaped spout and sweeping handle as well as by its nicely stepped molded foot. Engraved within fine mantling are the arms of Sir William Pepperell, hero of Louisburg. Refinements such as the turned drop under the spout and the engraved scrolls,

masks, and foliate designs make this an exceptional example of the globular teapot form.

Hurd was one of Boston's most prolific silversmiths and public esteem for his work is clear from the number of important commissions he received. While one of his most famous pieces is the mace of the Admiralty Court of Massachusetts (Massachusetts Historical Society), Hurd also made quantities of church silver (65), presentation silver (69), and tutorial plate.

Refs.: Buhler and Hood, no. 140. R. Campbell, *The London Tradesman* (1747; reprint, Newton Abbott, England: David and Charles, 1959), p. 142. Phillips, *American Silver,* pp. 76-77.

154 Sugar Bowl, New York, ca. 1738-1745
Simeon Soumain (1685-1750)
D. lip 4 11/16″ (119 mm); WT. 9 oz, 6 dwt (288 gm)
Mabel Brady Garvan Collection   1930.1056

By the early eighteenth century, sugar was no longer prohibitively expensive and could be stored in covered dishes rather than in locked boxes. At the same time, the growing popularity of the tea ceremony placed a new importance on such accoutrements as sugar dishes. One of the most felicitous results of this new set of circumstances is a superlative sugar dish by Simeon Soumain, based on the shape of the Oriental porcelain bowls much prized by contemporary collectors. Here Soumain has achieved a beauty of line and a harmony of proportions which far excel those of related examples. The graceful, flaring bowl stands atop a reel-shaped foot which is echoed, on a slightly reduced scale, by the handle on the lid. These reel-shaped extremities reflect, in turn, the round shape of the bowl itself and the circular format of the ciphers on the silver's surface; the piece thus becomes an integrated interplay of circles on various planes. The two ciphers, taken from Figure 100 in Colonel Parson's *A New Book of Cyphers,* bear the initials EC for Elizabeth Cruger, who came to New York from Jamaica with her husband Henry in 1738.

Refs.: Buhler and Hood, no. 603. Louise C. Avery, *Early American Silver* (New York: The Century Company, 1930), p. 329. Colonel Parsons, *A New Book of Cyphers* (London, 1704), Fig. 100.

155

156

155 Candlestick, New York, ca. 1745-1755
George Ridout (Freeman 1745)
H. 6⅝″ (168 mm); WT. 14 oz, 11 dwt (451 gm)
Mabel Brady Garvan Collection   1930.1053a

On 17 October 1743, George Ridout registered his mark as a "largeworker" at Goldsmith's Hall in London. In 1745, George Ridout, presumably the same man, was admitted as a freeman in New York. Little else is known of the maker of this beautiful candlestick, one of a pair in the Garvan collection. Free from any elaborate ornamentation, the candlestick relies for its visual success on the graceful curves and elegant proportions of its baluster stem and molded foot.

Other pairs of similar candlesticks by New York makers are known, all closely related to slightly earlier English examples.

Refs.: Buhler and Hood, no. 694. Arthur G. Grimwade, *London Goldsmiths, 1697-1837* (London: Faber and Faber, 1976), p. 642. Joseph T. Butler, *Candleholders in America, 1650-1900* (New York: Crown Publishers, Inc., 1967), pp. 27-37.

156 Caster, New York, ca. 1725-1740
Simeon Soumain (1685-1750)
H. 7⅜″ (187 mm); WT. 10 oz, 7 dwt (321 gm)
Mabel Brady Garvan Collection   1950.788

Usually taller than casters for mustard, pepper, or other spices, sugar casters such as this example were used for "casting" sugar onto food. The earliest casters made in America were straight-sided cylinders (**144**), but in the Queen Anne period this shape was often replaced by either the pear shape or the baluster shape. Simeon Soumain's octagonal baluster-shaped sugar caster is an acknowledged masterpiece of this form, and indeed, of American silver in general. Related to Peter Van Dyck's octagonal teapot (**152**), this caster has superb proportions which give it an air of poise and command. Ornament on the piece is limited to the beautifully engraved cartouche containing the arms of Joshua Maddox, the original owner, and the delicate piercing of the lid. However, a myriad of deftly handled edges, subtle but not soft, strong but not sharp, fracture and reflect light and serve to elaborate the caster. The strong vertical thrust of the caster is punctuated by the rhythm of its horizontal elements—the foot, the midband, the cover flange, and the band below the finial—to give further refinement to this extraordinary object.

Refs.: Buhler and Hood, no. 604. Graham Hood, *American Silver: A History of Style, 1650-1900* (New York: Praeger Publishers, 1971), p. 107. Fales, *Early American Silver,* pp. 68-69.

157 Spout Cup, Boston, ca. 1715-1725
Nathaniel Morse (ca. 1685-1748)
H. 5⅛″ (130 mm); WT. 6 oz, 18 dwt (214 gm)
Mabel Brady Garvan Collection   1930.1288

Nathaniel Morse's rotund little spout cup in the Queen Anne style is one of the most graceful examples of this rare form in American silver. Seemingly simple, its pear-shaped body, rising to a domed cover and with a spout and strap handle set perpendicularly to one another, is an elegant composition created by the rhythmic interplay of reverse curves.

Used for feeding liquids to invalids, small children, and the elderly, the spout cup is said to have originated in East Anglia in the mid-seventeenth century. Most surviving American examples were made during the first quarter of the eighteenth century in New England, a part of the country populated with many immigrants from East Anglia and their descendants.

Refs.: Buhler and Hood, no. 97. V. Isabelle Miller, "American Silver Spout Cups," *Antiques* 44, no. 2 (August 1943): 73-75. Mrs. G. E. P. How, "Seventeenth-Century English Silver and Its American Derivatives," in Ian M. G. Quimby, ed., *Arts of the Anglo-American Community in the Seventeenth Century* (Charlottesville, Virginia: The University Press of Virginia, 1975), p. 212.

158 Pepper Box, Boston, ca. 1720-1730
William Cowell, Sr. (1682-1736)
H. 3 5/16″ (84 mm); WT. 2 oz, 16 dwt (87 gm)
Mabel Brady Garvan Collection   1930.964

This diminutive pepper box is a fine example of a form which enjoyed great popularity in New England but is seldom found elsewhere in the colonies. Its seamed octagonal body is visually organized by the use of a thin applied band above each handle juncture, a formal device also found on tankards beginning at about this time. The band is echoed by the molding below the cover, a feature which was not only decorative, but allowed the silversmith to hide the break between the body and the cover. What makes the design of this particular example so pleasing is the slight flare to the base, which reflects the detail of the cover and is well suited to the fluid nature of the metal. Later examples of the form have raised domed covers and elaborate piercing. The slight scroll handle is cast.

From inventory references it appears that "pepper box" was the contemporary term for this type of small dredger, although several authors have suggested that they may have been used for a variety of spices. The form seems to have declined in popularity during the late rococo period as matched sets of casters for sugar, mustard, and pepper became increasingly common.

Refs.: Buhler and Hood, no. 91. Kathryn C. Buhler, *Massachusetts Silver in the Frank L. and Louise C. Harrington Collection* (Worcester, Massachusetts: Privately Printed, 1965), pp. 37-38, 57.

159 Two-handled Covered Cup, New York, ca. 1730
Charles Le Roux (1689-1745)
H. 10¼″ (260 mm); WT. 55 oz, 18 dwt (1733 gm)
Mabel Brady Garvan Collection   1935.229

The cut-card ornament and harp-shaped handles of this cup are in the tradition of the French Huguenot craftsmen who left France to settle in England and America after the Revocation of the Edict of Nantes (1685) forced them from their native land. Charles Le Roux's cup, very similar to cups made by his fellow Huguenots in England, was probably

made as a christening gift for Frederick de Peyster, son of Abraham de Peyster and his wife Margaret Van Cortlandt. Frederick's father was the treasurer of New York, so it is fitting that his silver cup was made by Le Roux, the official goldsmith of that city.

The cup balances outward thrusts with self-containment. The acorn finial strives upward but is firmly rooted to the cup by the cut-card strapwork which reaches downward toward its counterpart on the body of the cup. This vertical tension is balanced by the horizontal midband and by the

handles, which push outward only to curl back toward the center at the cup's broadest point.

Cups of this type were traditionally called grace cups, a name which derives from the English practice of passing a drink around the table after the saying of grace at the end of the meal.

Refs.: Buhler and Hood, no. 612. Louise C. Belden, "The Verplanck Cup," *Antiques* 92, no. 6 (December 1967): 840-842. John Marshall Phillips, "Additions to the Garvan Collection of Silver," *Bulletin of the Associates in Fine Arts at Yale University* 8, no. 1 (June 1937): 8. John F. Hayward, *Huguenot Silver in England* (London: Faber and Faber, 1959), pl. 6.

160 Salver, Boston, ca. 1740-1750
Jacob Hurd (1703-1758)
D. 12 9/16″ (319 mm); WT. 34 oz, 8 dwt (1066 gm)
Mabel Brady Garvan Collection   1940.125

By the middle of the eighteenth century, low, footed salvers were common. Used variously to serve wine, sweetmeats, and tea, they were an important ornament of the dining room or parlor when not in use.

Basically octagonal in shape, the outline of this salver is softened and yet emboldened by the rhythmic broken curves of its molded edge. The deeply engraved shells, scrolls, rosettes, and diaperwork just inside the molding are skillfully blended into the overall design. The scrolls and shells are repeated in the delicately engraved cartouche surrounding the Clarke family coat of arms, making the object a well-integrated whole.

There is little doubt that Jacob Hurd was one of the masters of the Queen Anne style in America. Although he died at an early age, being "Seiz'd with an Apoplexy"

161 Porringer, Boston, ca. 1720-1740 (detail)
George Hanners (ca. 1696-1740)
D. bowl 5 5/16" (135 mm); WT. 7 oz, 12 dwt (235 gm)
Gift of Mr. and Mrs. H. W. Maxwell   1952.13.1

Although porringers, or bleeding bowls as they are called in England, began to go out of style in the mother country after 1700, the form persisted in America well into the nineteenth century. Bowl forms changed little over time, but stylistic evolution is evident in the piercings of early cast porringer handles. This example by George Hanners of Boston has an unusual handle design made up of the gentle S-curves and C-scrolls so well known in Queen Anne silver.

Porringers enjoyed unusual popularity in New England, where hardly a household of substance existed which did not include one or more made either of silver or pewter. It has been suggested that the frequency with which the form appears may be due to certain traditional customs. It seems that porringers, often engraved with the initials of married couples, were common gifts which carried wishes for fertility and family prosperity to the recipients. It is possible, however, that this one, which is engraved with only a single set of initials, may have been presented to a young child. Today, porringers are still thought of as gifts for children.

Refs.: Buhler and Hood, no. 122. Fales, *Early American Silver*, pp. 52-53. Kathryn C. Buhler, *Masterpieces of American Silver* (Richmond, Virginia: The Virginia Museum of Fine Arts, 1960), pp. 32-33. Anthony N. B. Garvan, "The New England Porringer: An Index of Custom," *Annual Report of the Board of Regents of the Smithsonian Institution . . . for the Year Ended June 30 1958,* Publication 4354 (Washington, D.C.: United States Government Printing Office, 1959), pp. 543-552.

(*Boston News-Letter,* 23 February 1758), he was a prolific craftsman and trained two of his sons, Benjamin (1739-1781) and Nathaniel (1730-1777), in the art of silversmithing.

When this piece was included in "Masterpieces of American Silver," an exhibition held at the Yale University Art Gallery in 1939, it was still in a private collection. In 1940 it was purchased and given to the Gallery as a memorial to Francis P. Garvan through the generosity of his classmates and friends.

Refs.: Buhler and Hood, no. 151. Lady Grisell Baillie, *The Household Book of Lady Grisell Baillie, 1692-1733* (Edinburgh: The Scottish History Society, 1911), pp. 273-277, 289-299. Hollis French, *Jacob Hurd and His Sons Nathaniel and Benjamin, Silversmiths, 1702-1781* (1939; reprint, New York: Da Capo Press, 1972), pp. 3-11.

162 Tankard, Philadelphia, ca. 1730-1740
Philip Syng, Jr. (1703-1789)
H. 8⅝″ (219 mm); WT. 44 oz, 2 dwt (1367 gm)
Mabel Brady Garvan Collection   1930.1194

Philip Syng's monumental tankard has been called "one of
the foremost objects of the Queen Anne style in Philadelphia
silver." Its form, featuring a capacious body rounded at the
base, a domed top, and a cast double-scrolled handle, is
unusual for an American tankard, nor is it common in
English work. It has been theorized that the high degree of
sophistication seen in this object and other examples of
Syng's work is a reflection of his visit to London in the 1720s
after the completion of his apprenticeship in Philadelphia.
The excellent quality of the elaborately engraved Maddox
arms suggests that they are the work of Lawrence Herbert, a
London-trained engraver who was employed in Syng's shop
as early as 1748. The original owner, Joshua Maddox
(1687-1759), an influential member of Philadelphia society
and one of the founding trustees of the University of Pennsylvania, owned some £200 worth of silver at the time of his
death. A number of pieces originally owned by him have
survived, including this tankard and a caster (156) by Simeon Soumain, also in this exhibition.

Refs.: Buhler and Hood, no. 825. *Philadelphia: Three Centuries of American Art* (Philadelphia: Philadelphia Museum of Art, 1976), pp. 30, 52-53.

163 Candlestick, New York, ca. 1760-1775
Myer Myers (1723-1795)
H. 10⅛″ (257 mm); WT. 19 oz, 13 dwt (609 gm)
Mabel Brady Garvan Collection   1936.148a

Candlesticks, especially those of rococo design, are rare in
early American silver. This example, part of a set which
includes four candlesticks and a snuffers and tray, is one of
the finest American expressions of the form to survive. The
candlesticks, in fact, rated special mention in the will of their
original owner, Catherine Livingston Lawrence, who in
1807 bequeathed "to Louisa E.F. Patterson Wife of my
Grand Nephew John W. Patterson one pair of my Silver
Candlesticks and the sum of Two Hundred and fifty Dollars
& the other pair of Silver Candlesticks I leave to my Niece
Lady Mary Watts." The candlestick shown here is one of the
pair inherited by Mary Watts.

Above the spreading base of this object a beautifully
proportioned baluster, subtly enriched with shells and
foliage, rises to the flaring, scalloped drip pan, tracing out a
form delicate and refined. This type of candlestick is closely
based on contemporary English examples; Myers may even
have cast this candlestick from a mold made directly from an
imported English model. Another pair of candlesticks made
by Myers bear the faint outline of London hallmarks, an
obvious indication that their mold was made directly from
an English prototype.

Refs.: Buhler and Hood, no. 658. Jeanette W. Rosenbaum (with technical
notes by Kathryn C. Buhler), *Myer Myers, Goldsmith, 1723-1795* (Philadelphia: The Jewish Publication Society of America, 1954), pp. 103-104.
Edward Wenham, "Candlesticks and Snuffers by American Silversmiths,"
Antiques 18, no. 6 (December 1930): 491-493. Bernard and Therle Hughes,
Three Centuries of English Domestic Silver (New York: Wilfred Funk, Inc.,
1952), pl. 4.

163

164 Dish Ring, New York, ca. 1760-1770
Myer Myers (1723-1795)
D. base 8⅞″ (225 mm); WT. 14 oz, 6 dwt (443 gm)
Mabel Brady Garvan Collection   1936.136

Made for the Honorable Samuel and Susannah Cornell of New York and inscribed with their monogram, this dish ring by Myer Myers is apparently the only surviving example of the form in early American silver. Designed to support a hot dish or bowl and thus protect the tabletop from damage, dish rings were made in other materials as early as 1667, when (as Kathryn Buhler notes) "wicker rings to sett Dishes on" were listed in a Boston inventory. The form was not popular in English silver, although many Irish dish rings made during the last half of the eighteenth century exist.

The pierced fretwork and interlaced scrolls of this example mark it as a major expression of the American rococo style, a style of which Myers was a master. In his long career, however, Myers kept abreast of the latest fashion, and silver by him in the earlier Queen Anne and later neoclassical styles is also extant. A prominent member of the

Jewish community in New York, Myers is the only colonial silversmith known to have made *Rimonim* (scroll ornaments, sometimes called Torah bells) for Jewish synagogues. Five pairs of these ornaments have survived and are still owned by their original congregations, including two made for the Touro Synagogue in Newport, Rhode Island, two for the Congregation Mikveh Israel in Philadelphia (Fig. 25), and a single pair for the Congregation Shearith Israel in New York.

Refs.: Buhler and Hood, no. 659. Jeanette W. Rosenbaum (with technical notes by Kathryn C. Buhler), *Myer Myers, Goldsmith, 1723-1795* (Philadelphia: The Jewish Publication Society of America, 1954), pp. 111-112. Douglas Bennett, *Irish Georgian Silver* (London: Cassell & Co., Ltd., 1972), pp. 101-103, 122-123, 130. Kurt Ticher, *Irish Silver in the Rococo Period* (Shannon, Ireland: Irish University Press, 1972), pl. 66-94.

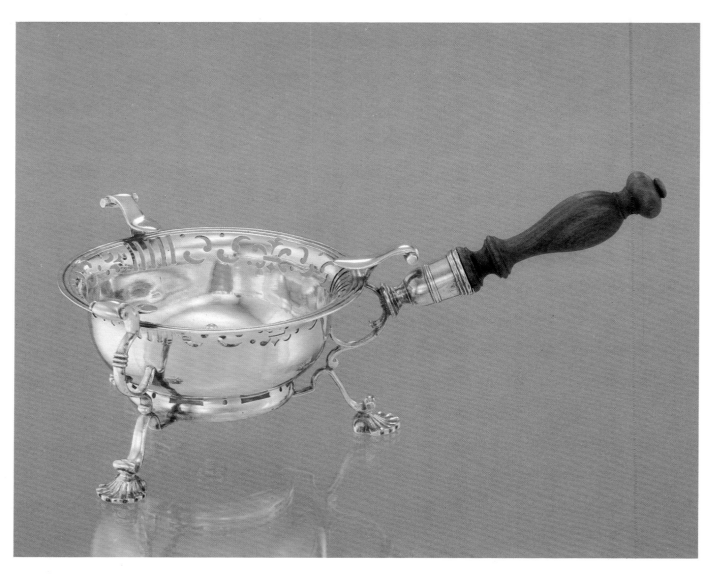

165 Chafing Dish, Stratford or Durham, Connecticut,
ca. 1745-1755
Robert Fairchild (1703-1794)
L. 11 11/16″ (297 mm); WT. 10 oz, 19 dwt (339 gm)
John Marshall Phillips Collection   1953.10.5

It is somewhat surprising that one of the most sophisticated
American rococo chafing dishes to have survived was made
in relatively rural Connecticut. Although it has counterparts
made in urban centers, particularly Boston, none surpass in
grace or elegance this example by Robert Fairchild. The
fleur-de-lis, lunette, and geometric piercings on both the
body and the inset rim (which allowed heat to dissipate from
the burning coals within) combined with the scroll supports
and the unusual shell feet give this object great expressive
quality. According to tradition, it was made for William
Samuel Johnson (1696-1772), Yale College 1714, later the
first president of Columbia University.

Refs.: Buhler and Hood, no. 340. Peter Bohan and Philip Hammerslough,
Early Connecticut Silver, 1700-1840 (Middletown, Connecticut: Wesleyan
University Press, 1970), p. 80.

166 Snuff Box, Philadelphia, ca. 1750-1770
Joseph Richardson (1711-1784)
L. 3 1/16″ (78 mm); WT. 2 OZ, 4 dwt (68 gm)
Mabel Brady Garvan Collection   1930.1281

The use of snuff in eighteenth-century America never
reached the level of popularity that the habit enjoyed in
England, where the taking of snuff was an elaborate social
ritual frequently satirized by English authors. In the 1790s,
Moreau de Saint-Méry commented that "an American of
either sex who uses snuff is a sort of phenomenon, and the
women never deform or dirty their noses by using this
powder so cherished by Europeans." The Frenchman overstated the case, however, for snuff was commonly used by
both men and women in colonial America at least as early as
1700. This mid-eighteenth-century snuff box by Joseph
Richardson is one of the most elaborate American boxes in
the rococo style. The asymmetrical chased decoration on the
top incorporates the full vocabulary of rococo ornament,
including shells, scrolls, garlands, and a basket of flowers.
As Martha Gandy Fales notes, this box and a very similar
example by Richardson now at the Philadelphia Museum of
Art embody the same spirit of the rococo that animates
Philadelphia furniture and woodwork of this period.

Refs.: Buhler and Hood, no. 837. Clare Le Corbeiller, *European and
American Snuff Boxes, 1730-1830* (New York: The Viking Press, 1966), pp.
7, 49-51. Fales, *Richardson*, pp. 132-135.

167 Cann, Boston, ca. 1760-1775
Benjamin Burt (1729-1805)
H. 5¾″ (146 mm); WT. 15 OZ, 3 dwt (470 gm)
Mabel Brady Garvan Collection   1930.951a

The influence of the rococo style on this cann, one of a pair
in the Garvan collection, is most readily apparent in the
asymmetrical Moore family arms and crest on its front and
in the double scroll handle which accentuates its sinuous,
pear-shaped body. Benjamin Burt, son of the silversmith
John Burt (1693-1746), was a well-known figure in late
eighteenth-century Boston, perhaps as much for his impressive girth (he is said to have weighed three hundred and eighty
pounds) as for the high quality of his silver.

Refs.: Buhler and Hood, no. 218. Flynt and Fales, p. 173.

168 **Sauceboat,** Boston, ca. 1760-1790
      Benjamin Burt (1729-1805)
      L. 8 5/16″ (211 mm); WT. 13 oz, 5 dwt (411 gm)
      Mabel Brady Garvan Collection   1930.1222

Also by Benjamin Burt is this commodious sauceboat, probably made for Nathan and Rebecca Pierce of Boston. Its
beaded edge, shell feet and knees, and gracefully curved
handle and flaring spout are characteristic of the restrained
New England rococo style, yet the engraving surrounding
the Pierces' initials is in a distinctly neoclassical style. Such a
combination of motifs from two overlapping stylistic periods is not unusual in American silver. Burt, like other Boston silversmiths, continued to be influenced by the rococo
style during and after the Revolution. A closely related
example by Burt, lacking only the beaded edge to be nearly
identical, is at the Museum of Fine Arts, Boston, and has
been assigned a date of ca. 1790.

Refs.: Buhler and Hood, no. 219. Kathryn C. Buhler, *American Silver,
1655-1825, in the Museum of Fine Arts, Boston,* 2 vols. (Greenwich,
Connecticut: New York Graphic Society, 1972), I, 350.

169 Sugar Bowl, New York, ca. 1760-1770
John Burt Lyng (Freeman 1761)
H. 4⅞″ (124 mm); WT. 8 OZ, 12 dwt (266 gm)
Mabel Brady Garvan Collection   1934.302

This sugar bowl by John Burt Lyng shares the inverted pear shape and high center of gravity which also mark teapots and coffee pots in the rococo style. The chased floral bands on both the body and the cover are characteristic of New York silver in the rococo period, and are reminiscent of the style of chasing found on earlier New York silver (**143**). The bowl is topped by a finial in the form of a pinecone or perhaps a pineapple; the pineapple was a symbol of hospitality in the eighteenth century.

Ref.: Buhler and Hood, no. 727.

170 Teapot, Baltimore, Maryland, ca. 1760-1770
Gabriel Lewyn (w. ca. 1768-1780)
H. 6″ (152 mm); WT. 18 oz, 7 dwt (569 gm)
John Marshall Phillips Collection   1955.10.4

171 Coffee Pot, Philadelphia, ca. 1765-1775
Thomas Shields (w. ca. 1765-1794)
H. 12 15/16″ (329 mm); WT. 39 oz, 1 dwt (1211 gm)
Mabel Brady Garvan Collection   1932.59

One of the most fully developed statements of the rococo aesthetic in America is made by this teapot by Gabriel Lewyn of Baltimore. Unlike some American rococo pieces, in which conservative and restrained ornament is tightly controlled within boundaries and applied fortuitously to the object, this teapot has fluid repoussé which is woven into the very fabric of the form. The asymmetrical sprigs of flowers and foliage sweep across the surface of the teapot, organically integrated with the bulging instability of the inverted pear-shaped form beneath. The sophistication and refinement of this piece are all the more remarkable when it is noted that it was made in Baltimore, a city which in this period was but an artistic province of Philadelphia.

Refs.: Buhler and Hood, no. 959. Montgomery and Kane, pp. 193-194. J. Hall Pleasants and Howard Sill, *Maryland Silversmiths, 1715-1830* (Baltimore: Lord Baltimore Press, 1930), pp. 156-157.

Made in his shop at the Sign of the Golden Cup and Crown, Thomas Shields's coffee pot is a superb example of the "double-bellied" form popular during the rococo period. In addition to the swirling shells and other decoration on its cast spout, this pot has gadrooning on its foot and cover, a form of ornamentation popular during the baroque period and reintroduced in the 1760s. Shields scratched the original price, "£27-7-6," and the original weight, "38 oz 5 dwt," on the bottom of the pot. The present weight of 39 oz, 1 dwt, includes the wooden handle, which Shields omitted from his total.

Ref.: Buhler and Hood, no. 872.

172 **Teapot,** Boston, ca. 1790-1795
Paul Revere, II (1735-1818)
H. 6″ (152 mm); WT. 19 oz, 12 dwt (608 gm)
Mabel Brady Garvan Collection   1930.959

In sharp contrast to the elaborately ornamented rococo style, the neoclassical style marks a return to elegant simplicity, with an emphasis on geometrical forms and ornament inspired by the art and architecture of antiquity. The earliest known piece of American neoclassical silver was made in 1774, and the style remained fashionable into the second decade of the nineteenth century. Technological innovation is also evident in this period in American silver, as the first steps toward the transformation from craft to industry took place.

In common with other craftsmen, silversmiths eagerly adopted labor-saving methods and materials as quickly as they became available. When making this fluted neoclassical teapot, one of numerous examples known, Revere made use of rolled sheet silver, which had begun to be widely available at this period. He simply shaped the sheet silver to the desired form and soldered it together to the left of the handle. This method of manufacture involved considerably less time and effort than raising the pot from an ingot with countless hammer blows, yet produced a form perfectly suited to the neoclassical style. The addition of a pine-cone finial and bright-cut drapery swags and tassels completed one of Revere's most successful designs.

Refs.: Buhler and Hood, no. 253. Montgomery and Kane, p. 211.

173 Footed Bowl, Alexandria, Virginia, 1790-1810
James Adam (1755-1798) or John Adam
(ca. 1774-1848)
D. lip 8¾″ (222 mm); WT. 31 oz, 11 dwt (978 gm)
Mabel Brady Garvan Collection   1934.351

The shape of this otherwise plain footed bowl derives great
expressive quality from its gently contoured, fluted and
chamfered corners. It has been published as a punch bowl,
but it is more likely that it is a slop bowl from a tea set; an
entire set in this style by James Musgrave of Philadelphia is
in the Winterthur Museum. Marked "J·Adam," the bowl

may have been made by either James Adam or his son John;
it is usually attributed to the latter. Father and son were the
first two in a line of five successive generations of Adam
silversmiths or allied artisans in Alexandria.

Refs.: Buhler and Hood, no. 968. George B. Cutten, *The Silversmiths of Virginia* (Richmond, Virginia: The Dietz Press, Inc., 1952), pp. 3-5. Worth Bailey and William Robert Adam, "Silversmiths of Alexandria," *Antiques* 47, no. 2 (February 1945): 93-95. Anne Stuntz, "The Adam Family of Alexandria, Virginia Silversmiths," *Journal of Early Southern Decorative Arts* (forthcoming).

174 Bread Basket, Baltimore, Maryland, ca. 1810-1815
George Aiken and E. Brown (w. ca. 1807-1816)
L. 14⅞″ (378 mm); WT. 36 oz, 15 dwt (1139 gm)
Mabel Brady Garvan Collection   1930.1402

While in Philadelphia in the 1790s, Moreau de Saint-Méry observed that "before dinner and all during dinner, as is the English custom, all the silver one owns is displayed on the sideboard in the dining room." One specialized object which frequently appeared on sideboards during the Federal period was the bread basket, sometimes called a cake basket. George Aiken (1765-1832), a Baltimore silversmith, made this example in partnership with one E. Brown, possibly John Eden Brown or more likely Edward Brown, both listed as silversmiths in Baltimore directories. Its boat-shaped body has the clean lines and smooth surfaces typical of the neoclassical style. Bright-cutting (a technique in which the silver is notched or gouged to create facets) is also characteristic of neoclassical silver and is used here to form a decorative border inside the lip.

Refs.: Buhler and Hood, no. 966. Jennifer F. Goldsborough, *Eighteenth- and Nineteenth-Century Maryland Silver in the Collection of the Baltimore Museum of Art* (Baltimore: The Baltimore Museum of Art, 1975), pp. 59-66. J. Hall Pleasants and Howard Sill, *Maryland Silversmiths, 1715-1830* (Baltimore: Lord Baltimore Press, 1930), pp. 84-86.

175 **Ladle,** Philadelphia or New York, ca. 1780-1800
Daniel Van Voorhis (1751-1824)
L. 15⅝″ (397 mm); WT. 5 oz, 16 dwt (180 gm)
Mabel Brady Garvan Collection   1946.257

It is somewhat difficult to determine exactly where this magnificent ladle by Daniel Van Voorhis was made. During the last two decades of the eighteenth century, when the ladle was probably crafted, the peripatetic Van Voorhis was working in at least three, or possibly four, locations.

Van Voorhis seems to have served his apprenticeship in New York, but by 1780 he had moved to Philadelphia and established his business. In 1782 he moved to Princeton, New Jersey, announcing in the *New-Jersey Gazette* of 4 December 1782 that he had opened his shop and was ready to carry on his trade "at a lower price than it can be done in

Philadelphia." His advertisement also notes that he made and sold, among many other things, silver "soupe ladles" and "punch ladles." By the summer of 1784, Van Voorhis had gone on to Brunswick, New Jersey, a temporary stopover on his way to New York City. He is known to have worked in New York from 1785 until his retirement in the early nineteenth century.

A mixture of stylistic features are evident in this example of his work. The chased floral designs in the deep, fluted bowl of the ladle are reminiscent of the late rococo style, but the bright-cutting on its handle relates more closely to the neoclassical style.

Refs.: Buhler and Hood, no. 712. Carl M. Williams, *Silversmiths of New Jersey, 1700-1825* (Philadelphia: George S. MacManus Company, 1949), pp. 117-122. Helen Burr Smith, "Van Voorhis, Peregrinating Silversmith," *The New York Sun,* 14 December 1940.

176 Tea Set, Philadelphia, ca. 1785-1795
   Abraham Dubois (w. ca. 1777-1807)
   H. teapot 11⅜″ (289 mm); WT. teapot 26 oz, 3 dwt
   (810 gm)
   Mabel Brady Garvan Collection   1930.1002a-c

This neoclassical tea set consists of a matching teapot,
creampot, and sugar bowl, all with classically inspired urn-
shaped bodies placed diagonally on square bases and
capped with urn-shaped finials which repeat the form of the
body. Lines of beading define the forms and accent the
otherwise plain surfaces. In addition, the sugar bowl features a pierced scalloped band around its top, a characteristic of silver from the Philadelphia area (**32**).

   In the neoclassical period, matching tea services such as
this became fashionable; some sets contained as many as
nineteen pieces. According to tradition, Aaron Burr (1756-
1836) was the original owner of this elegantly restrained set.

Refs.: Buhler and Hood, no. 888. Montgomery and Kane, pp. 208-210.

Figure 39
Bone ash porcelain inkstand, Eng-
land, possibly Worcester, ca. 1810.
Indianapolis Museum of Art, gift of
Richard M. Pelham-Keller.

177 Inkstand, Philadelphia, ca. 1815-1825
Harvey Lewis (w. ca. 1811-1825)
H. 3⅝″ (92 mm); WT. 15 oz, 5 dwt (473 gm)
Mabel Brady Garvan Collection   1932.80

During the first decades of the nineteenth century the neo-classical style thickened into Empire and silver forms became weightier, both visually and in the actual gauge of the silver used. Profuse ornament inspired by ancient civilizations abounded. This inkstand, small in size yet monumental in character, is a superb example of the new style. The close diplomatic relations between America and France at this time are reflected in the borrowing of French motifs by American craftsmen, motifs strongly influenced themselves by Napoleon's recent campaign in Egypt. Such details as the crisply stamped applied bands of foliage and the winged sphinxes on this inkstand are closely related to the designs of Percier and Fontaine, who accompanied Napoleon on his Egyptian campaign, and to the interpretation of their designs by French silversmiths. Nonetheless, American aesthetic sympathies remained more akin to those of England,

politics notwithstanding, and French design often came to America via England. In its adaptation of a banded hemispherical form supported by monopodous winged sphinxes on a tri-cornered plinth, the Lewis inkstand is closer to a silver-gilt tea urn by the London silversmiths Scott and Smith than it is to anything purely French. Catherine Lippert of the Indianapolis Museum of Art has discovered that an English porcelain inkstand of about 1810 (Fig. 39) is even closer in form to the Lewis inkstand. Both the Lewis inkstand and its English counterpart emphasize the feathered headdresses of the female figures, a feature suitably used in both to hold quills. Thus the Egyptian sphinx is transformed into an American princess, long the allegorical symbol of the rich new continent. In the metamorphosis an exotic image and a foreign style gain a familiar native reference.

Refs.: Buhler and Hood, no. 926. C. Percier and P. F. L. Fontaine, *Recueil de Décorations intérieures* (Paris: P. Didot L'Aine, 1812), pl. 18, no. 9. Faith Dennis, *Three Centuries of French Domestic Silver* (New York: The Metropolitan Museum of Art, 1960), pp. 65-77. John F. Hayward, "Rundell, Bridge and Rundell, *Aurifices Regis*," *Antiques* 99, no. 6 (June 1971): 860-865. Hugh Honour, *The New Golden Land* (New York: Pantheon Books, 1975), pp. 84-117.

178 Teapot, New York, ca. 1820-1828
William B. Heyer (1776-1828)
H. 10½" (267 mm); WT. 25 oz, 14 dwt (796 gm)
Gift of Mrs. William Crozier and William Williams
1947.310a

The development of the neoclassical style from its eighteenth-century form to its nineteenth-century version was
complete by the time this teapot was made. The elegant
classical form of the Dubois tea set (**176**) has swollen here
into the broad, rounded, lobed shape so popular in the early
nineteenth century, and the addition of heavy, eclectic ornament further marks the nineteenth-century character of this
piece. In yet another way the teapot, part of a set made for
Lucretia Woodbridge Perkins Williams, is a bridge between
the neoclassicism of the eighteenth century and the romanti-
cism of the nineteenth: the applied decorative band depicting a rustic landscape peopled with simple country folk is in
the classical pastoral spirit of Virgil's *Eclogues* and *Geor-
gics,* but has been romanticized to reflect the contemporary
yearning for a simple way of life already disappearing before
the spread of industrialism. William Cullen Bryant expressed the growing romantic desire to return to nature in
"Green River" (1818):

Yet fair as thou art, thou shun'st to glide
Beautiful stream! by the village side;
But windest away from haunts of men,
To quiet valley and shaded glen;
And forest, and meadow, and slope of hill,
Around these, are lonely, lovely, and still.

Ironically, this figural band, like the bands of foliage decoration on the piece, was stamped by machine, and is thus a product of the very industrialism it seems to shun.

Ref.: Buhler and Hood, no. 751.

179 Pair of Salts, Philadelphia, ca. 1825-1846
Robert and William Wilson (w. ca. 1825-1846)
D. bowl 2 9/16″ (65 mm); WT. 1 oz, 16 dwt (56 gm)
Mabel Brady Garvan Collection   1974.13

Nineteenth-century design was characterized by a rich medley of successive yet overlapping styles borrowed from the past, and many silversmiths worked in more than one revival style. William Wilson entered into partnership with his brother Richard at the latter's shop on the corner of Fifth and Cherry streets in Philadelphia in 1825. No doubt the

earliest productions of the two brothers were in the neoclassical style, and indeed they continued to produce silver in that style well into the nineteenth century. This rich and elaborate pair of salts, however, is in the more fashionable rococo revival style of the mid-century. In the form of scallop shells lifted in sprightly fashion above ornate bases, these salt cellars recall the animated use of irregular natural forms in the French rococo designs of a previous century, when similar shells were used for objects as diverse as salt cellars, plates, and drip pans for candlesticks.

Salt cellars were an indispensable part of the Victorian dining table. *The American Chesterfield* (1852), an influential book of manners, suggests, "At the corners of the table [place] table spoons, a salt cellar, and a small spoon for the salt. . . . If the table is large, the furniture of the corners should be likewise placed at short and convenient intervals." It goes on to warn, "Let no lady who wishes to earn a large share of credit, neglect, before dinner, to examine into the state of that most necessary appendage to a dinner table [i.e., the condiments, and to] . . . remember the salt spoons."

Refs.: *Philadelphia: Three Centuries of American Art* (Philadelphia: Philadelphia Museum of Art, 1976), pp. 336-337. *French Master Goldsmiths and Silversmiths* (New York: French and European Publications, Inc., 1966), pp. 127, 184, 208. *The American Chesterfield* (Philadelphia: Lippencott, Grambo and Co., 1852), pp. 240-241.

180 **Fork,** New York, 1855
William Gale and Son (w. ca. 1850-1865)
L. 7¾″ (197 mm); WT. 1 oz, 16 dwt (56 gm)
Gift of Stephen R. Parks, B.A. 1961   1973.44

The Gothic revival made its first major appearance as an
adjunct to the rococo style in eighteenth-century England.
By the nineteenth century the medieval style had gained
momentum in England due to the influence of its great
proponent, A.W.N. Pugin (1812-1852), who published designs for Gothic-style furniture and silver (including spoons)
at the same time that he was building his famous Gothic-
revival churches. In America the new style was introduced to
the public by the enthusiastic propaganda of A. J. Downing
(1815-1852), and was welcomed as creating a sense of roots
and a romantic association with a fictitious past in the rough
new land. By the 1840s the style had spread to all areas of
design, and Gothic motifs were adapted wholesale for manufactured items in both England and America. Pugin himself
was moved to comment in 1841: "if they only introduce a
quatrefoil or an acute arch, be the outline and style of the
article ever so modern and debased, it is at once denomi-
nated and sold as Gothic. . . . Like everything else, silverwork has sunk into a mere trade, and art is rigidly excluded
from its arrangements."

An example of Gothic decoration applied to a modern
form is this fork, replete with pointed arches, quatrefoil, and
crockets, made by William Gale and Son. The design was
patented in 1847 and made through the mid-1850s; this fork
is dated 1855.

Refs.: Katherine S. Howe and David B. Warren, *The Gothic Revival Style in
America, 1830-1870* (Houston: Museum of Fine Arts, 1976), pp. 70-71. A.
Welby N. Pugin, *The True Principles of Pointed or Christian Architecture*
(London: John Weale, 1841), pp. 29, 38. _____, *Designs for Gold and
Silversmiths* (London: Ackermann and Co., 1836), pl. 2. Robert Alan
Green, "William Gale and Son, New York," *Silver* 11, no. 2 (March-April
1978): 6-11.

181 **Coffee Pot,** New York, 1862
    William Gale and Son (w. ca. 1850-1865)
    H. 10⅝″ (271 mm); WT. 26 oz, 12 dwt (824 gm)
    Gift of Loomis Havemeyer to the Yale University
    President's House   1967.55.3

Some seventy years after Paul Revere and others introduced
the fluted, bright-cut neoclassical teapot (172) to America,
William Gale and Son of New York produced this coffee pot
in a style which is reminiscent of the earlier objects. The
Gales, however, were selective in their reinterpretation of
the earlier style, and their version differs considerably from
its neoclassical prototypes. For example, they retained the

basic fluted shape of the body, while increasing the height of
the object and using bright-cutting in a much more liberal
fashion, covering nearly every available surface with decoration. This coffee pot is part of a five-piece tea and coffee
service made in 1862 and given to Yale in 1967 for use in the
president's house. Although the "neoclassical revival" style
is characteristic of Gale and Son's work, they also made
silver in the rococo, Renaissance, and Gothic revival (180)
styles.

Refs.: Robert Alan Green, "William Gale and Son, New York," *Silver* 11,
no. 2 (March-April 1978): 6-11. Graham Hood, *American Silver: A History
of Style, 1650-1900* (New York: Praeger Publishers, 1971), pp. 239-241.

182 Two Pitchers, New York, ca. 1860-1870
Tiffany & Company
H. water pitcher 11 11/16″ (297 mm); WT. water pitcher
38 oz, 1 dwt (1180 gm)
Gift of George W. Pierson, B.A. 1926, in memory of
Charles F. Montgomery   1978.2.4, 1978.2.8

Although the strength of the neoclassical style began to
wane in the 1830s, the classical past continued to exert an
influence on design throughout the nineteenth century.
These two pitchers, the covered one for hot milk, the other
for water, are in the pattern called "Etruscan." Tiffany's
choice of this name reflects the freedom with which the
Victorians applied titles to their designs, for the pitchers are
primarily derived from Greek rather than Etruscan sources.
The shape of the pitchers is related to that of nineteenth-
century English pitchers based on the Greek *oenochoe* form;
the engraved decoration echoes the Parthenon friezes, decoration also found on English examples. The tentative nature
of this engraving, as opposed to the more careful rendering
on English examples, may be explained by the fact that

English designers could consult the Parthenon friezes directly in the British Museum, while the American engraver
knew them only at second hand, perhaps through engraving
on English silver or more probably through engravings published in books. Other classical motifs on the pitchers include acanthus and anthemion designs, Greek key borders,
the woman's head on the handles, and the helmet on the lid
of the milk pitcher, another feature found in English examples. Charles Carpenter's research in Tiffany's records re-
vealed that this pattern was first produced in 1858 and
continued to be made, under the direction of Edward C.
Moore, as late as 1873. Part of a set which also includes a
teapot, coffee pot, sugar, creamer, and slop bowl, these
pitchers were originally owned by William Slocum Groes-
beck, an Ohio lawyer who served as defense counsel to
President Andrew Johnson in his impeachment trial of 1868.

Ref.: Patricia Wardle, *Victorian Silver and Silver-Plate* (New York: Thomas
Nelson and Sons, 1963), pp. 105, 155-156.

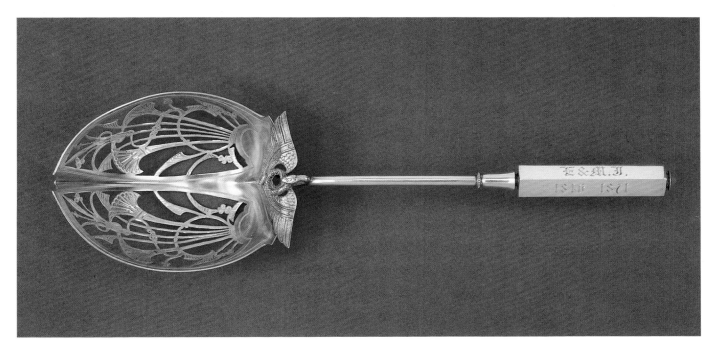

183 Serving Spoon, Providence, Rhode Island, ca. 1871
Gorham Manufacturing Company
L. 11" (279 mm); WT. 3 oz, 2 dwt (96 gm)
Carl R. Kossack Fund   1978.43

By the late 1860s Egyptian motifs, popular during the early
years of the century (**177**), again found their way into the
decorative arts.

1869 is an important date in the history of the Egyptian
taste in America, for it was in November of that year that the
governments of France and Egypt joined in the formal opening of the Suez Canal. Egypt became the playground of
dignitaries and people of fashion from all over the world
who assembled for the gala celebration, and the newspapers
and magazines covered their escapades with great enthusiasm. Apparently it was because of this fascination with
events in Egypt that the Gorham Company introduced a
new flatware pattern named "Isis" in the same year. As is the
case with many objects made in this style, the ornament has
been popularized and is not archeologically correct. Gorham's designers chose lotus blossoms and the winged snake
as motifs which would give the pattern a properly exotic
flavor. The elaborately pierced and bright-cut gilt bowl of
this large serving spoon makes it a particularly stunning
example of silver in the Egyptian taste.

Refs.: Turner, pp. 72, 97. *Frank Leslie's Illustrated Newspaper* 29, nos.
736-748 (6 November 1869-29 January 1870).

184 Tureen, Providence, Rhode Island, 1871
Gorham Manufacturing Company
w. 14½″ (369 mm); wt. 85 oz, 8 dwt (2647 gm)
Mr. and Mrs. Thomas M. Evans, b.a. 1931, Fund
1973.78

The fluid, sweeping expanses of smooth silver surfaces act as
a foil to the finely cast stag and satanic heads on this soup
tureen in the Renaissance revival style. The castings were
made by the army of highly skilled European craftsmen
recruited by Gorham during the presidency of Edward Holbrook (1865-1919). The use of animal heads with ring handles, ultimately derived from classical prototypes, was revived during the Renaissance, again in the eighteenth century by such designers as Robert Adam, and yet again during
the Renaissance revival of the middle of the nineteenth
century. The bands of strapwork which decorate this tureen
are also characteristic of the Renaissance revival style.
Gorham made salad bowls, vegetable dishes, oyster tureens,
and sauce boats to match this tureen, and they also produced objects in which castings identical to those on this

piece were used with goat heads, standing cows, and other
decoration.

Refs.: *Nineteenth-Century America,* no. 172. McClinton, p. 55.

185 Set of Fruit Knives, Providence, Rhode Island, ca. 1880
Gorham Manufacturing Company
w. box 14½″ (368 mm); l. knife 7¾″ (197 mm)
Gift of Mrs. Samuel Schwartz 1972.134.4a-l

Commodore Matthew C. Perry's intimidating show of naval
strength in the Bay of Uraga in 1854 paved the way for the
opening of trade between Japan and the United States; almost immediately thereafter the Western world began to
take notice of Japanese art. Such books as Adalbert de
Beaumont and Eugene V. Callinot's *Recueil de Dessins pour
l'Art et l'Industrie* (1859) made Japanese design readily
available to Western craftsmen, and objects imported directly from Japan were much praised: "One of the chief
differences now between Chinese and Japanese articles is

that the homogeneity of the Japanese has not yet been injured by European demands; and in buying a Japanese article we are tolerably sure of getting something according to the aboriginal idea, and not according to the idea of what the European purchaser may require." If the Japanese were not producing objects specifically altered for the Western market, Westerners were certainly turning out their own designs in the Japanese taste. In the United States, the taste for things Japanese was given a boost by the great success of the Japanese exhibit at the Centennial Exhibition in Philadelphia, where Japanese art was praised as being "so subtile, free, and varied in decorative expression, so full of delicious coquetries and surprises, that it never becomes stale or monotonous."

These fruit knives, whose bright-cut silver blades conform to the nineteenth-century belief that steel should not touch fruit, are based on *hari kari* knives brought back from the Orient by Edward Holbrook, president of the Gorham Company. Their asymmetrical composition of insects, animals, plants, and figures combines Japanese taste with the observation of nature so important to nineteenth-century theorists. In a departure from the complicated inlay process used by the Japanese, however, the handles of these knives are cast in silver, then parcel-plated with copper and gold of varying purity to create different colors.

Refs.: Harriet Spofford, *Art Decoration Applied to Furniture* (New York: Harper and Brothers, 1878), p. 162. George T. Ferris, *Gems of the Centennial Exhibition* (New York: Appleton and Company, 1877), p. 78. *Japonisme* (Kent, Ohio: Kent State University Press, 1975).

186 Coffee Pot, North Attleboro, Massachusetts, or
Newark, New Jersey, 1875-1890
Whiting Manufacturing Company
H. 9¼" (235 mm); WT. 15 oz, 18 dwt (493 gm)
Gift of Alexander O. Vietor, B.A. 1936   1974.22.3

By the 1880s designers of silver had revived nearly every
earlier period of Western art and had also been heavily
influenced by the Japanese style. The continuing desire for
the exotic caused designers to turn toward the Near East.
The novel "Moorish" shape of this coffee pot parallels the
popularity of the "Turkish corner" in interior decoration,
but its all-over floral repoussé is a familiar design element
which had been popular since the 1820s. Such Victorian
repoussé differs significantly from the eighteenth-century
rococo form from which it was derived. The best eighteenth-century rococo repoussé is organic, seeming actually
to grow around the form it decorates (170). By contrast,
Victorian rococo repoussé is conceived as a three-dimensional decoration on a flat surface, and seems to be
wrapped around the object it decorates like a skin of
embossed printed paper.

Ref.: Dorothy T. Rainwater, *American Silver Manufacturers* (Hanover,
Pennsylvania: Everybodys Press, 1966), p. 199.

187 Bowl, Newark, New Jersey, 1890-1900
Whiting Manufacturing Company; retailed by
Theodore B. Starr, New York
D. lip 7 15/16" (202 mm); WT. 16 oz, 4 dwt (502 gm)
Gift of Mrs. Samuel Schwartz   1972.134.2

For several decades before this bowl was made, Americans
had been flocking to summer resorts by the sea in search of
the simpler life. One side effect of this fascination with the
ocean and with nature in general was a renewed impulse to
apply natural motifs to the more formal accoutrements of
city life. The use of naturalistic shells to ornament silver
objects was not a new idea, but a practice which dated back
to the rococo period and which had already been revived in
nineteenth-century America (179). But with the awakening

of American self-consciousness and pride, the shells took on a new significance. Pride in native American flora and fauna led to the creation in 1879 of a set of china for the Rutherford B. Hayes White House using naturalistic renderings of native species, including shellfish. Patented and put on the public market in 1880, the china was a popular success, inspiring imitation and further development of the theme.

This gilt-lined silver bowl, which bears the marks of both its maker (Whiting Manufacturing Company) and retailer (Theodore B. Starr), can be related to this development.

The bowl, whose lip and body are shaped to give an impression of a rude and rocky coast, is encircled by a band of finely chased shells of various types—oyster, scallop, and mussel. The opposition thus created between the rustic nature of the decorative motif and the richness of the material is both disarming and delightful.

Refs.: Margaret Brown Klapthor, *Official White House China* (Washington, D.C.: Smithsonian Institution, 1975), pp. 97-121. *Nineteenth-Century America*, no. 241.

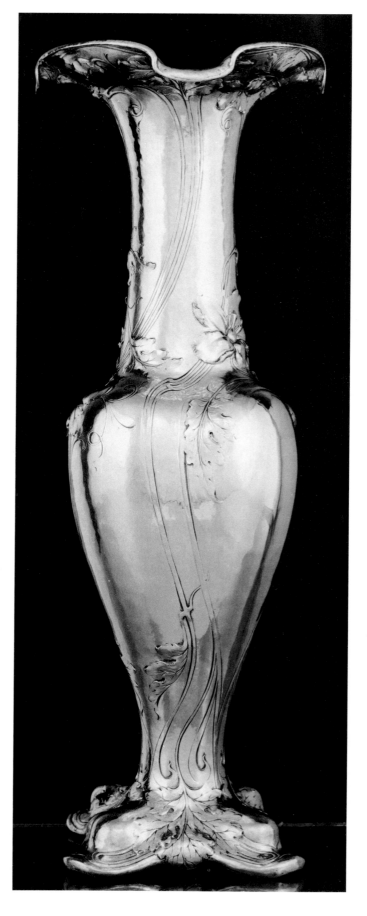

188 **Vase,** Providence, Rhode Island, ca. 1900
Designed by William C. Codman (1839-1921)
Gorham Manufacturing Company
H. 19⅜″ (492 mm); WT. scratched on bottom 50 oz
(1550 gm)
Gift of Dr. Louis J. Camuti   1974.102.1

William Christmas Codman, chief designer of the Gorham
Manufacturing Company from 1891 to 1914, was perhaps
the most important designer to work in the art nouveau style
in America. Born and trained in England, he was already an
accomplished craftsman when he was enticed to come to this
country by Gorham's president, Edward Holbrook.

   This vase is signed by Codman himself and may well be
the work of his own hammer. Monumental in scale, it is
designed to resemble the languid lines of a huge flower;
vines, leaves, and blossoms culminate in a graceful floral
rim. Certainly in every particular this vase follows the aims
of its designer and his colleagues as expressed in a company
publication of 1912: "The form is the important thing, and
the decoration, far from being conventional, partakes almost wholly of naturalistic forms: waves of the sea, natural
flowers, mermaids, fishes, cloud effects,–almost anything
can be used provided it is treated in a naturalistic manner."
Nature, rather than styles of past eras, now became the
primary inspiration for works of art in silver, and there is no

doubt that these objects were meant to be works of art. As one contemporary admirer noted: "The method frankly meets the material and conforms itself to it, as all art must. . . . He [Codman] never for a moment loses sight of the fact that he is designing for metal, and though he takes his motives from many natural forms, he expresses them only in metallic terms." There is no question that this piece and the others produced with the Martelé trademark express in their design the marvelous fluidity of silver when worked under the hammer. Made of 950 fine silver, Martelé pieces were in fact "softer" than objects made of sterling silver, which is 925 fine.

All Martelé pieces were made by special order, and new designs were developed for each commission to insure that no two pieces would be exactly alike. The silversmith left hammer marks evident on the surface to give the metal "a soft misty texture" and to emphasize the handcraftsmanship which went into each object.

Refs.: John S. Holbrook, *Silver for the Dining Room, Selected Periods* (Cambridge: Printed for the Gorham Company by the University Press, 1912), pp. 112-119. Charlotte Moffit, "New Designs in Silver," *The House Beautiful* 7, no. 1 (December 1899): 55-58. McClinton, pp. 96-121.

189 **Cigar Case,** Newark, New Jersey, 1901-1910
     Unger Brothers
     L. 5″ (127 mm); WT. 2 oz, 1 dwt (64 gm)
     American Arts Purchase Fund   1973.25.5

The Newark, New Jersey, firm of Unger Brothers produced thousands of objects in the art nouveau style during the first decade of the twentieth century. Heavily influenced by French work, much of their art nouveau silver featured swirling, twisting floral decoration and images of women with long, flowing hair in various states of undress. This cigar case depicts a woman encircled by the smoke from her cigarette. Her image also appears on slightly smaller cigarette cases, ash trays, match-holders, flasks, tape measures, and many other small objects and novelties illustrated in the Unger Brothers 1904 catalogue.

Refs.: Robert Koch, "Unger Brothers Art Nouveau Silver," *The Antiques Journal* 28, no. 5 (May 1973): 16-18. Dorothy T. Rainwater, ed., *Sterling Silver Holloware* (Princeton, New Jersey: The Pyne Press, 1973).

190 Loving Cup, Providence, Rhode Island, ca. 1906
Gorham Manufacturing Company
H. 16⅜″ (416 mm); WT. 109 oz, 7 dwt (3390 gm)
Department of Athletics, Yale University

The opulence characteristic of the turn of the century is
readily evident in this large, gilt-lined loving cup, made by
Gorham to serve as the Inter-Collegiate Golf Association
Team Championship Trophy. Naturalistic repoussé ornament, including oak leaves, acorns, and thistles, frames the
blank spaces left open for engraving. The Scottish thistles,
alluding to the land where golf was invented, probably represent an attempt to use meaningful decoration, as do the
fluid lines of ivy which appropriately twist and move around
the college seals on the foot. Harvard, Pennsylvania, Cornell, Columbia, Princeton, and Yale, the members of the
Association, are represented. This trophy was awarded to
Yale in 1908 after it had been won by members of its team
for three successive years.

191 Coffee Service, New York, ca. 1917
Tiffany & Company
H. coffee pot 5 11/16″ (144 mm); WT. total 59 oz, 15 dwt
(1852 gm)
Gift of Dorothy Scudder Black in memory of
Henry H. Scudder, B.A. 1917   1977.34a-d

By the first decade of the twentieth century the Arts and
Crafts movement, which had been conceived and born in
England, was firmly established in America. This diminutive
coffee set exemplifies the Arts and Crafts aesthetic, yet at the
same time incorporates elements of the fading art nouveau
style in the lines of the strapwork handles. The simple,
low-bellied forms and the surfaces which retain evidence of
hand-raising are characteristic of the movement and are
related to features of silver work being done at this time in
Chicago (193). The graceful lines of the pot's spout, the
gentle swelling of the hexagonal bodies of the various pieces,
and the contrast between these heavy bodies and their tiny
pierced galleries combine to create a most pleasing effect.
Although this pattern was entered in the Tiffany pattern
books as early as 1907, this set was probably not made until
1917, the year it was given as a wedding gift to Dorothy
Weeks Scudder, whose monogram appears on it.

Refs.: Sharon S. Darling, *Chicago Metalsmiths* (Chicago: Chicago Historical Society, 1977), nos. 48, 49. C. R. Ashbee, *Modern English Silverwork*
(London: Essex House Press for B. T. Batsford, 1909).

192 Punch Bowl, New York, ca. 1925
Tiffany & Company
D. lip 10⅜″ (264 mm); WT. 54 oz (1674 gm)
Gift of Philip Skinner Platt, B.A. 1912   1972.110.1

During the early twentieth century one of Yale's secret societies, Scroll and Key, commissioned Tiffany's to design a punch bowl which would be presented to each member at the time of his marriage. This particular bowl was given to Philip Skinner Platt and Annetta Joanna Nicoll in 1925 and is inscribed with the names of Platt's fellow society members. The form is classic in its simplicity, but reflects the concern for functionalism and purity of line which has characterized modern American design. The applied ornament of the base is especially notable for its strong geometric quality and interlacing strapwork.

193 Coffee Pot, Sugar Bowl, and Creamer, Chicago, ca. 1925-1935
Chicago Silver Company; retailed by Lewy Brothers, New York (?)
H. coffee pot 10⅛″ (257 mm); WT. coffee pot 24 oz, 2 dwt (747 gm)
Bradford F. Swan, B.A. 1929, and American Arts Purchase Funds   1978.82

From about 1890 to the end of the First World War, Chicago was a center of silversmithing in the Arts and Crafts style. The tradition of handcrafted silver begun during this period was carried further into this century by the Kalo Shop and a number of other firms, including the Chicago Silver Company, which was founded in 1923 by the Swedish-born and trained Knut L. Gustafson (1885-1976).

These three pieces are part of a set which also includes a teapot, tea kettle on stand, and tray. Their top-heavy, lobate bodies are made of sheet silver, seamed to the left of the handles and self-consciously hammered. The form is probably derived from Kalo Shop silver of the same period. Each piece in the set bears the Chicago Silver Company trademark, a pattern number, and the words "HAND WROUGHT"; the name of Lewy Bros. Co., probably a New York retailer, is also stamped on each object.

Refs.: Sharon S. Darling, *Chicago Metalsmiths* (Chicago: Chicago Historical Society, 1977), pp. 88-89. _____, "Chicago Metalsmiths," *American Art Review* 4, no. 4 (January 1978): 65.

194 Compote, Meriden, Connecticut, ca. 1953-1960
Designed by Alphonse La Paglia (d. 1953), ca. 1952
International Silver Company
D. lip 10″ (254 mm); WT. 30 oz, 13 dwt (951 gm)
Gift of Dr. Louis J. Camuti   1974.120.8

In 1952 the International Silver Company opened a separate
craft shop under the name of Sterling Craft Associates, in
which Alphonse La Paglia, who had studied silver design
under Georg Jensen in Denmark, played an active part.
Unfortunately, La Paglia's death the following year ended
his fledgling venture, but International Silver did acquire his
designs and adapted them for machine production. This
compote, based on La Paglia's design and so marked on the
base, was probably put into production by International
Silver about 1953. The play of the smooth, shallow flare of
the compote's bowl against the stem (composed of spherical
forms above a band of open stylized floral ornament) is
reminiscent of Jensen's work of the 1910s and also repre-

sents the enduring appeal of the streamlined and geometric
aesthetic of the art deco style.

Ref.: Walter Schwartz, *Georg Jensen: En kunstler—hans tid og slaegt*
(Copenhagen, 1958), pp. 189, 191, 199.

195 Coffee Pot, Rochester, New York, ca. 1960
(designed ca. 1956)
Hans Christensen (b. 1924)
H. 9⅝″ (244 mm); WT. 22 oz, 5 dwt (690 gm)
American Arts Purchase Fund   1978.90

A native of Denmark, Hans Christensen served his appren-
ticeship in the firm of Georg Jensen and later studied at the
School for Danish Craftsmen and the Art Academy of
Goldsmiths in Copenhagen. In 1954 Christensen came to
the United States to teach at The School for American
Craftsmen at the Rochester Institute of Technology, where

he is currently the Charlotte F. Mowris Professor of Contemporary Crafts. The clean, smooth, free-flowing lines of his work show an indebtedness both to the innovative forms produced by the Jensen firm and to Danish design of the early 1950s. The subtle curves of his objects and the care taken to achieve the perfection of a plain surface are testimony to Christensen's high regard for the attributes of silver as a material. In addition, Christensen is an artist who nevertheless believes that function is of the utmost importance, and his designs reflect this concern. This particular coffee pot was designed to pour with ease and efficiency. Its delicate balance is such that when it is lifted by the vertical rosewood handle it tips, practically pouring itself. Exhibited at the Brussels World's Fair in the late 1950s, this unusual design attracted great interest and was widely reproduced in popular magazines and newspapers.

Refs.: "Hans J. Christensen," *Design Quarterly* (1957): 6. Harold J. Brennan, "Three Rochester Craftsmen," *American Artist* 22, no. 6 (June-August 1958): 36-43, 87-90.

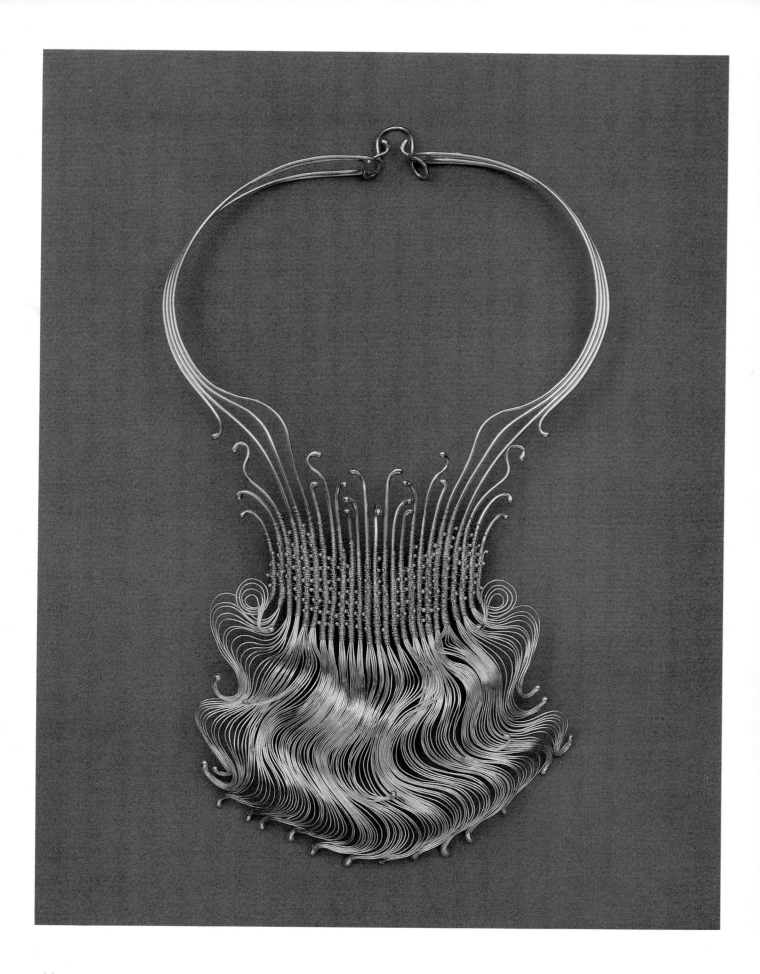

196 Neckpiece #26, East Lansing, Michigan, 1976
Mary Lee Hu (b. 1943)
L. 11¼″ (286 mm); WT. 4 oz, 10 dwt (139 gm)
Bradford F. Swan, B.A. 1929, Fund   1978.94

Today's artists working in metal are constantly experimenting with the many ways, both traditional and modern, in
which their medium can be manipulated. Mary Lee Hu is
one of a group of artists intrigued with forms which are most
effectively made using weaving and other textile techniques.
Although most of her work is in jewelry, she has also created
a remarkable array of fantastic and complex forms.

Like much of Hu's work, this neckpiece has a fluid
grace which seems at first impossible in metal but is in fact
evidence of the singular malleability of silver and gold.
Beautifully flexible and organic, her design complements
and enhances the human body. It is composed of gold and
sterling silver wire, woven together and fused. The free-
flowing quality of this piece is characteristic both of her
work and of the current concern of many artists with natural
forms. Always interested in animal structure, Hu has recently produced a number of sculptures inspired by the
physiology of sea creatures.

Hu received her undergraduate training at the Cran-
brook Academy of Art and her graduate degree from Southern Illinois University, where she studied under Brent
Kington. She is currently Assistant Professor of Metalsmithing and Jewelry at Michigan State University.

Refs.: Elizabeth Breckinridge, "Mary Lee Hu: High on the Wire," *Craft
Horizons* 37, no. 2 (April 1977): 40-43, 65. Arline M. Fisch, *Textile
Techniques in Metal, for Jewelers, Sculptors, and Textile Artists* (New
York: Van Nostrand Reinhold Company, 1975), pp. 10-51, 59, 70, 95, 133,
147-159.

Selected Bibliography

The following bibliography parallels the organization of the catalogue section of this book and is designed as an introductory guide to the voluminous literature on American silver. For other references, see the extensive bibliographies included in many of the books listed here and the works cited after each catalogue entry. In addition, Charles F. Montgomery and Catherine H. Maxwell, *Early American Silver: Collectors, Collections, Exhibitions, Writings* (Portland, Maine: Southworth-Anthoenson Press, 1969), a compilation first published in the 1968 Walpole Society Note Book, is a rare but invaluable handbook.

Silver, Its Sources and Uses

Bateman, Alan M. *Economic Mineral Deposits.* New York: John Wiley & Sons, Inc., 1950.

Butts, Allison, and Coxe, Charles D., eds. *Silver: Economics, Metallurgy, and Use.* Princeton, New Jersey: D. Van Nostrand Co., Inc., 1967.

De Quille, Dan. *The Big Bonanza.* 1876. Reprint. New York: Thomas Y. Crowell Company, 1947.

Paul, Rodman W. *Mining Frontiers of the Far West, 1848-1880.* Albuquerque, New Mexico: University of New Mexico Press, 1963.

Roberts, Willard Lincoln; Rapp, George Robert; and Weber, Julius. *Encyclopedia of Minerals.* Princeton, New Jersey: D. Van Nostrand Reinhold Company, 1974.

Watkins, T. H. *Gold and Silver in the West: An Illustrated History of an American Dream.* New York: Bonanza Books, 1971.

Coins and Medals

Buttrey, T. V., Jr. *Coinage of the Americas.* New York: The American Numismatic Society, 1973.

Crosby, S. S. *The Early Coins of America.* Boston: Estes and Lauriat, 1878.

Noe, Sydney P. *The New England and Willow Tree Coinages of Massachusetts.* New York: The American Numismatic Society, 1943.

————. *The Oak Tree Coinage of Massachusetts.* New York: The American Numismatic Society, 1947.

————. *The Pine Tree Coinage of Massachusetts.* New York: The American Numismatic Society, 1952.

Vermeule, Cornelius. *Numismatic Art in America.* Cambridge, Massachusetts: The Belknap Press of Harvard University Press, 1971.

Traditional Craft Practices

Abbey, Staton. *The Goldsmith's and Silversmith's Handbook.* 2nd rev. ed. London: The Technical Press Ltd., 1968.

Badcock, William. *A New Touchstone for Gold and Silver Wares.* 1679. Reprint. New York: Praeger Publishers, 1971.

Buhler, Kathryn C. *Colonial Silversmiths, Masters and Apprentices.* Boston: Museum of Fine Arts, 1956.

Campbell, R. *The London Tradesman.* 1747. Reprint. Newton Abbot, England: David and Charles, 1969.

Cuzner, Bernard. *A Silversmith's Manual.* London: N.A.G. Press, Ltd., 1965.

De Matteo, William. *The Silversmith in Eighteenth-Century Williamsburg.* Williamsburg, Virginia: Colonial Williamsburg, 1956.

Fales, Martha Gandy. "English Design Sources of American Silver." *Antiques* 83, no. 1 (January 1963): 82-85.

————. *Joseph Richardson and Family, Philadelphia Silversmiths.* Middletown, Connecticut: Wesleyan University Press, 1974.

Maryon, Herbert. *Metalwork and Enamelling.* 5th rev. ed. New York: Dover Publications, 1971.

Mass Production and Craft Revival

MASS PRODUCTION

Freeman, Larry. *Victorian Silver: Plated and Sterling, Hollow and Flatware.* Watkins Glen, New York: Century House, 1967.

————, and Beaumont, Jane. *Early American Plated Silver.* Watkins Glen, New York: Century House, 1947.

Gibb, George S. *The Whitesmiths of Taunton.* Cambridge, Massachusetts: Harvard University Press, 1943.

Hogan, E. P. *An American Heritage: A Book About the International Silver Company.* Meriden, Connecticut: International Silver Company, 1977.

May, Earl Chapin. *Century of Silver, 1847-1947: Connecticut Yankees and a Noble Metal.* New York: Robert M. McBride and Co., 1947.

Rainwater, Dorothy T., and Rainwater, H. Ivan. *American Silverplate.* Nashville, Tennessee: Thomas Nelson, Inc.; Hanover, Pennsylvania: Everybodys Press, 1968.

Turner, Noel D. *American Silver Flatware, 1837-1910.* New York: A. S. Barnes and Co., 1972.

United States Tariff Commission. *Silverware, Solid and Plated.* Washington, D.C.: United States Government Printing Office, 1940.

CRAFT REVIVAL

Darling, Sharon S. *Chicago Metalsmiths.* Chicago: Chicago Historical Society, 1977.

Eaton, Allen H. *Handicrafts of New England.* New York: Harper and Brothers, 1949.

Fisch, Arline M. *Textile Techniques in Metal, for Jewelers, Sculptors, and Textile Artists.* New York: Van Nostrand Reinhold Company, 1975.

Hall, Julie. *Tradition and Change: The New American Craftsman.* New York: E. P. Dutton and Co., 1977.

Leighton, Margaretha Gebelein. *George Christian Gebelein, Boston Silversmith, 1878-1945.* Boston: Privately Printed, 1976.

Philbrick, Helen Porter. "Franklin Porter, Silversmith (1869-1935)." *Essex Institute Historical Collections* 105, no. 3 (July 1969): 143-214.

Precious Metals: The American Tradition in Gold and Silver. Miami, Florida: Lowe Art Museum, University of Miami, 1976.

Untracht, Oppi. *Metal Techniques for Craftsmen*. Garden City, New York: Doubleday & Company, Inc., 1968.

Silver and Society

Ball, Berenice. "Whistles with Coral and Bells." *Antiques* 80, no. 6 (December 1961): 552-555.

Belden, Bauman L. *Indian Peace Medals Issued in the United States*. 1927. Reprint. New Milford, Connecticut: N. Flayderman & Co., 1966.

Church Silver of Colonial Virginia. Richmond, Virginia: The Virginia Museum, 1970.

Cummings, Abbott Lowell. *Rural Household Inventories*. Boston: Society for the Preservation of New England Antiquities, 1964.

Fales, Martha Gandy. "The Early American Way of Death." *Essex Institute Historical Collections* 100, no. 2 (April 1964): 75-84.

————. "Some Forged Richardson Silver." *Antiques* 79, no. 5 (May 1961): 466-469.

Franco, Barbara. *Masonic Symbols in American Decorative Arts*. Lexington, Massachusetts: Scottish Rite Masonic Museum of Our National Heritage, 1976.

Garvan, Anthony N. B. "The New England Porringer: An Index of Custom." In *Annual Report of the Board of Regents of the Smithsonian Institution . . . for the Year Ended June 30 1958*, Publication 4354. Washington, D.C.: United States Government Printing Office, 1959.

Garvan, Anthony N. B.; Kringold, Arlene; Stone, Philip; and Jones, Robert. "American Church Silver: A Statistical Study." In *Spanish, French, and English Traditions in the Colonial Silver of North America*. Winterthur, Delaware: The Henry Francis du Pont Winterthur Museum, 1968.

Gere, Charlotte. *American and European Jewelry, 1830-1914*. New York: Crown Publishers, Inc., 1975.

Holloway, H. Maxson. "American Presentation Silver." *The New-York Historical Society Quarterly* 30, no. 4 (October 1946): 215-233.

Jones, E. Alfred. *The Old Silver of American Churches*. Letchworth, England: Privately Printed for the Colonial Dames of America, 1913.

Nygren, Edward J. "Edward Winslow's Sugar Boxes: Colonial Echoes of Courtly Love." *Yale University Art Gallery Bulletin* 33, no. 2 (Autumn 1971): 38-52.

The Odd and the Elegant in Silver. Newburyport, Massachusetts: The Towle Silversmiths, 1956.

Peterson, Harold L. *The American Sword, 1775-1945*. Philadelphia: Ray Riling Arms Books Co., 1973.

Phillips, John Marshall. "Faked American Silver." In *Antique Fakes and Reproductions*, by Ruth Webb Lee. Wellesley Hills, Massachusetts: Lee Publications, 1966.

Prucha, Francis P. *Indian Peace Medals in American History*. Lincoln, Nebraska: University of Nebraska Press, 1971.

Rainwater, Dorothy T., and Felger, Donna H. *American Spoons, Souvenir and Historical*. Camden, New Jersey: Thomas Nelson and Sons; Hanover, Pennsylvania: Everybodys Press, 1968.

Roth, Rodris. "Tea Drinking in Eighteenth-Century America: Its Etiquette and Equipage." In *United States National Museum Bulletin 225, Contributions from the Museum of History and Technology*. Washington, D.C.: Smithsonian Institution, 1961.

Scott, Kenneth. *Counterfeiting in Colonial America*. New York: Oxford University Press, 1957.

Shoenberger, Guido. "The Ritual Silver Made by Myer Myers." *Publication of the American Jewish Historical Society* 43, no. 1 (September 1953): 1-9.

Sommer, Frank H., III. "The Functions of American Church Silver." In *Spanish, French, and English Traditions in the Colonial Silver of North America*. Winterthur, Delaware: The Henry Francis du Pont Winterthur Museum, 1968.

Whitehill, Walter Muir. "Tutor Flynt's Silver Chamber-pot." *Publications of the Colonial Society of Massachusetts* 38 (Transactions 1947-1951): 360-363.

A Gallery of American Silver

GENERAL WORKS

Avery, C. Louise. *Early American Silver*. 1930. Reprint. New York: Russell & Russell, 1968.

Bigelow, Francis Hill. *Historic Silver of the Colonies and Its Makers*. New York: Macmillan Company, 1917.

Buck, John H. *Old Plate, Ecclesiastical, Decorative, and Domestic: Its Makers and Marks*. New York: The Gorham Manufacturing Company, 1888.

Buhler, Kathryn C. *American Silver*. Cleveland: The World Publishing Company, 1950.

————. *Masterpieces of American Silver*. Richmond, Virginia: The Virginia Museum of Fine Arts, 1960.

Clayton, Michael. *The Collector's Dictionary of the Silver and Gold of Great Britain and North America*. New York: The World Publishing Company, 1971.

Fales, Martha Gandy. *Early American Silver*. New York: E. P. Dutton and Company, Inc., 1973.

Hood, Graham. *American Silver: A History of Style, 1650-1900*. New York: Praeger Publishers, 1971.

Hughes, Graham. *Modern Silver*. New York: Crown Publishers, Inc., 1967.

Jones, E. Alfred. *Old Silver of Europe and America from Early Times to the Nineteenth Century*. Philadelphia: J. B. Lippincott Co., 1928.

McClinton, Katharine Morrison. *Collecting American Nineteenth-Century Silver*. New York: Charles Scribner's Sons, 1968.

Montgomery, Charles F., and Kane, Patricia E., eds. *American Art, 1750-1800: Towards Independence*. Boston: New York Graphic Society, 1976.

Nineteenth-Century America: Furniture and Other Decorative Arts. New York: The Metropolitan Museum of Art, 1970.

Phillips, John Marshall. *American Silver*. New York: Chanticleer Press, 1949.

REGIONAL STUDIES

Avery, C. Louise. *An Exhibition of Early New York Silver*. New York: The Metropolitan Museum of Art, 1931.

Beckman, Elizabeth D. *An In-depth Study of the Cincinnati Silversmiths, Jewelers, Watch and Clockmakers Through 1850*. Cincinnati, Ohio: B. B. & Co., 1975.

Bohan, Peter, and Hammerslough, Philip H. *Early Connecticut Silver, 1700-1840*. Middletown, Connecticut: Wesleyan University Press, 1970.

Brix, Maurice. *List of Philadelphia Silversmiths and Allied Artificers from 1682 to 1850*. Philadelphia: Privately Printed, 1920.

Burton, E. Milby. *South Carolina Silversmiths, 1690-1860*. 1942. Reprint. Rutland, Vermont: The Charles E. Tuttle Co., 1968.

Carpenter, Ralph E., Jr. *The Arts and Crafts of Newport, Rhode Island, 1640-1820*. Newport, Rhode Island: The Preservation Society of Newport County, 1954.

Cutten, George Barton. *The Silversmiths of Georgia*. Savannah, Georgia: The Pigeonhole Press, 1958.

————. *The Silversmiths of North Carolina*. Raleigh, North Carolina: State Department of Archives and History, 1948.

_____. *The Silversmiths of Virginia.* Richmond, Virginia: The Dietz Press, Incorporated, 1952.

Gerstell, Vivian S. *Silversmiths of Lancaster, Pennsylvania, 1730-1850.* Lancaster, Pennsylvania: Lancaster County Historical Society, 1972.

Goldsborough, Jennifer F. *An Exhibition of New London Silver, 1700-1835.* New London, Connecticut: Lyman Allyn Museum, 1969.

Gourley, Hugh J., III. *The New England Silversmith.* Providence, Rhode Island: Museum of Art, Rhode Island School of Design, 1965.

Halsey, R. T. Haines. Introduction to *Catalogue of an Exhibition of Silver Used In New York, New Jersey, and the South.* New York: The Metropolitan Museum of Art, 1911.

Hiatt, Noble W., and Hiatt, Lucy F. *The Silversmiths of Kentucky, Together with Some Watchmakers and Jewelers, 1785-1850.* Louisville, Kentucky: The Standard Printing Company, 1954.

Hindes, Ruthanna. "Delaware Silversmiths." *Delaware History* 12, no. 4 (October 1967): 247-308.

Knittle, Rhea Mansfield. *Early Ohio Silversmiths and Pewterers, 1787-1847.* Cleveland: The Calvert-Hatch Company, 1943.

Miller, V. Isabelle. *Silver by New York Makers, Late 17th Century to 1900.* New York: Museum of the City of New York, 1937.

Miller, William Davis. *The Silversmiths of Little Rest.* Kingston, Rhode Island: Privately Printed, 1928.

New Haven Colony Historical Society. *An Exhibition of Early Silver by New Haven Silversmiths.* New Haven, Connecticut: New Haven Colony Historical Society, 1967.

Paul Revere's Boston, 1735-1818. Boston: New York Graphic Society, 1975.

Philadelphia: Three Centuries of American Art. Philadelphia: Philadelphia Museum of Art, 1976.

Pleasants, J. Hall, and Sill, Howard. *Maryland Silversmiths, 1715-1830.* Baltimore: Lord Baltimore Press, 1930.

Roach, Ruth Hunter. *St. Louis Silversmiths.* Privately Printed, 1967.

Southern Silver: An Exhibition of Silver Made in the South Prior to 1860. Houston, Texas: Museum of Fine Arts, Houston, 1968.

Williams, Carl M. *Silversmiths of New Jersey, 1700-1825.* Philadelphia: George S. MacManus Company, 1949.

BIOGRAPHIES OF INDIVIDUAL SILVERSMITHS

Buhler, Kathryn C. *Paul Revere, Goldsmith, 1735-1818.* Boston: Museum of Fine Arts, 1956.

Clarke, Hermann Frederick. *John Coney, Silversmith, 1655-1722.* Boston: Houghton Mifflin Company, 1932.

_____. *John Hull, A Builder of the Bay Colony.* Portland, Maine: The Southworth-Anthoenson Press, 1940.

_____, and Foote, Henry Wilder. *Jeremiah Dummer, Colonial Craftsman and Merchant, 1645-1718.* Boston: Houghton Mifflin Company, 1935.

Failey, Dean Frederick. "Elias Pelletreau, Long Island Silversmith." Master's thesis, University of Delaware, 1971.

Forbes, Esther. *Paul Revere and the World He Lived In.* Boston: Houghton Mifflin Company, 1942.

French, Hollis. *Jacob Hurd and His Sons Nathaniel and Benjamin, Silversmiths, 1702-1781.* Cambridge, Massachusetts: The Walpole Society, 1939.

Rosenbaum, Jeanette W. (with technical notes by Kathryn C. Buhler). *Myer Myers, Goldsmith, 1723-1795.* Philadelphia: The Jewish Publication Society of America, 1954.

Wroth, Lawrence C. *Abel Buell of Connecticut: Silversmith, Type Founder, and Engraver.* 2nd. rev. ed. Middletown, Connecticut: Wesleyan University Press, 1958.

CATALOGUES OF COLLECTIONS

Avery, C. Louise. *American Silver of the XVII and XVIII Centuries: A Study Based on the Clearwater Collection.* New York: The Metropolitan Museum of Art, 1920.

Buhler, Kathryn C. *American Silver, 1655-1825, in the Museum of Fine Arts, Boston.* 2 vols. Greenwich, Connecticut: New York Graphic Society, 1972.

_____. *Massachusetts Silver in the Frank L. and Louise C. Harrington Collection.* Worcester, Massachusetts: Barre Publishers, 1965.

_____. *Mount Vernon Silver.* Mount Vernon, Virginia: The Mount Vernon Ladies Association of the Union, 1957.

_____, and Hood, Graham. *American Silver, Garvan and Other Collections in the Yale University Art Gallery.* 2 vols. New Haven, Connecticut: Yale University Press, 1970.

Fales, Martha Gandy. *American Silver in the Henry Francis du Pont Winterthur Museum.* Winterthur, Delaware: The Henry Francis du Pont Winterthur Museum, 1958.

Flynt, Henry H., and Fales, Martha Gandy. *The Heritage Foundation Collection of Silver, With Biographical Sketches of New England Silversmiths, 1625-1825.* Old Deerfield, Massachusetts: The Heritage Foundation, 1968.

Goldsborough, Jennifer F. *Eighteenth-and Nineteenth-Century Maryland Silver in the Collection of the Baltimore Museum of Art.* Baltimore: The Baltimore Museum of Art, 1975.

Hammerslough, Philip H. *American Silver Collected by Philip H. Hammerslough.* 4 vols. Hartford, Connecticut: Privately Printed, 1958-1973.

Hipkiss, Edwin J. *Eighteenth-Century American Arts: The M. and M. Karolik Collection.* Boston: Museum of Fine Arts, 1941.

_____. *The Philip Leffingwell Spalding Collection of Early American Silver.* Cambridge, Massachusetts: Harvard University Press, 1943.

Warren, David B. *Bayou Bend: American Furniture, Paintings, and Silver from The Bayou Bend Collection.* Houston, Texas: Museum of Fine Arts, Houston, 1975.

MARKS

Currier, Ernest M. *Marks of Early American Silversmiths.* Edited by Kathryn C. Buhler. Portland, Maine: The Southworth-Anthoenson Press, 1938.

Ensko, Stephen G. C. *American Silversmiths and Their Marks, III.* New York: Robert Ensko, Inc., 1948.

French, Hollis. *A Silver Collectors' Glossary and A List of Early American Silversmiths and Their Marks.* 1917. Reprint. New York: Da Capo Press, 1967.

Green, Robert Alan. *Marks of American Silversmiths.* Harrison, New York: Robert Alan Green, 1977.

Jewelers Circular Publishing Company. *Trade Marks of the Jewelry and Kindred Trades.* 1915. Reprint. Ironton, Missouri: American Reprints Company, 1977.

Kovel, Ralph M., and Kovel, Terry H. *A Directory of American Silver, Pewter, and Silver Plate.* New York: Crown Publishers, Inc., 1961.

Rainwater, Dorothy T. *Encyclopedia of American Silver Manufacturers.* New York: Crown Publishers, Inc., 1975.

Index

Index of Silversmiths, Designers, Manufacturers, and Retailers whose work is included in the exhibition. Numbers refer to catalogue numbers.

Photograph Credits

Unless otherwise noted below, all original photography for this book was done by E. Irving Blomstrann, New Britain, Connecticut. Numbers without prefix are catalogue numbers.